TOUCH AND GO

Died 96 years old

ALSO BY STUDS TERKEL

TOUCH AND GO

A Memoir

Studs Terkel
with Sydney Lewis

THE NEW PRESS

NEW YORK
LONDON

Requests for permission to reproduce selections from this book should be mailed to:
Permissions Department, The New Press, 38 Greene Street, New York, NY 10013.

Published in the United States by The New Press, New York, 2007
Distributed by W. W. Norton & Company, Inc., New York

LIBRARY OF CONGRESS CATALOGING-IN-PUBLICATION DATA

Terkel, Studs, 1912–
Touch and go : a memoir / Studs Terkel.
p.   cm.
Includes index.
ISBN 978-1-59558-043-6 (hc.)
1. Terkel, Studs, 1912–   2. Broadcasters—United States—Biography.
3. Authors, American—20th century—Biography.   I. Title.
PN1990.72 T4A3 2007
384.54092—dc22

[B]   2007018673

The New Press was established in 1990 as a not-for-profit alternative to the large,
commercial publishing houses currently dominating the book publishing industry.
The New Press operates in the public interest rather than for private gain,
and is committed to publishing, in innovative ways, works of educational,
cultural, and community value that are often deemed insufficiently profitable.

www.thenewpress.com

Composition by dix!

Printed in the United States of America

2   4   6   8   10   9   7   5   3   1

To my son, Dan

And every evening at sun-down
I ask a blessing on the town
For whether we last the night or no
I'm sure it's always touch and go.

—Dylan Thomas

You see, there's such a thing as a feeling tone.
One is friendly and one is hostile.
And if you don't have this, baby, you've had it.

—Nancy Dickerson

Contents

Part III

Part IV

Editor's Note

At the age of ninety-four, Studs Terkel finally sat down to write a memoir of his life. After a lifetime of talking to others, he has set down his thoughts about his own past. Much of the book has been written directly by Studs on his old typewriter. Other parts were the result of conversations with his old friend and associate Sydney Lewis. I suspect that for many readers the two parts of the book will blend together easily. They both capture Studs' voice, his humor, and his life.

In a few instances, Studs has decided that he'd already written about the people he wanted to incorporate in the book. Therefore there are some brief passages that are excerpted from his earlier books, all of which are clearly marked. The longest excerpt comes from *Chicago,* which, due to complicated copyright reasons, is the only one of his books that is currently out of print. Everything else by Studs is available from The New Press, and an excellent selection has been made in the recently published *The Studs Terkel Reader.*

Having worked with Studs for over forty years, I'm delighted that he's finally written this book. I'm also very impressed to see that his feistiness, his humor, and his incredible memory have been totally undiminished by age. This book will give the reader the experience of sitting next to Studs and hearing him talk, discovering what a fantastic raconteur he is. The reader will also see that he is still the same idealist, fighter, and chronicler of American life that he's always been.

—André Schiffrin

Acknowledgments

My luckiest break: Sydney Lewis as my collaborator. She heard my thoughts as well as my spoken words. JR Millares was more than a caregiver. He was hip to all the nuances; his help was immeasurable. My son, Dan, saw the whole thing through.

My three medicine men, Dr. Quentin Young, our family physician and friend for half a century; Dr. Joseph Messer, cardiologist; Dr. Marshall Goldin, cardiovascular surgeon.

Garry and Natalie Wills, Lois Baum and David Krupp, Robert and Laura Watson, Garrison Keillor, Tony and Valentine Judge, Tom Geoghegan, Alex Kotlowitz, Jamie and Patsy Kalven, M'Loo Kogan and Rick Kogan, Amy Greene Andrews, Eleanor Bron, Ursula Bender, Moni Foreman, Calvin Trillin, Haskell Wexler, Roger and Chaz Ebert, Judy Royko, Vic Navasky, Michael and Cheli Dibb, Bill Young, Franklin and Penelope Rosemont, Dr. Marvin Jackson, Connie Hall, Magda Krance, Jack Clark, and Jonathan Cott.

Also, Jay Allison, Samantha Broun, and Viki Merrick of Atlantic Public Media.

My longtime colleagues at WFMT: Norm Pelligrini, the late Ray Nordstrand, the late Bernie and Rita Jacobs, Jim Unrath, Linda Lewis, Don Mueller, Steve Jones, Andrea Lamoreaux, Kay Richards, Don Tait, Steve Robinson.

Russell Lewis, director of the Chicago Historical Museum, and his associate, Luciana Crovato; and Usama Alshaibi.

Of course, André Schiffrin, my publisher through the years; his associates Joel Ariaratnam and Ina Howard; and the rest of the New Press staff.

My apologies to those friends whom I have unintentionally neglected.

Prologue

I have, after a fashion, been celebrated for having celebrated the lives of the uncelebrated among us; for lending voice to the face in the crowd.

This, I imagine, is what much of oral history is about. It has been with us long before the feather pen and ink, and certainly long before Gutenberg and his printing press. It's been with us since the first shaman, at the communal fire, called upon the spirits to recount a tribal tale.

It is no accident that Alex Haley, in writing *Roots*, first visited the land of his forebears, Gambia, to search out the *griots*, the tribal storytellers.

It was Henry Mayhew, a contemporary of Dickens, who sought out the needle workers, the shoemakers, the street criers, the chimney sweeps; all those etceteras; and, in one year, 1850, poured forth a million words, *their* words, in the *Morning Chronicle*. He lent voice to these groundlings who were so often seen, but, like well-behaved children, seldom heard. The Respectables of London, Manchester, and Birmingham, in reading their morning newspaper, were astonished. They had no idea these etceteras, who had for so long submissively and silently served them, thought such thoughts; and what's more, felt that way.

E.P. Thompson pointed out that Mayhew rejected the temptation to "varnish matters over with sickly sentimentality, angelizing or canonizing the whole body of workers of this country, instead of speaking of them as possessing the ordinary vices and virtues of human nature."

Listen to this man at a public gathering of tailors in October, 1850:

> It is easy enough to be moral after a good dinner beside a snug sea-coal fire, and with our hearts well warmed with a fine old port. It is easy enough for those that can enjoy these things daily to pay their poor's rates, rent their pew and love their neighbors as themselves; but place the self-same "highly respectable" people on a raft without sup or bite on the high seas, *and they would toss up who would eat their fellows*. Morality on 5000 pounds a year in Belgrave Square is a very different thing to morality on slop-wages in Bethnal Green.

It is no accident that Nelson Algren, winner of the very first National Book Award for Fiction precisely one hundred years later in 1950, often expressed his admiration for Mayhew's classic, *London Labour and the London Poor*. As for me, that book has been scripture. Mayhew has been my North Star.

Nor was Henry Mayhew the last so engaged in this adventure we call oral history. It was Zora Neal Hurston, already established as a folklorist and anthropologist (she was a disciple of Franz Boas★), who, during the Great Depression, as a member of the WPA Writers Project in Florida, at the pay of $37.50 every two weeks, engaged in a similar adventure. She tracked down former slaves, children of slaves and their children, sharecroppers. She celebrated their lives, in their own words. There were scores of such writers so occupied throughout the country.

What distinguishes the work in our day from the efforts of these pioneers is the presence of a machine, a ubiquitous one—the tape recorder. I know of one other person as possessed by the tape

---

★ A pioneer of modern anthropology; often referred to as "the father of American anthropology."

recorder as I have been these past thirty years—a former president of the United States. Though our purposes may have been somewhat different, the two of us have been equally in its thrall. Richard Nixon and I could be aptly described as neo-Cartesians: I tape, therefore I am. I hope that one of these two so possessed may be further defined by a paraphrase: I tape, therefore *they* are. Who are *they*, these etceteras of history, hardly worth a footnote? Who are *they* of whom the bards have seldom sung?

> Bertolt Brecht, in a series of questions, put it this way:
> Who built the Seven Gates of Thebes . . . ?
> When the Chinese Wall was built, where did the masons go
>   for lunch?
> When Caesar conquered Gaul, was there not even a cook in
>   the army?
> When the Armada sank, we read that King Philip wept.
> Were there no other tears?

That's what I believe oral history is about. It's about those who shed these other tears. Or who laughed that other laugh, during those rare moments of rebellious triumph. Consider some of these heroes of our day, whom I've had the good fortune to encounter. They are an arbitrary few I've chosen out of a multitude of such heroes.

E.D. Nixon, former Pullman car porter, president of the NAACP, Montgomery, Alabama. It was he who chose Rosa Parks, his secretary, to do what she did one afternoon. It was he who chose a young pastor from Atlanta, Martin Luther King Jr., to head the Montgomery Improvement Association and drum-major the bus boycott in 1954. The rest, as they say, is history.

C.P. Ellis, former Grand Cyclops of the Ku Klux Klan, Durham, North Carolina. A poor white; all his life having a hard time of it. One piece of bad luck after another; barely making it from one day to the next.

"I began to get bitter. I didn't know who to blame. I had to hate somebody. Hatin' America is hard to do because you can't see it to hate it. You gotta have somethin' to look at to hate. I began to blame it on black people. So I joined the Klan. My father told me it was the savior of the white race."

It was one daily revelation after another. He'd worked as a janitor at Duke University; member of the union; 80 percent black, mostly women. He ran for the full-time job of business agent; his opponent, a black man. As he began his campaign speech, the women shouted him down. "Sit down, Claiborne Ellis. We know all about you." He took a long pause in recounting the moment. It was almost a whisper. "They elected me, four to one." He sobbed softly. "Those women. They knew my heart. You feel so good to go to a plant with those black women and butt heads with professional union busters, *college men*. And we hold our own against them. Now I feel like somebody for real."

In neither of these cases was there that one overwhelming moment of epiphany. It was no Damascan road they traveled; nor was any one of them struck by a blinding light. It was an accretion of daily revelations and the discovery of where the body was hid. Moments of daily astonishments.

The story is told of Sergei Diaghilev, the ballet impresario, who was never satisfied. A desperate Vaslar Nijinsky cried out: "What do you want of me?" Diaghilev is reputed to have replied, in a world-weary fashion: "*Ettone-moi.*" Astonish me.

My moment of ultimate astonishment happened about thirty years ago. It was at a public housing project. A young mother. I don't remember whether she was white or black. The place was mixed. She was pretty, skinny, with bad teeth. It was the first time she had encountered a tape recorder. Her little kids, about four of them, demanded a replay. They insisted on hearing mama's voice. I pressed the button. They howled with delight. She put her hands to her mouth and gasped. "I never knew I felt that way." She was astonished, sure, but no more than I was. Such astonishments have always been forthcoming from the etceteras of history. Ever since the Year One.

Part I

1

Street Scene

Natacha Rambova, Rudolph Valentino's wife, is tousling my hair. Gently, fondly. Or was it Pola Negri? She, too, has something to do with the Sheik of Araby. No, it was not Pola, whose two eyebrows furrowed into one like those of Frida Kahlo, who had been married to Diego Rivera. That put Frida out of the running, the insatiable Mexican painter keeping her much too busy. Who else might that dark lady have been at that delightful moment eighty-six years ago when I was a heaven-touched eight?

Theda Bara? She was the pioneer, the first sultry temptress of our silent films. How could one forget that most memorable of subtitles? Sidling across the Persian rug with serpentine grace, certain of her kill, the hapless WASPy dolt in her encircling arms from which only Houdini could have escaped, we saw the words which she so stunningly synched: "Kiss me, my fool."

No. Not only was she slightly before my time, she was beyond the pale. She was aka Theodosia Goodman, daughter of a Cincinnati tailor. Cincinnati. Not a touch of the Arabian Nights in these quarters. It is true the Cincy baseball club had a sidearm pitcher bearing the exotic name Eppa Jeptha Rixey, a perfect one for a Jesus-obsessed sinner in a Flannery O'Connor short story—but not exotic enough to match my fantasy moment.

Though the ninety-four-year-old mind's eye sees the name,

Hannah Stein, let the eight-year-old's impression prevail. It was Natacha of the raven locks parted in the center, with her fingernails painted blood-red, fooling around with my small boy's pompadour. It was a Sunday afternoon in the early spring of 1920. And oh, how I was enjoying the chocolate ice cream soda.

It was but a year or two before that, on the steps of the Forty-second Street Library, that my father was holding me high on his left shoulder, as we watched our soldier boys marching in the Armistice Day parade, having triumphed Over There in the war to end war. For some reason, my father paused a long time before shifting me to his right shoulder. A few years later, we were told that he had a case of angina pectoris and that his heart was failing fast. I, though a sickly, frail child, may have weighed sixteen tons to him, though you'd hardly have known it. He happened to be enjoying the moment because he felt I was enjoying the moment.

So it is this Sunday afternoon, so many months after the celebratory march, we three are seated at a tiny round table on an East Side sidewalk café: Natacha Rambova, my father, and I. It didn't take me long to discover that he had arranged it. I had never seen her before, yet in no way did her delicate ministrations diminish my delight as my straw slurped away my sweet repast.

I had neither the time nor the inclination to ask about other things. Why was she here? And behaving in so familiar a manner? It really didn't matter. Let's be realistic, first things first. The chocolate ice cream soda was what it was all about.

Statistic: I was born in 1912, three weeks after the *Titanic* blithely sailed into the tip of that iceberg. Make of it what you will.

And yet—what was she, the strange dark lady, doing here as my father's companion? True, I was a child of eight, fast going on nine, yet I may have been preternaturally endowed with a keyhole view of carnal knowledge. Somehow, I had a slight suspicion that something illicit was going on. Did I or did I not recall the moment I saw their fingers tentatively reach out and touch as I was downing the good stuff? All in all, it was A-OK with me. Call me a pragmatist.

Why didn't I feel as Biff Loman did when he discovered his father, Willy, in that Boston hotel room with a woman not his wife? "What happened in Boston, Willy?" was the recurring refrain in *Death of a Salesman*. Why was what was so devastating to Biff Loman so delightful an experience for me as a merry go-between? In short, why did I enjoy my first moment as a small boy pander? It was simply a matter of my own happiness, at that moment, being dependent upon my father's happiness. I was, I feel certain some eighty-six years later, aware of the burdens wearing him into a premature gray.

By the time we three, Natacha, my father, and I, sat that Sunday afternoon at the sidewalk café with the chocolate soda never tasting sweeter, my father's mustache was a bit too roughly trimmed and turning a portentous ash-gray. It was the cloudy color of trouble ahead. Still, it was Sam's mustache, no matter how it shaped up, that distinguished him from others.

The earliest movies I saw lacked my kind of hero; the one with a mustache; someone whose hallmark would approach that of my father; who would bear a signature that would afford me comfort. Unfortunately, in the movies, only the villains wore the telltale handlebars. Invariably. Slick. And rotten to the core, Maud.

Lowell Sherman immediately comes to mind. He was among the first. Brilliantined, patent-leather black hair, with a mustache that also appeared patented; evil-eyed; a cad in a class by himself. Lew Cody, a fair-skinned, craven toady up to no good. Their mustaches gave them away. What the scarlet letter was to Hester Prynne, the damnable facial adornment was to them. There was a note of redemption and hope in the saga of Warner Baxter. Oh, he was a bad one, twirling his mustache until the day an imaginative producer transformed him into the Cisco Kid. Now he was a Mexican, but a good one, a greaser who did not throw knives at gringos. With talking pictures, the biggest transformation occurred in the person of one actor: William Powell.

Remember the two-day silent blockbuster, *Beau Geste*? (Sure, its hero Ronald Colman had a growth, but he was a Brit, so it didn't count.) Remember how this movie opens? There are louts, clods, and poltroons whom the screen offers us as heroes: the French Foreign Legion. Their fortress has guns pointed out of each turret, aimed at the advancing Arabs. We realize that in a moment the outnumbered Legionnaires will be dead. Among the Legionnaires, especially the Geste brothers were true Kiplingesque heroes . . . "Theirs not to reason why, theirs to do or die." Among them is a wretched coward, Boldini, played by William Powell, mustachioed, of course.

Comes the first full-length talking picture, *Interference*. We now hear the plum-rich voice of Powell; no villain this one. He, indubitably a good guy, gives up his life to knock off the troublesome Evelyn Brent and thereby save the marriage of Doris Kenyon, the woman he loves. We think further of Powell and his incredible good luck with talkies. He is teamed up with the wondrous Myrna Loy as Nick and Nora Charles in the *Thin Man* series; cold martinis and the witty stuff of Dashiell Hammett.

The one I best and most reverently remember as my mustachioed hero of the silents, aside from the Little Tramp of Charlie Chaplin, is Raymond Griffith. He was aptly described as Chaplin in a top hat, white gloves, and cape; with a slight buzz that added to his charm. I have no idea how talkies may have affected his career as an actor. But I shall never, ever forget him in a talking movie, an adaptation of *All Quiet on the Western Front*. He didn't utter a word, yet his quite brief scene still astonishes me. How long ago was it? Would you believe seventy-five years?

It is during World War I. Lew Ayres plays the lead, a young German soldier, Paul. During an horrendous battle Paul finds himself in a foxhole with a French *poilu*, played by Raymond Griffith. Remember, it's the first time I've seen this iconic comic actor in years. Here he is, stabbed to death a moment ago by Paul. As Lew Ayres, the actor, looks over the letters and notes of the dying Griffith, he bursts into uncontrollable sobs and begs forgiveness. Ayres was great, but it is the mute performance of Griffith that haunts me even as I type these words. His look is one of wonderment. Bewilderment. *I never met this handsome young German kid in my life. Why has he bayoneted me to death as I had been taught to do unto him?* That brief moment, lasting but a few seconds, his death pose in the trench, his eyes open yet unseeing—is that a world-weary Griffith smile pasted onto a corpse?—tells us all we need to know of the absurdity of war.

We had known Griffith as the cheery, generous-hearted, slightly plastered peace courtier. It was peace at any cost. Consider, in a long-forgotten farce, the two attractive young women who love him and seek marriage. He loves them both. Equally. How did the Raymond Griffith modus vivendi work out in this instance? He packed both women into his roadster and off they drove. The film ends with a rear bumper sticker: BOUND FOR SALT LAKE CITY.★

There are a number of memorable scenes in *All Quiet*, yet this is the one that's hung on to me. Lewis Milestone, the director, chose the perfect actor for that tragic cameo role, a grand comic with a mischievous mustache.

A long-delayed confessional. Call it contrition, though it warrants no forgiveness. Lew Ayres, as a result of his role in the film (still one of the strongest of antiwar movies) was converted into a conscientious objector. He took a public stand that no doubt may have disturbed his career. World War II had begun. I was conducting a local commentary series on a Chicago radio station. There were no tapes then. I have recently searched for a copy of the script, yet somehow I've lost it. Fortunately. It may have been the most craven thing I've ever done. I'm sure the loss was Freudian.

I was criticizing Ayres, gently, of course (making it all the worse; I should have worn the mark of T for toady as Hester wore A for adultery). I was righteously addressing Ayres, in sorrow, of course (this sounds worse and worse as I type it) for his hurting the efforts

★ *The Silent Clowns* by Walter Kerr (Knopf, 1975).

to recruit soldier boys. I am fairly certain he never heard it. Mine was a limited local audience.

I had the effrontery to call him years later while I was working on the oral history "*The Good War.*" I had intended to apologize and ask if he'd appear in the book as a conscientious objector. I had no chance to tell him my dirty little secret (he fortunately never found out). He was remarkably gracious, though by this time weary of the subject and planning a memoir of his own. I don't think he ever got around to it.

As NATACHA, oh so gently, touched my cheek—eighty-six years later, I'd say "sensually"—Sam lit his Turkish cigarette. Murad was his favorite brand. I've always wondered why Russian Jewish tailors preferred Turkish tobacco to all others. It was, I suspect, more expensive than, say, Camels, for which, said the billboard, you'd walk a mile. I remember the popularity as well as the aroma of Helmar and Melachrinos among his collegial craftsmen.

As a prelude to his lighting up, he invariably tapped the elegantly long cigarette against the hard Murad case. He was at the moment Noël Coward; but once he lit up and blew smoke rings in the air, the cigarette poised between thumb and index finger, he was transformed into Uncle Vanya. He offered Natacha one, of course. Her smoke rings matched his. They needed no Chesterfield ad to tell them what to do.

The most popular billboard of them all was the Chesterfield ad: a pretty girl—was she a John Held Jr. lovely?—invited the unseen other to "Blow some my way." As the smoke wafted in, hers was a more satisfied smile. No Mona Lisa, that one. I don't recall whether she had as yet removed her earrings.

Of all the works of billboard artistry, the ones that still impress me most were devoted to the delightfulness of cigarettes. From time to time, there were the scolds and Cassandras whom the tobacco industry had to deal with. The Lucky Strikers and the others did not have as rough a time as they do now, but there were troublemakers.

During the resurgence of the suffragist movement, early in the century (the twentieth), the tobacco companies discovered an astonishing spokesman who was master of his craft. I had the enthralling experience of meeting Edward Bernays a number of times. Always there was the professorial air: the graying well-trimmed mustache; the spectacles; the easy, witty conversation. He was a pioneer, in fact; a revolutionary in his field. He had a reputation as a free thinker on the liberal side. But a job is a job is a job. He was the master of his. It was he and his way with words who transmuted "press agent" into "public relations counselor."

When we think of the press agent, we think of a cigar chosen from the lobby counter, of the medicine man hawking Lydia Pinkham's Vegetable Compound, or a jolly backslapping as a matter of reflex. A genial drinking companion.

Edward Bernays, in the manner of a medieval alchemist, had transmuted dross into the semblance of gold. It doesn't matter that the work itself hasn't altered. They are still coat holders for their clients. What Bernays had done, in fact, was to affect our daily working vocabulary. When I was in the tall grasslands of Inner Mongolia some twenty years ago, I heard the Chinese interpreter teach his Mongolian colleague what a PR man does. He used the actual English initials. I realized in that revelatory moment that, among words or phrases universally understood, whether you are in Inuit country or Tierra del Fuego, "PR" rates along with "Taxi!" and "No problem." Some years later, in reflecting on the pretty girl in the Chesterfield ad pleading "Blow Some My Way," I thought of Bernays. It may have been a sign that the wind was blowing his way.

The last time I saw Bernays, he was approaching the century mark. He was frail and hard of hearing, and his memory played hide-and-seek at times, but he still had almost all his marbles.

I put the earphones on him. It was a tape recording we had done years before. Immediately on hearing his younger voice, his face glowed with the wonder of a child. The subject was the nature of his work and, in this instance, of his powerhouse client—the tobacco industry. He was recounting an early moment in the twentieth century, when the feminist movement was in its resurgence. Names come to mind. Margaret Sanger. Helen Keller. Alice Paul. Jane Addams. Florence Kelley. They were advanced in many areas. Certainly the evils of tobacco were among them. Bernays himself was pro-suffragist as well as a peace and civil-rights advocate. But he did have a job to do, one of his biggest as a public-relations counselor: to make smoking cigarettes not only acceptable to the suffragists but a sign of liberation! And, to some extent, he succeeded. As I remember our conversation, to which he was listening at that moment, pressing the earphones tighter to himself, eyes wonder-wide, he had talked some of the spokeswomen, militant and courageous, into smoking during their celebratory march on Fifth Avenue. Puffing away publicly, lighting small fires of flaming tobacco, was their symbol of emancipation. As I relieved him of his earphones, he looked up at me. Mouth slightly open; a small boy bewildered by something. Was he aware of his giftedness and triumph? Did he realize the nature of his works, his expertise?

Parenthetically, Edward Bernays was the nephew of Sigmund Freud. Whenever he visited his uncle in prewar London he always presented him with a box of Havana cigars.

MY FATHER was a master of his craft, too. He was a men's tailor. I look at the gilt-edged daguerreotype of my two brothers, about four and six, in fancy woolen winter clothes sewn by Sam. What stand out are the earlaps, of identical corduroy fabric and design. They add just the right panache to the classy attire. You'd think the photo had been snapped by a Slavic Margaret Cameron. Oh, he was good, my father. I'm still much moved when I come across the picture of the three of us boys. There I am, in my little white nightgown, two years old, looking somewhat bewildered. I am standing on a stool as my two brothers (each in short pants, made by my father, of course) pose protectively on each side of their darling baby brother. When my father and his young wife, Annie, arrived in New York from the Russian-Polish border city, Bialystok, they were both good at what they tackled. She was a nimble-fingered seamstress. When she was not at the factory during a strike or slack time, I still see her, in our living room, on her knees, pins in her mouth, fitting a neighbor woman into a new dress.

It may have been in 1902 or '03 when they arrived. It was quota time instituted by the Brahminesque Henry Cabot Lodge, a quota aimed primarily at Italian immigrants. A shoemaker, Nicolo Sacco, and a fish peddler, Bartolomeo Vanzetti, may have been among them.

I look, from time to time, at an old-world gilt-framed daguerreotype of my mother, Annie, and my father, Sam. It is so obviously unlikely a pairing, and the photograph says it all. His curly-cued flowing jet-black mustachio gives him an Italian look: a Calabrian or Sardinian. He is Mateo Falcone of Sardinia's best credentials for honesty, courage, and above all, sanctuary to all seeking to escape from authority.★ His eyes appear bright, blazing and ready to face the day, whatever it may bring.

She wears a pince-nez, which instantly adds an air of anxiety to her eyes that appears at odds with her piercing, squinty look. Could it be fear, for which I could sense no reason? I was about to say there was a wild touch to her portrait, but that would be redundant.

These two were not born to be a vaudeville team. They were certainly no clones of George Burns and Gracie Allen. No, not even Broderick and Crawford, with the acerbic Helen and the easy-does-it Lester. HE: "Do you mind if I smoke?" SHE: "I don't care if you burn." How often had my brother Ben and I seen their act and how many times had we fallen out of our second balcony seats at the Palace on hearing that line as though for the first time?

★ Mateo Falcone is the hero of a short story of the same name by Prospero Merimee (who wrote the libretto for *Carmen*). Falcone shoots his beloved young son, who has betrayed a fugitive hiding in their barn.

No, Sam and Annie were creatures of different spheres whom some God of the perverse had blessed and cursed into union.

It was my father's popularity among his landsmen and the women that I remember best. He was the one they all sought as a guest at gatherings. He was easy and quiet in speech and small matters, avoided gossip, admired Gene Debs because he thought all union people did that. It was Gene's style of speech, easy as well as fervent, that won them over. My old man puffed away at his Murads, sipped tea and sampled cakes—life was paradise now. Of the mother of us all, Annie, he said little in public; though there was much commiseration offered, he accepted none. The words he would say of her: "She's a nervous woman." He was right. She had from the moment she first appeared anywhere—a weekend *vereins* party, a neighborhood gathering—added not so much a spark as a blast to the proceedings.

Consider a jovial gathering at the home of my wealthy uncle (the one who lent us money for our Chicago adventure, money which we returned), general laughter, sighs of contentment. It all changes in an eyeblink. She appears at the threshold. A sudden silence possesses the parlor. A tension. She merely poses, all 5'1" of her, smiles softly. The hostess timidly approaches her and offers tea and cakes. My mother demurely accepts. The festivities resume, but there is always the fear of some sort of outburst. It could be as mild as a narrowing of the eyes, or of slightly more dramatic intensity.

Often Dora and Herb would appear at these gatherings of landsmen from the shtetl near Bialystok. Dora, working day and night running a bakery, is something of a lackey. Herb, always, always looking for work, somehow never finds any that suits him. Herb's favorite pastime is puffing away on a Charles Denby ten-cent cigar. (Thomas Marshall, Woodrow Wilson's vice president, memorably commented: "What this country needs is a good five-cent cigar.") While Herb is looking heavenward, admiring the smoke rings, my mother simply takes the cigar from his hand. As he watches, she smashes it into the standing ashtray, grinding and grinding until it is bereft of smoke. "So much for you and your ten-cent cigar. Go help Dora in the kitchen. What is she, your slavey?" Perhaps she saw her own mother, Fanny, in Dora. Fanny, the widow baker, her hands huge from kneading, calloused and bruised.

The story goes that Annie had once been engaged to a dentist. It was he who had been her first shot at the brass ring. Though nothing like a great beauty, she was lively, in her quicksilver Ruth Gordon way, but his family had rebuffed her. Not of the same class. On the rebound, she married the easygoing, genial Sam.

Late on Friday nights, still awake though pretending sleep, I'd await my father's return.

I shared my bed with my father. There was a weekly poker game at the Harkaveys'. Usually, my father lost. In no way did that prevent my mother from going through his tossed-aside trousers and searching the pockets. When, on rare occasions, he wound up a winner, she mumbled, "Well, well, well," and extracted a few bills. On the usual empty night of the hunter when the pheasant was not there, she cursed to herself. It was nothing loud, not even bitter; merely further proof that her life was one of wasted chances. As for Sam and Annie, how did these ill-matched two ever share a bed? More to the impertinent point, how did they ever cohabit? Helen Morgan, an iconic singer of American musicals, the ideal torch singer, is, in my mind, seated on the piano top. She sings "Why Was I Born?" Of course. I am guessing that my brothers had joined me in asking the most pertinent of all questions: How were we conceived?

Annie doesn't live here anymore and yet she does in me. I am genetically more hers than his. The imp of the perverse has come to possess me and has had a pretty good run of it. From time to time, a touch of contrition may appear. It is the best way of paying tribute to Annie.

MY HEAD was often swathed in bandages due to my bouts of mastoiditis. It was described as an inflammation of the middle ear and frequently afflicted small boys. Abscesses came uninvited, aches that led us to tightly cup our diseased ears. I have noticed in recent years—say, 2006—young girls and boys walking the streets in like manner; hand over ear, intently listening, oblivious to all surrounding them, including fellow humans. Oh, my God, is there a recurrence of mastoiditis, as may be the case with tuberculosis? No, dearie, it is our young using their cell phones.

I was a constantly sick child. I had a case of whistling asthma. It had its whimsical as well as its traumatic moments. At night, with my whistle-as-I-breathe especially clear, my eldest brother, Meyer, seven years up on me, would sing along, "I'm Forever Blowing Bubbles" or an ethnic pop song, "Lena is the Queen of Palestina." And where did Meyer pick up "I Shook the Hand of the Man Who Shook the Hand of John L. Sullivan"? Ben, five years my senior, would croon "My Gal Sal" or "I Wonder What's Become of Sally." Sally was, hands down, the most popular lost heroine of song and story.

Aside from a foggy memory of being in a Manhattan hospital ward, the mastoid kid, with my bandaged head, my more graphic childhood memories lay in Clinton, an ever-busy street in the Bronx. There was often a moment of awe, and also a show of respect for our betters.

It was usually in the late afternoon that an electric automobile made its ten-miles-an-hour tour of the block. Two elegant elderly ladies were seated up front. They wore Queen Mary hats. Had we worn hats, we'd have doffed them. Our tiny caps did come off. A matter of reflex. What I remember best is the silver lever in place of the steering wheel, so serenely handled. The confident manner— an up, down, and away motion—was an art form wholly strange to the children on the street.

Ours was a triply diverse neighborhood: Irish, Italian, and Jewish. There was the occasional Dutch boy whom we reflexively called Van. He was no child of a wealthy patron. His father was a sanitation employee doing the best he could with the city's considerable detritus. Yet the boy always called on his family's escutcheon: "I am a descendant of Peter Stuyvesant." Unfortunately, his constantly running nose, always wiped clean by his left sleeve (he was a southpaw) didn't help his case.

There was the usual ethnic slurring among the neighborhood's youngbloods (eight, nine, ten were their ripening ages). And there was 1920, when a tripartite understanding overcame. It was the time of the troubles in Ireland; the time Yeats celebrated the birth of "a terrible beauty." It was a time when all the kids on the block became Irish. Terence MacSwaney, Sinn Fein's Lord Mayor of Cork, was on a prison hunger strike of which the whole world was aware. We all wore huge buttons that covered the lapels of our tight little jackets three times over: FREE TERENCE MACSWANEY. After seventy-five days of fasting while in Brixton Prison, he died of starvation and the troubles multiplied. Nonetheless, we had done our bit for Irish freedom. Had we known "Kevin Barry," we'd have sung it out, with more fervor than the Clancy Brothers and Tommy Makem. There was a worldwide protest, no demonstrator more fervent and fiery than my brother, Ben, a flamboyant ten, displaying as many buttons as a cockney pearlie. No shining scholar at school, he astonished all with his eloquence: "A nation which has such citizens will never surrender." Was this our street-talk Ben or a young William Jennings Bryan? My mother immediately touched his forehead to make certain his temperature was 98.6 though she'd settle for 102. Ben had picked up the lingo from his nonscholarly buddy, Quinton Moore, who'd had it smacked into his head by his scholarly brother, Jerry. Jerry had read the item somewhere in a Sinn Fein sheet. It was a comment of Ho Chi Minh, a young dishwasher at a London restaurant just before he latched onto the job as pastry chef for Escoffier at the Ritz of Paris.

The ones we most respected on the block were the big boys on the corner. Getting on their good side was our prime desideratum. They bore their names with a tribal pride: Irish, Dutch, Blackie, Greek. (In fact, though the two left fielders of the Giants and the

Yankees, the Mueller brothers, Emil and Bob, were German, they were popularly known as "Irish" and "Dutch." My brother Ben was a true neighborhood boy. Schooling was not his true love; his mentors and patrons were the big guys on the corner. There was little doubt that of all the kids Ben was their runaway favorite. I can still hear their requests for his throbbing rendition of "Break the News to Mother." They tossed nickels and dimes at him, though there was nothing patronizing about the gesture. It was as though sentimental passersby were paying tribute to a street singer. He picked up enough change in that manner to occasionally take me to a Saturday feature and a Pearl White serial. The Civil War song was to Ben what "Casey at the Bat" was to DeWolf Hopper, or "Over the Rainbow" to Judy Garland.

> Just break da noos to mudder
> Y'know how deah I love 'er
> Tell her not tuh wait fer me
> F'r I'm not comin' ho-o—me.

Now and then, Dutch or Irish or Greek would engage Ben and Quinton, the ten-year-old wonders, to box a wild round or two. Winner take all—a dime. It would usually wind up in a draw and each warrior would be a buffalo nickel richer. Neither Ben nor Quinton knew of the Marquis of Queensberry rules nor did they much care. They aimed for each other's groin; they rabbit punched. And even pivot punched, a maneuver that was outlawed a half-century before.

Meyer was respectfully recognized as the family scholar. He was known in the neighborhood and respected by Irish, Greek, Blackie, and Dutch. It was a case of all being neighborhood boys. He had college in mind and they knew he'd become a teacher. The fact that he enjoyed and understood baseball and was a Giants fan didn't hurt matters. There were few Yankee fans in the community, even among the Italian kids. This was in the pre-DiMaggio days and Tony Lazzeri was the only recognized name.

Bulldog was our baseball aficionado. I, not much for anything physical, merely a good listener, was his perfect audience. Thanks to him I could rattle off the million-dollar infield—George "High-pockets" Kelly; Frankie Frisch, the Fordham Flash; Davey Bancroft; and Heinie Groh, recently acquired with his bottle bat from the Cincy Reds; he was the bunting artist. John McGraw was of course our god.

Bulldog didn't mind his block-given name because he did indeed bear a remarkable resemblance to the species. Bill Mauldin recalls his encounter with General George Patton and his most dear companion, his bulldog. Bill, a kid combat correspondent in World War II, was a cartoonist; his protagonists being Willie and Joe, a couple of footsloggers. On occasion, Mauldin had some masterpieces ribbing the pompous brass. Who was better meat than Patton? One day, the general, furious, demands the presence of Mauldin. The kid peeks into the office and recalls: There was Patton, in one chair, glaring; there was his bulldog in the other, usually fearsome. "I looked into two pair of the meanest eyes I'd ever seen in my life."

No, my baseball mentor was a progressive kid, more of the John Dewey type. When I hesitated in guessing the name of a baseball manager, he'd break a branch off a tree. "Branch Rickey," I'd exclaim.

What I best remembered as we left New York for Chicago was a play Bulldog told me about. It was during the Cleveland Indians–Brooklyn Dodgers World Series of 1920. A second baseman of the Indians pulled off an unassisted triple play. It was the only time ever it occurred in a World Series. Bill Wambsganss was his name. Every fan called him Wamby.

There was one more celebrated name I remember from our journey to Chicago. How could I disremember Professor Émile Coué, who made the front page for months? His credo for good health: Simply think and repeat, "Every day in every way, I'm feeling better and better."

As I recall, Professor Coué had a well-trimmed beard and a per-
petual smile. Fifty years later, I ran into his kindred spirit, W.
Clement Stone. He headed what was probably the country's most
successful insurance outfit, the Combined Insurance Company. He
owned the building plus just about everything else within reach.
He contributed more to Richard Nixon's "Four More Years" campaign than any other American.

Behind a mahogany desk, huge, sits the ebullient CEO. He is little, wears a pencil-thin mustache and a wide bow tie. He is in *Fortune* magazine as one of America's new centi-millionaires. The
corridors are enriched with familiar, beloved waltz and foxtrot
tunes. He immediately presents me with several books: *Success
Through a Positive Mental Attitude*; *The Success System That Never
Fails*; and *Think and Grow Rich*. He refers to the last.

> That's the greatest book that came out of the Depression, by
> Napoleon Hill. That motivated more people to success than any
> book you could read by a living author.
>
> As for me, first of all I thank God for my blessings. Then I'd use
> a very simple prayer: Please God, help me sell. Please God, help me
> sell. Please God, help me sell. I say it at least four times each morn-
> ing, facing the mirror. This did many things, the mystic power of
> prayer; it got me keyed up. I threw all the energy I had into it. Im-
> mediately, I'd relax and go to a movie—and then, r-r-r-ight.

"So you recall any of those sad moments during those hard
days?" I asked.

"I don't believe in sadness. I believe if you have a problem it is
good. Maybe I had a poor day. I'd rest, go to movie. The next day
would be a rrrrecorrrrrrd day." He and Professor Coué were true
kindred spirits. Kindred spirits. I like that. Rrrrright. And so with
Mr. Stone's kindred spirit and the miracle of Wamby's triple play in
mind, I was on my way Chicago, The City of I Will. (I'd neither
heart nor mind to ask Nelson Algren's question: "What if I can't?")

2

Bound for Glory*

Bound for Glory (1920)
Away up in the northward,
Right on the borderline,
A great commercial city,
Chicago, you will find.
Her men are all like Abelard,
Her women like Heloise [rhymes with "noise"]—
All honest, virtuous people,
For they live in Elanoy.

So move your family westward,
Bring all your girls and boys,
And rise to wealth and honor
In the state of Elanoy.
   —A nineteenth-century folk song

When Abe Lincoln came out of the wilderness and loped off with the Republican nomination on that memorable May day, 1860, the Wigwam had been resonant with whispers. Behind cupped hands, lips imperceptibly moved: We just give Si Cameron Treasury, they

---

* Parts excerpted from *Chicago* (Pantheon, 1985 and 1986).

give us Pennsylvania, Abe's got it wrapped up. OK wit'chu? A wink. A nod. Done. It was a classic deal, Chicago style.

As ten thousand spectators roared on cue, Seward didn't know what hit him. His delegates had badges but no seats. Who you? Dis seat's mine. Possession's nine-tent's a da law, ain't it?

Proud Seward, the overwhelming favorite, was a New Yorker who had assumed that civilization ended west of the Hudson. He knew nothing of the young city's spirit of I Will.

When, in 1920, Warren Gamaliel Harding was similarly touched by Destiny, there had been no such whisperings in the Coliseum. Just desultory summer mumblings (it was an unseasonably hot June: 100 degrees outside, 110 inside; bamboo fans of little use): Lowden, Wood, Johnson. Wood, Johnson, Lowden. Johnson, Lowden, Wood. Three frontrunners and not a one catching fire. How long can this go on? Four ballots are enough. C'mon, it's too hot for a deadlock. Shall we pick straws?

But this wasn't just any conversation city. This was Chicago. Never mind the oratory. Yeah, yeah, we know about the Coliseum where, in 1896, the cry was Bryan, Bryan, Bryan as the Boy Orator thundered eloquently of crowns of thorns and crosses of gold. Nah, nah, let's settle this Chicago style.

A hotel room not far away.

The Blackstone, so often graced by Caruso and Galli-Curci during our city's lush opera season, was on this occasion beyond grace. Nah, nah, it's too hot. Maybe the Ohio Gang ran things that day, but with blowing curlicues heavenward from H. Upmann cigars in the smoke-filled room, the deal—Harding, OK?—was strictly My Kind of Town, Chicago Is.

As for my city, Chicago, yet, along came Jane Addams. Was it in 1889 that she founded Hull House? The lady was out of her depth, they said. Imagine. Trying to change a neighborhood of immigrants, scared and lost, where every other joint was a saloon and every street a cesspool. And there was John Powers, alderman of the Nineteenth Ward, running the turf in the fashion of his First Ward colleagues, Bathhouse John and Hinky Dink. Johnny Da Pow, the Italian immigrants called him. He was the Pooh-Bah, the high muckety-muck, the ultimate clout. Everything had to be cleared through Da Pow. Still, this lady with the curved spine, but a spine nonetheless, stuck it out. And something happened.

She told young Jessie Binford: Everything grows from the bottom up. This place belongs to everybody, not just Johnny Da Pow. And downtown. No, she told Jessie, I have no blueprint. We learn from life itself.

So many years later, years of small triumphs and large losses, Jessie Binford, ninety, is seated in a small Blackstone Hotel room. The Blackstone again, for God's sake? It isn't a smoke-filled room this time. My cigar, still wrapped in cellophane, is deep in my pocket. It's an H. Upmann—would you believe it? The old woman, looking not unlike Whistler's mother, is weary and in despair. The wrecking ball had just yesterday done away with Hull House and most of the neighborhood. Even the beloved elm beneath her window had been uprooted and removed.

The boys downtown tried to buy off Jessie Binford. You can live at the Blackstone as our guest for the rest of your life, they told her. Anything to keep her quiet. She and a young neighborhood housewife, Florence Scala, were making a big deal out of this. Sshhh. But they wouldn't shush, these two.

THESE TWO.

Florence Scala, first-generation Italian-American. Her father, a tailor, was a romantic from Tuscany. He was a lover of opera, of course, especially Caruso records, even the scratchy ones. He had astronomy fever, too, though his longing to visit the Grand Canyon transcended his yen to visit the moon. He was to make neither voyage. The neighborhood was his world and that was enough.

For Florence, her father's daughter, the neighborhood reflected the universe, with its multicolors, its varied immigrant life, its circumambient passions.

Jessie Binford, of early Quaker-American stock. Her father, a merchant, trudging from Ohio to Iowa in the mid–nineteenth century, found what he was looking for. The house he built in 1874 "still stands as fundamentally strong as the day it was built," his daughter observed. At the turn of the century, she found what she was looking for: a mission, Hull House, and a place, Harrison-Halsted. She found the neighborhood.

For Florence Scala and Jessie Binford, Harrison-Halsted was Blake's little grain of sand.

They passed each other on early-morning strolls along these streets, not yet mean. They came to know each other and value each other, as they clasped hands to save these streets. They lost, of course. Betrayed right down the line. By our city's Most Respectable.

"I'm talking about the boards of trustees, the people who control the money. Downtown bankers, factory owners, architects, people in the stock market." Florence speaks softly, and that, if anything, accentuates the bitterness.

> The jet set, too. The young people, grandchildren of the old-timers on the board, who were not like elders, if you know what I mean. They were not with us. There were also some very good people, those from the old days. But they didn't count any more.
>
> This new crowd, these new tough kind of board members, who didn't mind being on the board for the prestige it gave them, dominated. These were the people closely aligned to the city government, in real estate and planning. And some very fine old Chicago families.

As Florence describes the antecedents of today's yuppies, she laughs ever so gently. "The nicest people in Chicago."

．　．　．

MISS BINFORD is leaving Chicago forever. She had come to Hull House in 1906. She is going home to die. Marshalltown, Iowa. The town her father helped found.

The blue of her eyes is dimmed through her spectacles. Her passion, undimmed. "Miss Addams understood why each person had become what he was. She didn't condemn because she understood what life does to people, to those of us who have everything and those of us who have nothing." It's been a rough day and her words, clearly offered, become somewhat slurry now. "Today we're getting further and further away from this eternal foundation on which community life must rest. I feel most sorry for our young people that are growing up at this time . . ." It's dusk and time to let her go. I press the STOP button of my Uher.

Our double-vision, double-standard, double-value, and double-cross have been patent ever since—at least, ever since the earliest of our city fathers took the Potawatomis for all they had. Poetically, these dispossessed natives dubbed this piece of turf "Chikagou." Some say it is Indian lingo for "City of the Wild Onion;" some say it really means "City of the Big Smell." "Big" is certainly the operative word around these parts.

Nelson Algren's classic *Chicago: City on the Make* is the late poet's single-hearted vision of his town's doubleness. "Chicago . . . forever keeps two faces, one for winners and one for losers; one for hustlers and one for squares . . . One face for Go-Getters and one for Go-Get-It-Yourselfers. One for poets and one for promoters . . . One for early risers, one for evening hiders."

It is the city of Jane Addams, settlement worker, and Al Capone, entrepreneur; of Clarence Darrow, lawyer, and Julius Hoffman, judge; of Louis Sullivan, architect, and Sam Insull, magnate; of John Altgeld, governor, and Paddy Bauler, alderman. (Paddy's the one who some years ago observed, "Chicago ain't ready for reform." It is echoed in our day by other, less paunchy aldermen.)

It is still the arena of those who dream of the City of Man and those who envision a City of Things. The battle appears to be forever joined. The armies, ignorant and enlightened, clash by day as well as by night. Chicago is America's dream, writ large. And flamboyantly.

PARADOX: Today's council members opposing the younger Mayor Daley are more diffuse, less cohesive, of all color, affording the son of the old Buddha more power than his old man had.

It has—as they used to whisper of the town's fast women—a reputation.

Elsewhere in the world, anywhere, name the city, name the country, Chicago evokes one image above all others. Sure, architects and those interested in such matters mention Louis Sullivan, Frank Lloyd Wright, and Mies van der Rohe. Hardly anyone in his right mind questions this city as the architectural Athens. Others, literary critics among them, mention Dreiser, Norris, Lardner, Algren, Farrell, Bellow, and the other Wright, Richard. Sure, Mencken did say something to the effect that there is no American literature worth mentioning that didn't come out of the palatinate that is Chicago. Of course, a special kind of jazz and a blues, acoustic rural and electrified urban, have been called "Chicago style." All this is indubitably true.

Still others, for whom history has stood still since the Democratic convention of 1968, murmur: Mayor Daley. (As Chicago's most perceptive chronicler, Mike Royko, pointed out, the name has become the eponym for "city chieftain"; thus, it is often one word, "mare-daley.") The tone, in distant quarters as well as here, is usually one of awe; you may interpret it any way you please. "Who's the mare-daley of your town?"

Hog Butcher for the World, Tool Maker, Stacker of Wheat, Player with Railroads and the Nation's Freight Handler; Stormy, husky, brawling, City of the Big Shoulders . . .

Carl Sandburg, the white-haired old Swede with the wild cowlick, drawled out that brag in 1914. Today, he is regarded in more soft-spoken quarters as an old gaffer, out of fashion, more attuned to the street corner than the class in American studies. Unfortunately, there is some truth to the charge that his dug-out-of-the-mud city, sprung-out-of-the-fire-of-1871 Chicago, is no longer what it was when the Swede sang that song. It is no longer the slaughterhouse of the hang-from-the-hoof hogs. The stockyards have gone to feedlots in, say, Clovis, New Mexico, or Greeley, Colorado, or Logansport, Indiana. It is no longer the railroad center, when there were at least seven awesome depots where a thousand passenger trains refueled themselves each day; and it is no longer, since the Great Depression of the 1930s, the stacker of wheat.

During all these birth years of the twenty-first century, the unique landmarks of American cities have been replaced by Golden Arches, Red Lobsters, Pizza Huts, and Marriotts, so you can no longer tell one neon wilderness from another. As your plane lands, you no longer see old landmarks, old signatures. You have no idea where you may be. A few years ago, while I was on a wearisome book tour, I mumbled to the switchboard operator at the motel, "Please wake me at six a.m. I must be in Cleveland by noon." Came the response: "Sir, you are in Cleveland." That Chicago, too, has so been affected is of small matter. It has been and always will be, in the memory of the nine-year-old boy arriving here, the archetypal American city.

One year after Warren G. Harding's anointment, almost to the day, the boy stepped off the coach at the La Salle Street depot. He had come from east of the Hudson and had been warned by the kids on the Bronx block to watch out for Indians. The Blackhawks. The boy felt not unlike Ruggles, the British butler, on his way to Red Gap. Envisioning painted faces and feathered war bonnets.

In Kiev, in 1963, I ran into kids who on hearing me say "Chicago" burst into laughter. They waved imaginary hockey sticks and howled out "Blackhawks!"

. . .

AUGUST 1921. The boy had sat up all night, but had never been more awake and exhilarated. At Buffalo, the vendors had passed through the aisles. A cheese sandwich and a half-pint carton of milk was all he had had during the twenty-hour ride. But on this morning of the great awakening, he wasn't hungry.

His older brother was there at the station. Grinning, gently jabbing at his shoulder. He twisted the boy's cap around. "Hey, Nick Altrock," the brother said. He knew the boy knew that this baseball clown with the turned-around cap had once been a great pitcher for the White Sox. The boy's head as well as his cap was awhirl.

There was expensive-looking luggage carried off the Pullmans. Those were the cars up front, a distant planet away from the day coaches. There were cool Palm Beach–suited men and even cooler, lightly clad women stepping down from these cars. Black men in red caps—all called George—were wheeling luggage carts toward the terminal. My God, all those bags for just two people. "Twentieth Century Limited," the brother whispered. "Even got a barbershop on that baby."

There were straw suitcases and bulky bundles borne elsewhere. There were all those other travelers, some lost, others excitable in heavy, unseasonable clothing. Their talk was broken English or a strange language or an American accent foreign to the boy. Where were the Indians?

This was Chicago, indubitably the center of the nation's railways, as the Swede from Galesburg had so often sung out. Chicago to Los Angeles. Chicago to Anywhere. All roads led to and from Chicago. No wonder the boy was bewitched.

Chicago has always been and still is the City of Hands. Horny, calloused hands. Yet, here they came: the French voyageurs; the Anglo traders; the German burghers, many of whom were the children of those dreamers who dared dream of better worlds. So it was that the Chicago Symphony Orchestra came into being; one of the world's most highly regarded. It was originally Teutonic in its repertoire; now it is universal.

They came, too, from Eastern Europe as hands. The Polish population of Chicago is second only to that of Warsaw. They came from the Mediterranean and from below the Rio Grande; and there was always the inner migration from Mississippi, Arkansas, Louisiana, and Tennessee. The African American journalist grandson of slaves spoke with a touch of nostalgia, memories of his hometown, Paris. That is, Paris, Tennessee. "Out in the fields, we'd hear the whistle of the Illinois Central engineer. OOOweee! There goes the IC to—Chica-a-ago!" It was even referred to in the gospel song "City Called Heaven."

The city called heaven, where there were good jobs in the mills and you did not have to get off the sidewalk when a white passed by. Jimmy Rushing sang the upbeat blues, "Goin' to Chicago, Baby, Sorry I Can't Take You."

It wasn't quite heaven. In 1919, an African American boy swam into a zone considered white and was stoned into the waves, setting off the riots of 1919.

Here I came in 1921, the nine-year-old, who for the next fifteen years lived and clerked at the rooming house, run by my mother, and the Wells-Grand Hotel. (My ailing father ran it for its first several years, and then my mother, a much tougher customer, took over.)

To me, it was simply referred to as the Grand, the Chicago prototype of the posh pre-Hitler Berlin Hotel. It was here I encountered our aristocrats as guests: the boomer firemen, who blazed our railroad engines; the seafarers who sailed the Great Lakes; the self-educated craftsmen, known as the Wobblies but whose proper name was the Industrial Workers of the World (IWW). Here in our lobby, they went head-to-head with their *bêtes noires*, the anti-union stalwarts, who tabbed "IWW" as the acronym for "I Won't Work."

Oh, those were wild, splendiferous debates, outdoing in decibel power the Lincoln-Douglas bouts. These were the Hands of Chicago making themselves heard loud and clear. It was the truly Grand Hotel, and I felt like the concierge of the Ritz of Paris.

There were labor battles, historic ones, where the fight for the eight-hour day had begun. It brought forth the song: "Eight hours we'd have for working, eight hours we'd have for play, eight hours for sleeping, in free Amerikay." It was in Chicago that the Haymarket Affair took place and four men were hanged in a farcical trial that earned our city the world's opprobrium. Yet it is to our city's honor that our governor, John Peter Altgeld, pardoned the three surviving defendants in one of the most eloquent documents ever issued on behalf of justice.

The simple truth is that our God, Chicago's God, is Janus, the two-faced one. One is that of Warner Brothers films with Jimmy Cagney and Edward G. Robinson as our sociopathic icons. The other is that of Jane Addams, who introduced the idea of the Chicago Woman and world citizen.

It was Chicago that brought forth Louis Sullivan, whom Frank Lloyd Wright referred to as "Lieber Meister." Sullivan envisioned the skyscraper. It was here that he wanted to touch the heavens. Nor was it any accident that young Sullivan corresponded with the elderly Walt Whitman, because they both dreamed of democratic vistas, where Chicago was the City of Man rather than the City of Things. Though Sullivan died broke and neglected, it is his memory that glows as he is recalled by those who followed Wright.

What the nine-year-old boy felt about Chicago in 1921 is a bit more mellow and seared. He is aware of its carbuncles and warts, a place far from heaven, but it is his town, the only one he calls home.

Nelson Algren, Chicago's bard, said it best: "Like loving a woman with a broken nose, you may well find lovelier lovelies. But never a lovely so real."

3

The Rooming House

The Gilded Age was coming to an end as a new century was beginning. The robber barons had a lush life, mostly at the expense of immigrant women slaving away at the textile mills and their men at the railroad yards.

The Republican, Warren Gamaliel Harding, had become president and promised an era of "back to normalcy."

The changes had taken place: the Jazz Age, the Stutz Bearcat, the pocket flask, the bobbed hair.

WE HAD FIFTY ROOMS, corner of Ashland and Flournoy, on Chicago's Near West Side. The area was primarily Italian, though there were several rooming houses around and about. Single-room occupancies were what they really were, though there were a couple of "suites" where hotplates and light housekeeping was in certain circumstances allowed.

Cook County Hospital, the biggest medical institution in the world, was only two years old and a few blocks away. Many of the dormitories had not yet been built. There was, you may imagine, a mingling of student nurses and interns in our establishment, and something considerably more than mingling on occasion. Laborers and semi-skilled workers, working for the city, were, by and large, our patrons.

One of them, an Italian railroad worker, brought in his maiden aunt Josefina, who had been raised in a Calabrian village and never had left it until this moment. She was a stranger in a strange land. He had paid her way to America and paid her rent at the rooming house. He made it clear to my mother, hoping she'd consent, that Josefina would need special attention. My mother was sympathetic enough to allow her light-housekeeping privileges. In fact, she helped her guest in shopping. And when there were occasional complaints about the exotic aroma of Italian food, Annie shushed them immediately. Annie treated her as a soft person in a hard world. This was the paradox that was my mother.

Annie was sympathetic to women who were in trouble. She was a crazy kind of feminist, a red-stocking feminist. This young hooker lived at the rooming house, though she didn't bring people up to her room. This little guy Froggy was the pimp who kept her, paid for her room. One day screaming is heard. Froggy is beating the hell out of her, smacking her around. Mother comes in and starts swinging at him. Bam, bam, bam. Not little scratches; tight little fists, bone-hard. He didn't know what the hell to do. "You touch her again, I'll kill you." Poor Froggy ended up all bloody, and that was the last we saw of him.

Among the other guests were single women doing secretarial work. One such was Helena Turner, the "protégé" of a successful florist, Jimmy Bonavaglia, who paid her weekly rent. At one time, he was delinquent for several weeks. My mother approached him and asked for the money. He was about Annie's height, and raised himself to his full five-feet-one. He said, "Do you know who you're talking to?"

"No, who am I talking to?"

"Jimmy Bonavaglia."

"Do you know who you're talking to?

"Who am I talking to?"

"You're talking to Annie Terkel." She collected.

There's a poignant postscript to the story of Helena Turner. She was obviously a lonesome dove. My brother Ben was then about eighteen and something of a precocious Don Giovanni. He had worked as a shipping clerk at a mail-order house nearby, as well as beginning a career as a shoe dog, a salesman. His big night was Friday, when he attended Paddy Harmon's Dreamland Ballroom. It's where young women who did the anonymous work of offices in tall buildings went—secretaries, operators, and file clerks. And sometimes, if my brother was fortunate, a nurse. Nurses were considered a cut above the others.

(I frequently followed Ben to the Dreamland Ballroom. I was caught by this music that so excited me—jazz. The patrons, lowly though their status in life may have been, were solely white. The musicians were all black. How could I forget Lottie Hightower and her High Steppers, and, on occasion, Charlie Cook? There was, of course, a quid pro quo to this privilege. As soon as I sensed a score on my brother's part, I'd rush back to the rooming house, make certain our mother was asleep, enter a vacant room, and prepare the bed with fresh linens. Oh God, when I think what I might have become. With these natural instincts of mine, I might have been a favored advisor to presidents, or a corporate executive knowing the thoughts and longings of the CEO. Think of it: suggest firing several thousand of the lowlies, pick up a million-dollar bonus, and make the front page of the business section of our favorite newspaper.)

Helena Turner never went to such ballrooms. I've a hunch she'd have delighted to dance with Ben; but Jimmy Bonavaglia kept a sharp eye on Helena as well as on his stockpile of gladioli. What I do know as a certainty: Ben visited Helena in her room more than now and then. Some years later, just before we sold the rooming house, Ben picked up the newspaper. He was casually having a look-see at the sports page when a notice in the obituaries caught his attention. His mumbling suddenly stopped; his easy-come, easy-go manner vanished as his face assumed a bloodless pallor. He showed me the obit notice: Helena Turner had committed suicide. "Do you remember who she was?"

"The name rings a bell." A pause; something of a sigh.

"She was someone I knew." And he knew I knew.

SOME YEARS LATER, when I came across *Look Homeward, Angel* by Thomas Wolfe, I associated Annie Terkel with Eliza Gant, the narrator's mother: small, bony, swift, and murder on deadbeats. Eliza ran Dixieland, a boarding house in Altamont (Asheville). American Style was its generic name: meals along with rooms. Ours was European Style: rooms only. Now and then, a guest working in the city's sanitation department, after the thankless job of keeping Chicago clean, was too weary to visit the all-night diner nearby. My mother, for two bits, would toss him a piece of lettuce, a thin slab of beef, and a boiled potato. On seeing the greenery, what little there was of it, an indignant howl was heard from the usually quiet man, "What am I, a rabbit?"

"Hetty Green"—Henrietta Howland Green, 1835–1916. My mother knew all about her when she took over the rooming house in 1921. I never could figure out how she came to know Hetty so much better than she knew Jane Addams, who founded Hull House only blocks away from us. How could this be, a matter of defying both geography and the calendar? I think I know. It was a sudden empathy my mother felt for a genius of her gender beating the male of the species at his own game.

Hetty Green, at the age of six, was immersed in reading the financial section of the newspaper to her ailing father. Yes, Annie knew of Mme. Curie and Rosa Raisa,★ but their giftedness is not what attracted Annie. Hetty became known as the richest woman in the world—her spheres were special: investment, real estate holdings, understanding of the market, free or free-fall. She also had a reputation for being the most miserly; that she was tight-fisted was obvious to anyone who had dealings with her. She never turned on

★ The celebrated opera singer who came from Annie's hometown of Bialystok.

the heat, nor used hot water. She wore one old black dress and undergarments that she changed only after they'd been worn out. Yet in the panic of 1907, she bailed out New York City with a million-dollar loan. It was not a philanthropist's gesture: she took it out in short-term bonds and picked up millions in repayment.

In defense of Annie, though in all business dealings she simply assumed she was about to be cheated, my mother never reached Hetty's level of parsimony. Though on occasion, Annie did try to save a penny or two in buying Octagon soap, a product quite abrasive and not meant for the human body. My father would sometimes sneak in a bar of Ivory soap: 99 and 44/100 percent pure. Annie could never have been indicted for undue philanthropy. She had a coin or two for the wayfaring mendicant, provided the unfortunate one was a woman. Males with outstretched hands were beggars and bums.

Of course, she knew of the Triangle Fire in Manhattan where management had locked exits while working girls died after flying through the air. Of course, she was for labor unions. She, as a matter of rote, even expressed admiration for Gene Debs. But it was the saga of Hetty Green that most enthralled her. She would not have minded being called the "Witch of Wall Street." Hetty caught the brass ring; my mother missed it, though she flew through the air. Luckily there was a net: the rooming house.

In seeing William Bolcom's opera *McTeague*, based upon the Frank Norris novel and Erich von Stroheim's film *Greed*, I thought of my mother, Eliza Gant, and Hetty Green. Catherine Malfitano, the soprano who played the role of Trina, the young charwoman who wins the lottery, sensed a real challenge.

"I feel uplifted by Alban Berg's Lulu, who is murdered by Jack the Ripper. Salome, after having this man decapitated and singing to that head, I felt uplifted, really. I did not feel so after *McTeague*." She spoke of a key scene in which Trina is in bed with the gold coins as though with a lover. "There is nothing uplifting in loving an inanimate subject, especially when it's money." [I'm reminded of current perverse and, to me, pornographic TV commercials, where flesh-and-blood actors court machines, usually cars.] "There is something empty in that emotional experience of being so in love with money and fearful of falling in love with other humans. Isn't that called a fetish? Trina is the embodiment of this kind of avarice. To have a scene where you can be in bed with all your golden coins and let them fall all over your body like the gentlest caress of a lover is frightening beyond belief. She is no longer with McTeague. She is just a cleaning woman . . . she forgets all about her exhaustion, her cares, as she gives herself to the magic sound of her golden babies."★

MEYER WAS BACK AND FORTH between Chicago and New York. Much of the time, he was absent from the family while in New York earning his degree in education at CCNY and courting his childhood sweetheart, Sophie, to whom he was to be married; their union would last thirty years.

My father's heart, by this time, was in worse shape than ever, and he was frustrated at being stuck to his bed. I had been, for most of my life, my father's bedmate. And again, we were together listening to the crystal set, which consisted of a piece of mineral and a thin wire you had to wind around and around. We'd hear KYW, with Wendell Hall at the ukelele. The red-headed music maker he was called, and of course, the song we knew:

> It ain't gonna rain, no more, no more.
> It ain't gonna rain no more.
> How in the heck are you gonna wash your neck
> if it ain't gonna rain no more?

It was 1925 and we listened to WGN, with Quinn Ryan at the microphone, broadcasting the Scopes Trial of Dayton, Tennessee—

★ *And They All Sang* (The New Press, 2005, pp. 73–74).

the Monkey Trial. A young teacher was being penalized for violating a state ordinance prohibiting the teaching of Darwin. His defense attorney was Clarence Darrow, the brilliant agnostic. The prosecution's most prestigious witness was William Jennings Bryan. We were listening as the world heard Darrow humiliating Bryan on the matter of Jonah and the whale; the Nebraskan claiming that Jonah set up light housekeeping in the belly of the whale. It was Bryan who said, "Instead of studying the age of rocks, sing 'Rock of Ages.' " The week after the trial ended, Bryan died. It was attributed to diabetes, but we know deep down it was the humiliation and the heartbreak he suffered. Therein lay the tragedy of the populist William Jennings Bryan. Out of Nebraska, he was known as the Boy Orator of North Platte. When he spoke, the audience was mesmerized. He was anti-corporate, anti–the Big Boys, and pro–the small farmer. During the 1896 Democratic convention at the Coliseum, he was at his most eloquent: "You shall not press down upon the brow of Labor this crown of thorns, you shall not crucify mankind on a cross of gold."

The profound tragedy of William Jennings Bryan was the conflict between his secular and religious beliefs; yet, he himself saw no such struggle. Even today, due in no small part to the success of the play and film *Inherit the Wind*, a great many of us see a fool KO'd by a witty man. He, as a mere congressman, three times candidate for president, represented the small, beleaguered farmers, those up against it. He fought against the Gilded Age robber barons, the corporate bigwigs, with an eloquence rare, and fervor unending, his battle waged in so soaring a manner that he caught fire as the populist hero of working stiffs everywhere. Remember, too, that he turned down President Wilson's offer of Secretary of State; in fact, he resigned on learning that Wilson was planning entry into World War I. His lucid eloquence, seemingly improvised, has hardly been matched.

Though to many of the intelligentsia (what a lovingly sadistic time H.L. Mencken had with Bryan) and the urban "learned," circumstances meant one thing; for the poor, bedraggled farmer, who sang "Poor Pilgrim of Sorrow," circumstances meant something else.

Now, some eighty years gone by and we still have a problem with creationism, without determining where the ache lies.

There were more country songs written about Bryan than about Abe Lincoln; at least twenty-five. Just about every country-song bard had one, including Vernon Dalhart, whom my father and I heard so often on the crystal set. Surely, you of an age remember "The Prisoner's Song"—"Oh, I wish I had the wings of an angel, over those walls I would fly."

Here's a Carson Robison song, written in grief shortly after Bryan's death. Years later, I heard a kid sing a few stanzas of this one in a Pennsylvania town, Girard.

> Oh, the folks in Tennessee are as faithful as can be,
> And they know the Bible teaches what is right.
> They believe in God above and his great undying love,
> And they know they are protected by his might.
> Then to Dayton came a man with his new ideas so grand
> And he said we came from monkeys long ago.
> But in teaching his belief, Mr. Scopes found only grief
> For they would not let their old religion go.
> Oh, you must not doubt the word that is written by the Lord,
> For if you do your house will surely fall.
> And Mr. Scopes will learn that wherever you may turn
> The old religion's better after all.

WHAT EXCITED MY FATHER MOST was that we were one block away from Lindlahr, the hospital where Eugene B. Debs, his number-one hero, was spending his last days. Debs was visited by those who were to us the celebrities of the time: Sinclair Lewis, Upton Sinclair, Theodore Dreiser, Ida Tarbell. Often we'd take a slow walk and hang around the corner outside Lindlahr, just as young groupies later waited for Mick Jagger, wondering who of our favorite muckrakers would be there. The irony was, Debs was no longer there. He had been moved to the hospital in Elmhurst, where he died.

Unfortunately, neither my father nor I knew too much of Bryan, being most ignorant of the farmers' trials and tribulations. Oh, we knew the phrases "Crown of Thorns," and "crucified on the Cross of Gold," but that's about all. It was Gene Debs whose glory possessed Sam. Of course, he knew the statement old Gene made on the day of his conviction for treason. Remember that? Oh, Jesus, how could you? Your grandmother had hardly been born. It was in Canton, Ohio, in 1916. Debs was challenging Wilson's plan to enter World War I. As he was sentenced to Atlanta Penitentiary for ten years, Gene spoke up: "While there is a lower class I am in it; while there is a criminal element, I am of it; while there is a soul in prison, I am not free."

It was President Harding, a Republican political toy, who, as one of his first acts in office, granted Debs his pardon. It so happened that the genial Harding and Gene were mutual admirers of the film cowboy hero Tom Mix. Was that a factor in Harding's inviting Debs to the White House? In fact, he not only invited Debs. He ordered Harry Daugherty, his attorney general, who escaped prison himself on a technicality, to put Debs on the train without a guard. Woodrow Wilson, our professorial chieftain, was a movie fan, too. According to Eric Foner, the American historian, Wilson found *Birth of a Nation* "as awful as lightning, but unfortunately true, quite true."

Eugene Salvatore, in his biography of Eugene Debs, reveals to us the deep affection and love Debs' fellow inmates of Atlanta felt for him, and what happened during his farewell as his old buddies met him at the Atlanta gates.

As they joyfully and tearfully embraced and fervently kissed one another, a low rumbling in the background intensified. Warden Fred Zerbst, in violation of every prison regulation, had opened each cell block to allow more than 2,300 inmates to throng to the front of the main jail building to bid a final good-bye to their friend. Turning away from the prison, Gene started down the long walkway to the parked car. As he did, a roar of pain and love welled up from the prison behind him. With tears streaming down his face, he turned and, hat in hand, stretched out his arms. Twice more, as he walked to the car, the prisoners demanded his attention. Twice more he reached to embrace them . . . ★

There is a grotesque epilogue to the story of Gene Debs and his life and meaning. The dean of the Yale Law School, who advised LBJ during his lowest days, the Vietnam War, continued as governmental wise man. He was LBJ's coldest warrior during the Vietnam War. His name was Eugene V. Rostow. His folks were admirers of old Gene; so was he. Did the irony of this escape the former Yale Law School dean?

Some years earlier, at the Wells-Grand Hotel, a guest, Harold Hanson Utterbach, swears he attended Debs' funeral; likewise that he had heard Bryan at his most eloquent at the Coliseum in 1896; and furthermore, that he saw Babe Ruth point to the right-field stands of Cubs Park in advance of the Bambino's long-flying home run to that very region. I've a hunch he was a liar, but what the hell, his stories made the day go faster. This information was offered in 1936, about a year or so before we ceased our hoteliers' life. I figured this one story might be truth; the arithmetic made sense. In any event, he was a fairly old gaffer and entitled to some poetic license. I know a little something about that.

I now roam back to the rooming house where the time had come for my father to demand a change in our lives. He could not spend his last days as an invalid. There was some work he had to do. My mother, astonishingly, agreed that a change was necessary. They decided on an amicable pro-tem split. My mother would join Meyer in New York and relax. My father, through a loan from his brother-in-law, raised enough to lease a men's hotel in Chicago.

★ *Eugene V. Debs: Citizen and Socialist* (University of Illinois Press, 1982, p. 328).

4

The Convention That Would Never End

A-*la-ba-ma! Twenty-foah votes fo Un-da-wood!* How clinically I re-member the sound and slight fury of that voice of the Deep South. Translated into English, the single language we should all speak, as our self-proclaimed philologists demand, it was: "Alabama, twenty-four votes for Underwood." His was, for 102 ballots, the first delegate's voice to be heard during each session. I don't know his name, simply that the same Southern voice spoke again and again. Tom Walsh, Senator from Montana, was the chairman of the 1924 convention. He was my hero. My elder brother had told me that Thomas Walsh, of the no-nonsense full black mustache, was the *bête noire* of Anaconda Copper, the corporation that ran Montana. So, too, it was with the junior senator from that state, his fellow populist, Burton K. Wheeler.

Let's go back a bit. It is summertime, 1924, and the living is fairly easy. I am the guest at a resort in South Haven, Michigan. My mother insisted that I was suffering from something called rheumatic heart fever and that fresh air of the lake would help. As well as the good food. In fact, the favorite—the only—question my fellow guests put to one another was: "What's for dinner?"

For some reason I cannot determine, even now, at ninety-four, what the attraction those radio voices had for me was. My interest in this convention simply happened because it was the same year that Senator Bob LaFollette was running for president on a Progressive Party ticket. Poetically enough, Burton K. Wheeler was his running mate. It seems I was interested in how major parties ran things. While my contemporaries were outside in the hot sun splashing cold water at one another, I was glued to the slightly worn easy chair, mesmerized by those orotund voices. Remember now, this had been going on for some time—in fact, for my whole vacation. It didn't bother me at all. It was in the nature of relief. Were it not for that delegate from Alabama and Tom Walsh, I'd be splashing water at another twelve-year-old and listening to my elders discussing their disappointment with the lunch they had just ravished, demolished, and consigned to their insatiable guts.

Intermittently, a well-appointed matron, for whom the least deadly of the seven sins was gluttony, would freight her way toward my throne. "You on a fast or something? If you don't eat, you die." I thanked her for her prescription as my attention wandered back to the Atwater-Kent and the prosecutorial voice of Tom Walsh.

Why did the contest last so long? There was a deadlock: William Gibbs McAdoo, Woodrow Wilson's son-in-law and the secretary of the treasury, versus Al Smith, the popular governor of New York. That Smith was the first Catholic ever put up for the presidency was the Roman candle that set off all those fireworks. The KKK was going crazy, white-sheeted all over the state of Indiana and a number of other border states.

The Teapot Dome scandal didn't amount to much in the campaign. It had happened during the administration of Warren Harding.*

---

* The scandal involved the leasing of oil-rich pieces of land in Wyoming and California to private interests. Harding's Secretary of the Interior, Albert Fall, went to the pokey; so did his multimillion-dollar buddy, Frank Doheny. What is astonishing in the midst of all this corruption is that President Harding took it upon himself to pardon Gene Debs, who still had about five years to go on his prison term. Cal Coolidge, Harding's VP, said nothing. In fact, Silent Cal was so silent that Dorothy Parker is reputed to have said on learning that Coolidge had died, "How can they tell?" The loss of money to small investors in the Teapot Dome scandal was considerable, but peanuts compared to Enron. Tom Walsh had been irreproachable as prosecutor of Teapot Dome. Ironically, he died shortly after the convention. Otherwise, he would have been Roosevelt's choice for attorney general.

Calvin Coolidge, VP under Harding, did not appear involved. He was, in fact, not involved in much of anything. Thus, he had nothing to say. He is best remembered in history for his memorable decision to distance himself from the 1928 race for his party's nomination. What school child doesn't remember Cal Coolidge's proclamation: "I do not choose to run"?

I shall always be that twelve-year-old remembering Tom Walsh, of the inflexible spine, who refused to "cool things down a bit." He saw that the people who picked others' pockets paid the price. Imagine how Tom Walsh as attorney general would have pinned down the Wall Street wise men, the Babsons, the others, and their waywardness—if not obtuseness—in impotently watching the free market fall so freely.

After the stock market crash, some New York editors suggested that hearings be held: What had really caused the Depression? The hearings were held in Washington. In retrospect, they make the finest comic reading. You read a transcript today and find them so unaware. The leading industrialist and bankers . . . they hadn't the foggiest notion.

> It was a mood of great bewilderment. No one had anticipated it, despite the fact that we had many severe panics in the past. The innocence of the business leaders was astonishing. There were groups at the time, arch-reactionary, almost Neolithic—the Liberty League, for instance. There was a bit of truth in it, but, by and large they were babes in the woods, or comedians . . .*

How CAN I FORGET an encounter with one of those Wall Street wise men? He was the Alan Greenspan of his day, though that may be going a bit too far. Sidney J. Weinberg, a senior partner of the Goldman Sachs Company, had served as an industrial adviser during the Truman and JFK administrations. Our conversation was in 1968.

---

* Carey McWilliams, at the time commissioner of immigration for California.

"October 29, 1929!—I remember that day very intimately. I stayed in the office a week without going home. The tape was running, I've forgotten how long that night. It must have been ten, eleven o'clock before we got the final reports. It was like a thunderclap. Everybody was stunned. Nobody knew what it was all about. The Street had general confusion. They didn't understand it any more than anybody else. They thought something would be announced.

Prominent people were making statements. John D. Rockefeller, Jr., announced on the steps of J.P. Morgan, I think, that he and his sons were buying common stock. Immediately, the market went down again. Pools combined to support the market, to no avail. The public got scared and sold. It was a very trying period for me. Our investment company went up to two, three hundred, and then went down to practically nothing. As all investment companies did.

I don't know anybody that jumped out of the window. But I know many who threatened to jump. They ended up in nursing homes and insane asylums and things like that. These were people who were trading in the market or in banking houses. They broke down physically, as well as financially.

Roosevelt saved the system. It's trite to say the system would have gone out the window. But certainly a lot of institutions would have changed. We were on the verge of something. You could have had a rebellion; you could have had a civil war."★

OH, I ALMOST FORGOT. There was a third-party candidate. Here was one campaign in which Gene Debs did not participate. In 1920, he polled a million votes while still in Atlanta Penitentiary. There was the last of his five runs at the presidency.

Fighting Bob LaFollette was the Progressive Party candidate in 1924, for the job over which McAdoo and Smith were battling all through my "vacation." Cal Coolidge was, of course, the Republi-

★ *Hard Times* (The New Press, 1986, pp. 72–73).

cans' mute candidate. As the spiritual goes, "He didn't say a mum-
blin' word." He didn't need to. He was in.

There was my unforgettable meeting with ex-Senator Burton
K. Wheeler. He had been Bob LaFollette's running mate on the
Progressive Party ticket in 1924, the year of the convention that
never ended. Remember, this was before his bitter contretemps
with FDR concerning Roosevelt's attempt to pack the Supreme
Court and his turn to the right. Remember, Wheeler had been the
eloquent and bellicose crusader, along with Tom Walsh, against the
Montana Big Boys.

Fast forward. 1978. Here I am in Washington, in the office of
ex-Senator Wheeler. He, as is true of many former Washington
politicos, had pursued a private law practice. The toll of the long
years since 1924 revealed themselves in his weariness and wrinkles.
His fire, though considerably banked, was still burning.

He knew I had been involved with the Progressive Party candi-
dacy of Henry Wallace in 1948, thirty or so years before. He knew
that his daughter, Frances, and her husband, Alan Saylor, had suggested this meeting. They had been devoted Henry Wallace workers. Wheeler at first appeared at loose ends, a touch lonely and out
of it. He seemed to come alive again remembering his run with
Bob LaFollette.

I remember telling Wheeler how my father and I had heard him
speak at the Ashland Auditorium, about three blocks from our
rooming house. It was a Sunday afternoon. And, he, Wheeler, to a
twelve-year-old, was Demosthenes and Abe Lincoln rolled into
one. And my father bought one of the gilded busts of Bob LaFollette
that were selling at five bucks a copy. Behind that desk, Wheeler became a different man; the glow replaced the glower. He obviously
got a kick out of his daughter and son-in-law still fighting for the
Progressive cause.

I remember some of the senator's tales out of school. Wheeler
was on a roll. Corruption, especially being bought off by the corporate biggies, was a natural political syndrome. Our public servants

had become the private servants of our CEOs. As I recall, Senator Wheeler was his younger self again, acting out those old-time encounters.

"Remember J. Ham Lewis of your state, Illinois? He grabbed me in the Senate cloakroom. Remember him?"

Of course. We called him Dr. Brush. He was my senator, and he had slaughtered Ruth Hanna McCormick, the colonel's cousin, in the senatorial race of '34. "Do you realize, Senator Wheeler, J. Ham was a dead ringer for Yellow Kid Weil, the master con artist?" As Louis Sullivan was Lieber Meister to Frank Lloyd Wright, the Yellow Kid was role model to all the imaginative youngbloods who wouldn't hurt a fly, though they would skillfully relieve "the greedy who had too much."

J. Ham and the Kid were each in a class by himself, well dressed. Oh, sure, there was Jimmy Walker, the one-time mayor of New York, and the Prince of Wales, who, with his great love, Wally Simpson, didn't think Hitler was quite that bad. In any event, I'll try to describe the Yellow Kid, and it could describe as well, spats and all, the august senator: a well-trimmed Van Dyke beard, a pince-nez, a pearl stickpin in a flash of tie, shoes that were far above Florsheim in style and value. Probably Italian. Each of them was possessed of a panache none of our young models in *Gentlemen's Quarterly* could touch.

A long time went by before I ran into the Yellow Kid. Dog days for him. I knew it because I spotted a slight egg stain on his onceexpensive jacket. It was on a streetcar that we met. His eyes were watery, he appeared weary; yet he was the same articulate, persuasive Yellow Kid Weil.

I'm still in Burton K. Wheeler's office and he's still, in memory, back in the cloakroom with J. Ham.

I had finished a hot assault on the big corporations that were short-changing all the hardworking people. Old J. Ham came up to me. He used to call out "Boy!" That made me mad. "Boy, give 'em the devil." I said, "Won't you make a speech on it?" He said, "No, I can't. I represent a damn bunch of thieves, I tell you, who want to reach their hand in the public coffers and pull all the money out. My God, if I were a free man, I'd tear this thing limb from limb." I was pretty much discouraged when the men in the cloakrooms would come up to me and say, "I agree with you!" Then go out and vote the other way.

I remember one piece of legislation I was interested in. It involved a challenge to the big money powers. A senator said to me, "I think you're right. I'm gonna vote with you." In the afternoon, he said, "I can't." "Why not?" "My bosses called me up. You've got one." I said, "The only boss I got is the people." He said, "Don't give me that stuff. You've got a boss somewhere."

When Tom Pendergast was indicted, Harry Truman came up to me. "Should I resign?" I said, "Why should you resign?" He said, "They've indicted the old man. He made me everything I am, and I've got to stand by him." [Pendergast ran the Democratic Party of Missouri.]

There was a distinct difference between Yellow Kid Weil, Wheeler's fashion-plate colleague, and other political figures. The Kid had only one boss—himself. His credo was a simple one: "I am an educator. I educate only those who can afford to pay for their education. They are either rich widows on an expensive cruise or well-heeled men in finance who are by their very nature greedy. They want more. Always. As a matter of fact, I once took Andrew Mellon's brother for half a million. It involved a silver mine in Colorado."

Remember that easy summertime of 1924, when I appeared to be in a catatonic state, bound to that Atwater-Kent and the never-ending dull, dull, dull convention—aside from the wondrous Tom Walsh's sternly comforting voice. The hard fact is that I was really invited to join the magic circle of politics by The Man himself. Non-Chicagoans, young ones, or those who suffer from Alzheimer's when it comes to politics, may need a guide. The Man to whom I'm referring was not the mayor. He was Bill Dawson, the congressman from the First Congressional District. It was an overwhelmingly African American community, whose votes were always delivered by The Man, something like nine to one Democratic.

This was pre–Martin Luther King Jr. time and Adam Clayton Powell had the idea that he was The Man. I'm sorry, he was the second-most powerful of African Americans. Bill was the most powerful of all straw bosses. As overseer of his people he won all sorts of pittances for them, while in the meantime serving Mr. Charlie very well indeed. He was in a sense the ideal overseer. The small favors offered to African American voters were more matters of gratuity than of gratitude.

Because of the sudden illness of an old acquaintance of mine, I was chosen to introduce Dawson to a liberal white middle-class audience. I remember the occasion well. I was in good form, and my debating experience and mastery of ambiguity released a flow of eloquent bushwa. Had Tom Paine heard himself so quoted, he'd have suffered a case of carbuncles far worse than those he did have.

Of course, I called upon the heritage of Frederick Douglass, Ida B. Wells, and Madame C.J. Walker. I introduced Bill Dawson shortly after mentioning the others. It was done so casually. Of course, the guest of honor, The Man, felt honored indeed. Said he to me, "Son, you should be in politics." You see, Bill Dawson recognized a con artist immediately.

My ill friend, an active African American, was deeply appreciative. He actually convinced me I had done the right thing. What the right thing was, I'm still trying to figure out. The fact is: I *coulda* been in Chicago politics. God, I *coulda* been a contender.

ONWARD AND UPWARD. There was a slight family split. A selling of the rooming house was in order. I accompanied my mother for a high school semester in New York. It was there that Meyer briefed me for the first month I'd missed at Morris High School in the Bronx. He was, hands down, the best teacher I ever had.

I remember one young teacher at Morris. His name was Bernard Drachman, a dead ringer for Robert Louis Stevenson. Tubercular; long, struggling mustache; and quite wonderful. I still remember a border ballad he taught—Sir Patrick Spens. Years later, as a disk jockey, I played a Burl Ives version. And damned if I didn't remember half the words.

But New York was not Chicago. I had become spoiled living in the archetypal American city. My father, medical advice or not, had to leave that bedside. He was in the men's hotel with Ben, awaiting the kid. Annie, of course, was welcome, but he'd run the hotel, not she.

How will this one work out? I sure liked that name: The Wells-Grand. It was, to me, a melding of two cultures. I remember the Wells-Fargo from all the movie references. And of course that posh pre-Hitler Berlin hotel, the Grand.

5

Teachers of the Gilded Age

I haven't mentioned my four remarkable old teachers at the McKinley High School in Chicago. Some had begun teaching in the nineteenth century, during the Gilded Age. All four were Edwardian in style and demeanor. George W. Powles Jr., teacher since 1800-and-something. Pince-nez balanced delicately on nose, white mustache overflowing; his daily mantra: a cigarette was "a light at one end, a fool at the other." He very much enjoyed my precise reading of Charles and Mary Lamb's *Children's Shakespeare*. "Oh, young sir, you could handle that Lady Macbeth all right. One day, I'll boast that I taught Shakespeare to a young Sir Henry Irving." I had no idea who Sir Henry was but obviously professor Powles put me in fast company.

Some of my fellow students were impish in nature—a few, members of the '42s, who were to the Mob what the Junior Chamber of Commerce members were to their elders. The '42s liked me because I always shoved my finished papers to my left while a certain '42 member-in-good-standing was seated behind me. He moved his chair to the left. His vision was apparently 20–20 because he'd always wind up with an A, much to his parents' surprise. There was in our class an ROTC chieftain, with medals brightening the sunshine where he was. He finked numerous times on his classmates. One, Louis Fratto, who won the Catholic Youth Organization

(CYO) featherweight title, beat the bejeepers out of the medal-lioned one. He asked me if he had gone too far. I kissed both his cheeks as General Foch did those of American soldiers in World War I.

As a parting gift, Mr. Powles offered me two books. I say "offered" because it was more than giving. Two books: *Roget's Thesaurus* and Olive Schreiner's novel *The Story of an African Farm*. The latter was written under the name of Ralph Iron, much as George Eliot found a name of her own. What astonished me so many years later, during a visit to South Africa, was that Nadine Gordimer told me that was one of the books she had read as a young woman in her family store near Johannesburg.

Now, the wondrous question: How did George W. Powles, an Edwardian schoolteacher, come across this book? Of course, after the two precious books had been many years in my possession, I lost both. (If there were time, I could heartbreakingly explain how I misplaced and never recovered a letter from Charles Chaplin in Vevey, Switzerland, and an astonishing note from Douglas Fairbanks Jr. on the horrors of ageism. Young Fairbanks was a grandfather at the time and I was his co-speaker. It was an assemblage of old guys and dolls, who gave him a standing ovation. I also lost a Western Union telegram from Sterling Hayden, its language so foul that the operator refused to repeat it other than to another woman. It was a lovingly hilarious note of congratulations on my having won the Debs Award.

The second of my McKinley mentors, Robert Potter, was rugged of face with a scraggly mustache. Though he and Powles were venerable contemporaries, their temperaments were somewhat at odds. Andrew Potter taught algebra. He was aware of my woeful weakness in anything involving numbers. Nonetheless, he maintained an air of patience. I found his kindness to me inexplicable, though as a quiet, shy boy, I was very well behaved. When he spoke of certain kinds of people, his speech was less than tender. I assumed he meant "Mediterraneans." It was the time of Italian and

Portuguese workingwomen first writing and then loudly singing
"Bread and Roses." No, Mr. Potter had discovered a people to be
disliked even more than Mediterraneans: the Jews. As an offering of
farewell, he gave me, all wrapped in thick rubber bands, the Dear-
born *Independent*. It was Henry Ford's beauty; he was publisher.
(There was much talk among affluent Jewish groups seeking to put
forth a car to rival the Model T. It was called the Star. To say that it
flopped is to say that Jack Dempsey defeated Billy Miske. The fight
lasted one round.) Not a bet was missed; the paper covered everything from the Protocols of Zion to the killing of Christ.

Perhaps Mr. Potter thought I was a Mel Gibson born a generation too soon.

I started reading them and they caught my attention and held it
fast. They contained the most virulent anti-Semitic speeches I had
ever encountered. It was so shameless; it approached an eloquence I
had never explored. Meyer told me to throw them into the stove,
but I hesitated, for I had seen nothing as sensational since Peaches
exposed everything about Daddy Browning.★ I regret that I was
never able to express my gratitude for Mr. Potter's largesse . . .

Our gym teacher was no Jack La Lanne, nor a Jane Fonda. He
was in his seventies, with the traditional mustachio, pocket watch in
jacket, suit, white shirt and tie—formal attire, except for well-worn
white sneakers. "George Commons, sir, is my name." They all had a
common attribute, ingenuity. Mr. Commons always wore heavy
sweaters because it was forever cold. The elves came through, the
'42s. They'd run by tossing hot pennies at him. Drawing himself up
to his full height, he'd threaten to take on "a dozen of you Mediterraneans."

My favorite of all was the gentle Miss Olive Leekley, who was
not merely our Latin teacher (she insisted it be pronounced softly
Lat-hin, which came easily because she was so thoughtful of every-

---

★ Bernard MacFadden published a scandalous tabloid, the *Telegraph*. One of its memorable exposés concerned the teenaged Peaches and her Daddy Browning. Peaches' Ma
approved.

one's feelings. She even passed the young oaf who suggested that Nero was a southpaw with the Boston Red Sox.).

Most important, she was our debating coach. Each school had an affirmative side and a negative. At McKinley, I had suddenly developed a case of logorrhea, and I was on both sides. The favorite topic was, of course: Resolved, the Death Penalty Shall Be Abolished. There was no honor. The students did the choosing and the '42s saw to it that I did well. They attended all the debates in which I appeared. I think of what I might have been, had I gone along with the law and maintained my friendship with the '42s. I might have been Sidney Korshak—Mr. Clout. When Senator Estes Kefauver, a genuine public servant, headed a committee investigating the Mob, Korshak saw to it that he stepped out. Korshak had everything on everyone. Oh, when I was on the negative, I was a small boy *Torquemada*. I'm not sure I came out for quartering or the rack, yet some of these buggers had to be punished. I do remember saying as a grotesque small-boy epilogue: "Of course, I didn't mean it." "Oh yeah?" said one my '42s classmates. "Why not?"

6

The Hotel

On the southeast corner of Wells Street and Grand Avenue is an imposing three-story building of condominiums: nine spacious, elegantly appointed apartments that frequently make the style sections of our daily newspaper. The occupants, a couple of indeterminate age, seated, oh, so casually, smile in the manner prescribed by a celebrated local photographer. (Once upon a time, I had run into the camera master and asked him if Cartier-Bresson had any influence on his work. "No," he replied. "Annie Liebowitz.")

Below is a four star Moroccan restaurant, whose fare is North African-cum-French—or it's changed hands and serves Italian-cum-Californian, but the prices are always high. Each time I passed this corner, I paused, trying to recall what this place once was, and kicked at the wall of the rather opulent entrance. The doorman always appeared discombobulated, as a seventy-five-year-old (the occurrences were twenty or so years before this writing) and obviously decrepit old bum limped away.

I was, at three score and fifteen, only performing what was the usual ritual. For me, what was once a native habitat had become alien turf. The transformation that had been happening gradually, SUVesque, seemed so sudden.

Yes, the Wells-Grand area had once been a near-north neighborhood of sorts. Italian was the predominant ethic, though it was ecumenical in the sharing of hard times. Yes, two blocks east was Clark. It was the strip that could reasonably be described as Skid Row East.

I stepped inside about thirty years ago, ages after we had sold the hotel, the lease; the building itself had been owned by H.L. Flentye, a rigid ultraconservative but an honest, decent landlord. The hotel had become SRO (single-room occupancy). I, for sentimental reasons, had visited from time to time and been quite satisfied. In the still quite neat lobby, I heard an elderly guest querulously wonder where "the jokes" were. The jokes. He didn't ask for "the funnies" or "the comics." I felt the place was in good hands. I was made aware of the SRO veterans being given three months' notice before being booted out. Where will they go? I had the temerity to ask this of one of the developers with whom I had become acquainted. "Out there." He pointed west, vaguely. It was more of a genial wave.

What, you may ask, made me, some twenty years ago, at seventy-five, sprain my foot against the brick of the wall? I realize the kicks made no sense; yet they brought back a memory. That obdurate wall had once upon a time been the glass-door entrance to the Wells-Grand Hotel. For years, after we had left, that entrance was unchanged. Gilt-edged letters across the glass proclaimed the name. On the fabled (for me) corner hung the neon sign bearing those sweet words—Wells-Grand.

During my last kick-time, I ran into a construction worker, the only one left, who was putting some last-minute touches to the masterwork. I said to him, with the prudishness of an old puritanical schoolteacher: "These were once fifty rooms. Do you know who lived there? Working people like you."

He simply looked at me for a good while. At last he replied, "Of course I know that. It's my job."

"Did you ever wonder about the people you kicked out—how many years ago? Did you ever wonder where they went?"

"One day," he casually responded, "these new people will be kicked out, too. This might become a great big office building."

He was now lecturing *me*. Obviously, I got more than I had bargained for.

The Wells-Grand Hotel of my memory, of my dreams, was not a flophouse. Let's get that straight. This was in the mid-twenties. There had been a rooming house, my mother, Annie, the proprietress. Now, we had the hotel, my father, Sam, the proprietor. The guests were what I remembered best. Remember, the times were still pretty good. The crash of '29 had yet to come. During the day, the lobby was empty, men at work: Some of them were old enough to be retired, ex's. There was Bill Brewer, the ex-carpenter. There was Teddy Tils, dapper and ex-mason: there was Ed Sprague, an ex-something; probably ex–boomer fireman.★ His work was mostly transient. Many of the guests were Wobblies.

On weekdays, the lobby was empty save for a few ex's playing cribbage or hearts, the rest off sauntering in Lincoln Park. Teddy was often kidded, due to his Old World courteous manners, of making time with the wealthy old dowagers of the Near North Side. Bill Brewer loved shooting pool at two and a half cents a cue.† "Billiards is my game. I once played with Willie Hoppe." (Hoppe was a billiards wizard; the world champion, for many years.) As for Sprague, his daily fare consisted of dead man's stew—a bowl of hot milk with bread dipped in it. Most of his teeth had been knocked out during the Seattle General strike of 1919. He had been a Wobbly, of course. At night, Saturday afternoons and Sundays, the guests crowded into our lobby. To me, at the time, the room seemed immense. When I visited it years later, I saw that the lobby was the size of an ordinary men's hotel room. The Abe Lincoln portrait (photographed by Matthew Brady) was still hanging askew. The September Moon calendar was still there. On Sundays, the men would express their worship of Eros rather than Jesus, with the girls on Orleans Street, two blocks west. On Sundays, those cribs were standing room only. Remember, my father ran the hotel, bum ticker or not,

★ Primarily transient workman who went from one railroad to another.
† An old pool hall phrase meaning "per game."

and Ben and I were his associates. My mother had to do something. For a time, she resumed dressmaking.

A guest whom we called Civilization was the center of our attention. He worked as a pearl diver—a dishwasher—during the day at Mike Legda's diner down below, the Victoria. All of Civilization's spare time, and I mean *all*, was expended in letter writing. He used a pencil whose nub was always wearing down, and his markings were something of an ordeal to make out. His stationery was lined paper torn from some old composition books. His letters, running to twenty or so penciled pages, were his prescriptions for a better world. He described himself as a Czech intellectual. Among his correspondents were Albert Einstein, George Bernard Shaw, Bertrand Russell, Henry Ford, Mahatma Gandhi, and Oscar Wilde. Not one had the courtesy to reply. Finally, he reluctantly concluded that civilization was doomed. Thus, his name.

What was remarkable and strangely moving was the show of respect the other guests afforded him. Oh, I imagine a good number had him down as a pistachio; but, nonetheless, they did not threaten to toss him out of the window. It is true there were occasions when Ben and I were urged to give him the heave-ho. Joe, whose real surname was Chch. It does look strange, no vowel, all consonants. All we could say was Joe Chuch. We had to include that one vowel in speech.

It was as Civilization that he brought forth our local notoriety. The moment that most irritated his fellow guests was when he'd go up to his room, number 35, on the third floor, dead, dead, dead drunk. As Ben or I tossed him onto his bed at, say, 1:00 a.m., the troubles began. As soon as we had descended to the clerk's desk three floors down, we heard the howl of a banshee. No, it was more of a cry for help. "Owww! Owww! Owww!" I'm sure the whole street resounded with this mayday howl. I expected the police at any moment.

Ben and I rushed back up those fifty, sixty steps, saw the man sprawled out, moaning. His mouth was wide open. We shut his mouth, pressing his lips tightly together. Again we descended. On reaching the desk, we heard that same chilling cry again. "Fuck! Fuck! Fuck!" Said Ben, "Let's get a safety pin." There was no need. Again we shut his mouth, but now we actually wedged his lower and upper teeth together until they interlocked. It worked. Thus, the nighttime passed.

I was for some time mystified by his baying at the midnight moon, "Owww! Owww!"

Suddenly it hit me. You needn't be a philological scholar to understand that Joe Chch, aka Civilization, was crying out for his missing vowel. "Owww! Owww!"

The one time Civilization did get into trouble involved me and a piece of zinc. We were always reading and hearing of non-physicians who had cures of some sort. I'm not referring to the obvious W.C. Fieldsian frauds and monkey-gland "doctors." I'm referring to thinkers like Civilization, who had an idea about increasing one's height. Civilization had experimented with zinc, so he informed me. A sliver of zinc under my heels would in one year increase my height by about two inches. I did as he advised and cut myself up pretty bad. My mother detected my bloody heels. On occasion, she arrived uninvited at the hotel. (We lived in an apartment some distance from the Wells-Grand.) She threatened to throw him out of the window. The man was unfazed. His thick accent added panache to his proclamations. He was advising her of a little known cure for ill-temperedness. Unfortunately, the world was not ready for that cure.

What really created the glory nights at the lobby were the debates between the retired Wobblies and the good "company men." "Company man" was the favorite good-behavior phrase for the fink or the three-dollar bill. The most favored of all the synonyms for the strikebreakers was "Scissorbill." He was the capitalist with a hole in his pocket.

I had no idea when my actions would turn political. As the favored child, I was an observer; I saw rather than did. I know that by

1933, just as I was finishing my last year at the U of C law school, I witnessed a demonstration. It was at the beginning of the Chicago World's Fair of 1933–34 that I saw Italo Balbo, Mussolini's minister of aviation, land with a flotilla of two dozen seaplanes from across the Atlantic. He came ashore to tumultuous greetings almost as lyrical as Lindy's. From then on, at the corner where the Hilton Hotel overwhelms all else, the street was no longer named Seventh. It became and remains Balbo—a small street, yet a vital thoroughfare in leading you to expressways.

Chicago may be the only large American city with a street named after a fascist. Oh, it has Goethe Street and Schiller and Mozart. You may not realize it, but early Chicago had many liberal Germans who came to be known as the Failed '48ers.⋆ The streets were so named in memory of a certain time in European history with ideals and dreams of a better world still in the hearts of men.

It was Bughouse Square, aside from the hot lobby disputes, plus the easy way of my father and older brother, that played a role in my political growth. Bughouse Square was much like London's Hyde Park, where free speech is the power and the glory. As in Hyde Park on a Sunday, the issues were openly and widely discussed. For years, India was the Hyde Park speakers' prime subject.

Here, in Chicago, is a small park known as Washington Square. It is much better known as Bughouse Square. In its heyday, during the 1920s and 1930s, there were five soapboxes on which the most celebrated speakers were allowed twenty minutes and then afforded the privilege of passing the hat. Among the speakers was Ben Reitman, renowned as the romantic clap doctor. He was world-celebrated for having been the favorite lover of Emma Goldman, the feminist militant, the articulate Anarchist, the star of so many tumultuous gatherings.

By the time I had discovered Bughouse Square, a short walking

---

⋆ In the 1840s there were numerous rebellions in Middle European countries among those seeking independence and thus a better world. They were henceforth known as the "Failed '48ers."

distance from the hotel, Reitman had seen his best days. His black fedora was there, his cape flamboyantly draped around his shoulders in the manner of Aristide Briant (remember the Toulouse-Lautrec portrait, with that red muffler stealing the show?). There appeared on Ben's black cape a telltale egg stain. By this time, old Ben R., somewhat frail and bent, was peddling books on sexual hygiene at fifteen cents a throw.

There was Frank Midney, Mayor of Bughouse Square (each year, the participants could choose among anybody present). Midney, an old Shakespearean actor we were told, hawk-nosed, John Gielgudian, bony hands, eloquent in speech, once withered a heckler, pointing his accusatory finger at the miscreant: "If brains was bedbug juice, you couldn't drown a nit."

There was the little cockney, Tom Sheridan, who claimed to have founded the British Labor Party along with Keir Hardie and George Bernard Shaw. When he grew weary after a half-hour nonstop monologue, his two froggy-voiced sons, John and Jim, took over.

And, of course, there was always One-Arm Cholly Wendorf. I was usually in attendance on a Friday or Saturday night. The workweek, five and a half days; the men at the hotel worked Saturday morning and were paid at noon. About one or so, a paycheck was shoved across the desk and the proper cash was doled out. I'd saunter toward the Cosmopolitan State Bank to deposit our weekly earnings.

On the north side of Bughouse Square stands the Newberry Library. Miss Polly Fletcher was there at the library, third-floor reading room. She was of Dorothy Parker's mien and, seeing a student hanging around Bughouse Square, suggested some book or other for me to fool around with. Upton Sinclair's *The Jungle* of course. Ida Tarbell on the Rockefellers. Dreiser's *Sister Carrie*. Miss Fletcher definitely played a role in my political growing-up.

The man who "once fought Battlin' Nelson," the sword swallower, Goodrich, Sister Grace, Midney, the Moody Bible people,

Doc Reitman, the Sheridan boys—all have their say. But it is One-Arm Cholly Wendorf whose peroration is the most memorable. (Cholly eventually succeeded Frank Midney as Mayor of Bughouse Square.)

Cholly holds up the stub of his right arm. "Know where the rest of this is? Somewhere in France. Somewhere in a trench near Cha-too Teary.* The French have it. Cholly Wendorf's arm is enrichin' the soil that grows the grapes that brings you da best Cognac money can buy. Coovahseer. Reemy Martin. Three-Star Hennessy. I touch nothin' else.

"Know what Omar said? What is it the vintner buys one half so precious as da stuff he sells? Lemme tell you somep'n, Omar. My arm. Only he didn't buy it. I gave it to him free of charge. When my president, Woodrow Wilson, says, Cholly, I need you. You gotta defend our free way of life. You gotta kill those Huns. You gotta save poor little Belgium. Will you do me dat favor?"

"What do ya think I tol' 'im? I said, 'You're my president, an' if you need me, I'll go. I'm a red-blooded American and I'm gonna save da world for democracy.' " He holds high his stub. "How da hell do you think I got this? I earned it. Look at it. Unique. I coulda been just an ordinary run-of-da-mill clown. Wit' two arms. Instead—look at me. One-Arm Cholly. A man of distinction."

"You tell 'em, Cholly." Another winner in the crowd. Cholly peers out. He indicates with his stub. "Can you imagine? Savin' democracy for *him*. Ain't it awful, Mabel?" Howls. The audience has come to expect call-and-response as eagerly as black parishioners do at a storefront church.

"I'm marchin' down Michigan Boulevard. I'm Douglas Fairbanks. You oughta see me in khaki. America, here's my boy. What a beautiful parade. It stirs my red-blooded American blood. There she is, da drum majorette leadin' da parade. Ain't she cute? Twirlin' her baton, her little fanny twitchin'. That trombone player's got a

---

* Château-Thierry was the site of one of the first American actions against the Germans in World War I.

hard time keepin' his mind on his work. An' here come da open cars. Da fat boys, with da stars and da chickens. And bringin' up da rear is us, da camels. Wit' sixty-pound bags on our back. And everybody wavin' at us. We're wit'cha, boys. All the way."

An open car passes through the square. The people reluctantly part, with much grumbling. An unwritten law is being violated. Only sightseeing buses are welcome. The guides and the speakers have an arrangement.

A young soldier and two girls are in the car. The boy calls out, "Go back to Russia."

Cholly turns toward the car. It's having a difficult time getting through. "Why, you pipsqueak! Look at him, ladies and gentlemen." We all look. The soldier, pale and bespectacled, grins weakly. Had he been a captain in his high school's ROTC? Give it to him, Cholly. The girls seem to have no idea what it's all about. Plainly, they'd rather be elsewhere. It's no use. The soldier honks his horn. Nobody moves. Well, he asked for it.

"Why, if you ever opened your yap over there at the Holy Name—" his stub indicates the Cathedral to the east, "—why, they'd fling the pee pot of the Virgin Mary at ya!" Cholly turns back to his audience. The car squeezes through.

"So, now we're on da ocean, on our way to prove we're da big muckety-muck. We land at Brest. Where's da parade? It's all in reverse. We're at da head of it, us camels. No open car, no brass band, no drum majorette wigglin' her fanny. Across da ocean, we hear 'em sayin', We're wit'cha, boys, far, far away.

"So I'm walkin' down the Champ de Leesee, have a few drinks, some Frenchman bumps into me. I say to him, 'Outa my way, you frog, I'm an American.' He says, 'I beg your pardohn, monsoor. You do not own Paris.' So I haul off to sock 'im. I'm an American, by God. Next thing I know, I'm flat on my back. Knocked cold. No more Stephen Decatur.

"There I am in the trench. Chatoo Teary. Next thing I know, I'm wounded. I holler. The Red Cross comes with a canteen of water. I say, What the hell is this? I want Three-Star Hennessy. And that's what they brung me. So here I am today, saved, thanks to demon rum."

On the steps of the Newberry Library, and along the curb, beehives form. Here, non-featured performers find their own coteries. Though lacking the credentials for the big league, the soapbox, one can attract as many as thirty, forty followers. There is a mild-mannered Finnish barber who has the widest of these circles. Nobody understands a word he says, but as soon as he appears, a small crowd gathers around him expectantly. He speaks softly. Could he be a guru from Helsinki? He is forever smiling, wisely. And sadly. He must know something. They look toward him for the answer.

Civilization appears in this arena. Of course. This is the evening of the big confrontation. Veterans of the beehive world tell me this has been a long time coming. I, naturally, am excited and proud. Our hotel is represented. The pearl diver and the barber. The Serb and the Finn. Never, before or since, have I heard conversation so recondite. The colloquy is as convoluted as it is profound. Editors of the *New York Review of Books* would go crazy. I, along with fifty others—there are more here than usual, the word has got around—crowd in close to the sages. We try to make out what they're saying . . .

I attended Bughouse Square as regularly as possible in the years that followed. I doubt whether I learned very much. One thing I know: I delighted in it. Perhaps none of it made any sense, save one kind: sense of life.

But this particular Saturday night was filled with more than life; it was overflowing. As the gathering was about to wind up and the speakers had counted all the small change in their hats, word spread that Lucy Parsons would appear.

The stars of the square were representatives of the Socialist Party, the Communists, the Vegetarians, and, of course, the Moody Bible Institute orators. To tell you the truth, they outspoke in fervor, and certainly outsang, their godless opponents.

Grace, of perfect posture and needing no soapbox, would sing of being cradled in the arms of Jesus all last night. She'd bring forth the obvious response from the atheistic printer: "What about me, Grace?" It fazed her not at all. Her singing, clear and pure, overcame.

The square itself and the library steps of Newberry were jampacked. These were the non-stars, who had appeared from the various hotels and the rooming houses of the neighborhood. Each one seemed to have a representative. Ours was of course Civilization. His opponent was usually the soft-spoken Finnish barber. All of us listened intently to the words, many of which we had never heard before, as, I suspect, the speakers themselves had not. The subjects were so arcane, none of us, least of all the participants, knew what it was all about.

Never mind. All became silence when it was announced that Lucy was here. She was the heroine of all of us, whom many had heard about but never seen in the flesh. She had a habit of suddenly appearing at Bughouse Square. Bam!

How to describe Lucy? This was in the late thirties. Several years later, destitute, she died in a 1942 stove fire. She had outlived her husband, Albert, by fifty-five years. He had been hanged in 1887, one year after the infamous Haymarket Affair trial of 1886. She was keeping alive the memory of Albert, his three martyred comrades, and the others who had barely survived. She was high of cheekbone, and she wore a worn old skirt and a fancy flowered hat. She was light black, part Indian, and even now you knew she had at one time been really beautiful. All of us gathered there: embattled old labor vets, hangers-on, wayfaring strangers. And a couple of curious "students" like me.

Who was Lucy? She and her gentle ex-Confederate soldier, Albert, along with August Spies, an eloquent German Anarchist advocate of the eight-hour day, and six others, had held a rally in front of the International Harvester Works.

It was the eight-hour day that working people the world over were singing and dreaming about. It was here in Chicago that it was first being celebrated. In fact, May Day had, until the time of the Cold War, become a holiday to millions everywhere.

The rally was set for a fine spring day in 1886. Mayor Carter Harrison was there on horseback to see that all was orderly. He was a highly respected figure, known for his sympathies with working people and small businessmen. Things were going along peacefully. He rode home.

The rains had come and most of the crowd had gone elsewhere. Each of the speakers, including the eight who were to be tried for stirring up the riot, and for murder, had retired to their homesteads. Hardly anyone was left. Suddenly, a bomb was thrown. Nobody knows who threw it or why. Even now it is a mystery. Several policemen as well as several civilians were killed, scores more were injured. The hysteria that caught the city had never, anywhere been so wild. All the establishment newspapers carried headlines urging the hangings of the culprits. To all the Respectables, the speakers were the villains who had planned the chaos, stirred the violent temper. The fact that none was there when the explosion occurred was of no consequence. It was the Respected—indeed the most Respectabled—whose language was the most hortatory.

There was a trial that history now regards as a farce. "Frame-up" is not the word. The trial would have been hilarious in the W.C. Fieldsian manner were it not so profoundly tragic. The jury was chosen from big-time employers in town, middle managers, many of them righteous in their fury. The judge was Joseph E. Gary, who really made a prosecutor unnecessary. Historians tell us that Judge Gary was more than prosecutorial; he was the jury. Four who were on trial were convicted, sentenced to be hanged. One killed himself in his cell. The other three were sentenced to imprisonment for life.

From all over the world came a stirring plea for the lives of the condemned. The trial was described as barbaric. Among the signatories of the eloquent petition were George Bernard Shaw, Oscar Wilde, John Ruskin, and William Dean Howells. Even more moving was the signature of Henry Demarest Lloyd, son-in-law of William Bross, co-owner of the Chicago *Tribune*, who disinherited him. Jessie Lloyd, Henry's wife, Bross's daughter, was also knocked off as a beneficiary. It was my honor and thrill to have walked the picket line on one or another issue—war, labor, color, or free speech—in the company of the son and daughter who bore their name.

Lucy, some forty-five years later, made old history once again aborning. With her frail old-woman's voice and her remarkable memory, she brought us back to the 1886 trial. She quoted August Spies, in his white gown, crying out through the muslin covering his hood before he was hanged: "The time will come when our silence will be more powerful than the voices you strangle today." During the trial, it was Spies' eloquence and ring of truth, as well as his appearance, that impelled a spectator, Nina van Zandt, a debutante of high societal degree, to fall in love with him. They married while he was on trial. Her mother sympathized and worked hard for the defense. They were at once ostracized in full by all their fellow socialites and crucified in the press. Both women died destitute.★

Lucy spoke of her beloved husband, whom she was not allowed to see on the day of his execution. Albert Parsons, during his slow walk to the rope, sang "Annie Laurie." In Scots dialect. It was not "The Marseillaise" he offered, simply a love song to Lucy.

A few days after Lucy died in '42, there was a funeral for her at Waldheim, where some of the Haymarket martyrs were interred. My good friend Win Stracke sang. He sang "Joe Hill," of course, but what knocked me completely out was his offering of "Annie Laurie."

There was one instant, one observation, I most remember about Lucy that Bughouse Square afternoon. Ed Sprague, who was standing beside me, dropped a dollar bill in Lucy's hat as it was passed around. A whole buck at that time of Great Depression, from a guy who'd surrendered his teeth for a better world. So he had one less

★ *Death in the Haymarket* by James Green (Pantheon, 2006).

dead man's stew to gum. To be fair, it must be pointed out that a fairly large group of Chicago industrialists, led by the highly respected Lyman Gage, had pleaded with Governor Oglesby, a friend of Lincoln, to commute the hanging sentences to life.

The plea appeared to have an effect until the Merchant Prince, Marshall Field I, intervened, in cold fury, his silvery mustache pointed heavenward. He called a meeting of all the Big Boys and, in effect, said, "Hang the Bastards." The Merchant Prince, it now appears, had more clout than dozens of philosophers and authors and scores of other industrialists.

Several years later, Governor John Peter Altgeld, a child of the "Failed '48ers," pardoned the survivors in an 18,000-word document. Clarence Darrow, who had begun his career as a corporate lawyer, described Altgeld's document as one of the most eloquent and telling he had ever read. It was certainly not the usual practice of a corporate lawyer such as Darrow to become an attorney for the have-nots. Attorney for the Damned, his biographers called him.

EVER SINCE MY MID-SIXTIES, I have had a habit of talking to myself. On the subject of Cubs, Sox, local corruption, international madness, and pampered dogs, any dogs, any subject. For years, and quite often while awaiting the number 146 morning bus to work, Monday through Friday. Though some in my neighborhood are aware of books I've put forth, it is for my logorrhea I am best recognized. However, there was one young couple with whom I did not score at all. I stood beside them each morning while bus-awaiting. But for them I was not there, wholly invisible. They were quite a handsome couple. He, in his Brooks Brothers or tailor-made suit, with the latest minted edition of the *Wall Street Journal* folded neatly beneath his arm. She, a stunner in Bloomingdale's or Neiman-Marcus, holding casually her *Vanity Fair*, could have been a model for *Vogue*.

I had in the past made advances to the pair. There was not even a lack of response; nobody was there. They may or may not have been aware of a pestiferous old goofball.

On this one morning, the bus was late. I saw my opportunity. "Labor Day is coming up." It seemed to be the phrase to do the trick.

He slowly, deliberately turned toward me as though seeing me for the first time. His face was unchanged, his manner fashionably cool. "We despise unions."

Oh, wow. I had a pigeon here. The bus had yet to make an appearance. He looked at me as Noël Coward might have looked upon a tiny bug he was flicking off the sleeve of his tailor-made shirt cuff. He turned away.

My self-esteem, as well as my ego, had been bruised. I took a step toward him. Looked back once more, no bus. Oh, goodie. I touched his back. He turned around. I was now the Ancient Mariner fixing him with my glittering eye. He was for this flick of a moment transfixed. "How many hours a day do you work?"

"Eight," he replied reflexively.

"How come you don't work fourteen hours a day? Your great-great-grandparents did. How come you only work the eight-hour day? Four guys got hanged fighting for the eight-hour day for *you*."

Unsettled as any young man on the make would be under such singular circumstances, he stepped back and bumped into the mailbox. I'd got him trapped. (The bus was still tardy. I thought: I must remember that driver come Christmas day.) She, the stunner, tremulously dropped her *Vanity Fair*. I courteously bent (ouch!) and handed it to her. No—no bus yet. God was in his heaven. Kismet was with me. I said, with some delightful malice I must admit, having pinned him against the metallic box, "There was something called the Haymarket Affair, and the hangings that resulted made your life so much easier." I'd had captive audiences before, but never one so anxious.

The bus was now in the distance but coming on fast. When it arrived, they scrambled onto it. I never saw them again. But I'll bet you that each morning she'd look out of the window of the twenty-second floor of their condominium. I just knew it faced the great lake and the small bus stop. After a moment, he'd call out: "Is that old nut still out there?"

I did not blame young Lochinvar and his bride for their ignorance of our history. Why should they be an exception? Yet I think the truth may be a bit more serious: The big A, Alzheimer, has taken over my own generation, or, for that matter, that of our sons and daughters. "What past? What happened yesterday? You know what happened yesterday, grandma, daughter, sonny boy? You mean you've forgotten that Tank Johnson was forgiven and taken back by the Bears? Tank's been on the front page of the papers all week and you've already forgotten?"*

As for me, my change from observer to activist is attributable to my Wells-Grand Hotel days. It was those loners—argumentative ones, deceptively quiet ones, the talkers and the walkers—who, always engaged in something outside themselves, unintentionally became my mentors. True, I did attend the University of Chicago law school, but whatever I am, for better or for worse, I owe to Ed Sprague, Teddy Tils, Bill Brewer, and even Civilization, Bughouse Square, and Polly Fletcher.

---

* Tank Johnson, a player for the Chicago Bears, spent several scandalous weeks in the headlines, charged with weapons possession, aggravated assault, and resisting arrest.

7

A Good Citizen*

As Glenn and Betty Stauffer approach the hotel desk, I sense trouble. I'm not sure why. It has something to do with her, I believe. The way she smiles and frowns and glances about. Her bobbed hair is Clara Bow. Why did they have to choose our place? There are others in the neighborhood. Damn.

Glenn Stauffer is a frail, small-boned, mild-mannered man. Come each Saturday, he pays his rent. My mother is delighted. Theirs is one of our few light-housekeeping rooms, and the most expensive. Eight dollars a week. With the early evening *Three-Star* under his arm, he offers no more than a brief comment about the weather as he urges the rent across the desk. Each morning at eight, he walks down the stairs. Each evening at six, he walks up the stairs. He never appears in the lobby. He is no trouble. Betty Stauffer is something else.

She is always in the lobby. She works but two days a week as a part-time waitress at the Victoria down below. Otherwise, time hangs heavy on her hands. The pensioners, busy at cribbage, pinochle, hearts, and the perusal of obituaries, pay her little attention.

I'm playing cribbage with John Barkie. Usually, I'm quite nimble at this game. Not this day. For some reason I'm having trouble.

Damn. Why does she have to cross her legs in that manner? True, I'm a hotelier and it's really none of my business. Still. The turn of

* Adapted from *Talking to Myself* (The New Press, 1995).

her calf is interfering with the turn of my card. How can a boy who has just turned sweet sixteen play a good game of cribbage under these circumstances? Damn this daughter of Eve.

I look up from my cards. Betty has gone. Uh-oh. Suppose Glenn Stauffer comes home unexpectedly. Ben, who should know, says, "Watch out for those little guys. The quiet ones. Don't ever cross a jockey. Murder." That's why Ben has never fooled around with Betty Stauffer. God knows she's made fat eyes at him often enough. Oh, yeah, I notice these things. And it doesn't help my cribbage game at all.

I toss in my cards. Mr. Barkie is surprised. I've never done that before, especially a sixteen hand. "I guess I'll go upstairs and study my catechism," I say. It's one of Horace Bane's catchphrases. He's full of such folksay. Another: "I guess I'll go get my ashes hauled." That's on Sunday morning, when he visits the girls on Orleans Street. Horace Bane is always bragging.

I find myself in the darkened corridor, near Glenn Stauffer's room. It's Betty's room, too. (I've never been an anti-feminist.) I rap, tentatively, on the door of the adjacent room. "Lucille, Lucille."

Our chambermaid, Lucille Henry, had earlier in the day asked for some fresh linen. On my arm are a Turkish towel, two pillowcases, and a sheet, all freshly laundered.

No response.

I pause before the Stauffer door. I call softly into the dark, "Lucille." Is that a bed squeak I hear? I have been blessed—or cursed—with keen hearing. Uh-oh. Suppose Glenn Stauffer appears at the head of the stairs. As Lord Arling did at the head of the bed. Returning unexpectedly from Henry VIII's coronation, he discovered his new-wedded wife under the sheets with Mattie Groves.

> Oh, he took his wife by the lily-white hand
> He led her through the hall
> And he cut off her head with his bitter sword
> And he stove it against the wall . . .★

★ One of three hundred medieval Border Ballads collected by Francis Child, Harvard Philologist.

Ben thought that was going a bit too far. Nonetheless, Betty, to him, was out of bounds.

How often have we read of mild little men who, on discovering betrayal, commit murder? Theirs is a sudden and gloriously gory transformation from bloodless vassal to bloody nobleman. In any event, Lucille did ask for fresh linen. Once again, I call out her name. My voice sounds so small and tight and far away.

I open the door. She looks up. Her face is sad. I stare at her. Imperceptibly, a slight smile appears. My Adam's apple is bobbing wildly. "If you happen to see Lucille . . ."

My voice trails off. I walk away from the open door toward the other end of the corridor, bawling out, louder than need be, the name of our chambermaid.

Betty hardly comes into the lobby any more. I barely glimpse her white dress as she flits up and down the staircase.

The following day, Ben appears to be in good spirits. I feel so much better.

"How you feelin', kid?"

"Fine," I say, feeling far from fine. Something tells me Betty Stauffer has a good deal to do with it. Daughter of Eve.

Years later, on hearing Cherubino's plaint, *Voi che sapete*, I get the drift. Cherubino, pageboy of the lovely countess, has that feeling. He's about sixteen, my age. No wonder it's my favorite of all Mozart arias. But if you think for one moment that I'll run Cherubino's risks, you're out of your mind. Imagine hiding in the closet of the countess's boudoir as the master returns. Okay, Count Almaviva, a dim-witted baritone, doesn't have too much to complain about, tomcatting around as he does. But suppose it were Lord Arling or, more to the point, Glenn Stauffer.

Ben is all business. "Kid," he says, "it's time we visited Orleans Street." He speaks glowingly of a girl named Laura. She's not too pretty but, he emphasizes, she's very understanding. Especially with novitiates. I have no idea what he's talking about, I tell him. All I want, as a young hotelier, is the avoidance of trouble. Ben insists on singing Laura's virtues. Who is Laura, I wonder, what is she, that all the swains commend her? Domestic tranquility is all I seek. Peace on the premises.

SOLLY WARD, the Dutch comic, is at the Star & Garter. It is one of our better burlesque houses. Was it 1926? '27? A sketch. He knocks on the door. The talking lady says, "Come in." She singsongs it. Solly enters. They embrace. Another knock on the door. "My husband!" she cries. Solly hides in the clothes closet. A man enters. He and the talking lady embrace. Another knock on the door. "My husband!" she cries. The man hides under the bed. Husband enters, a gun in his hand. "Where is he?" demands the outraged spouse. He discovers the man under the bed. They fire at one another. The talking lady screams. Blackout. Lights come on. Silence. The talking lady, as Fay Wray does in *King Kong*, trembles. Slowly, the door of the clothes closet opens. Solly Ward emerges. He sees the two dead men. He sees the terrified beauty. He studies the scene. At last, he says, "Iss ze var over? Goot. Now ve vill haff a little peace." Hands outstretched, he moves toward the talking lady. Blackout.

LUCILLE HENRY is laughing, too, as she makes the beds. My mother hired her six months ago. She and Bob Warner and Horace Bane and Ben are always laughing about something. I can guess. She's singing that dirty blues again.

> What is it smell like gravy
> Good if you really wanna know
> Well it ain't no puddin' an' it ain't no pie
> It ain't nothin' you don't have to buy . . .

Lucille descends the staircase and approaches the clerk's cage in which I sit. I pretend she's not there.

"Honey dripper."

Why does she call me that? She knows my name. As though I haven't troubles enough. I had rejected Ben's invitation. I shall never know what Laura looks like, let alone her charm. I court Lady Five Fingers rather than run the risk of Spanish ring. And now Lucille's laughter. Is there no right to privacy in these matters? They don't even have a warrant. Whatever happened to the Fourth Amendment of the Bill of Rights?

"She wants you to fix her radiator."

"Who?" As if I didn't know.

"The cute li'l girl. She says it's too hot."

"Why doesn't she turn it off?"

"Can't. Needs a wrench. Said for me to tell you to come up right away. She's meltin'."

I reach into the drawer and fumble for the proper tool. There is no need to hurry. I deliberately dawdle, determined not to be bullied by a chambermaid. Or a troublesome guest. Or Ben or Bob Warner or Horace Bane. I suspect they're all in on it. A conspiracy.

I tap on the door ever so lightly.

"Come in." Hers is the singsong of the talking lady at the Star & Garter. Am I Solly Ward?

She is in the middle of the double bed. Her knees are scrunched up against her chin. Her hands clasp her ankles, much in the manner of a little girl. She is smiling at me. I knew there'd be trouble the moment Glenn and Betty Stauffer mounted those stairs.

"Lucille said something about your radiator."

"Won't you turn it off for me? Please."

I turn off the radiator. There's no need for a wrench. A baby could do it. I show her. "It turns easily. See?"

As I walk toward the door, she shifts her position. Her legs are stretched out toward the edge of the bed. Her stockings are sheer, flesh-colored. There is a slave bracelet on her left ankle. There flashes through my mind the whispered innuendoes of Joe the Barber concerning women who wear slave bracelets. Ow! The wrench is cutting into the flesh of my hand. I'm gripping it too hard.

"Is this bandage too tight?"

She runs her hand down toward her right ankle, where a piece of adhesive tape is visible.

"Did you sprain it?" My voice is of a lower register than usual. Rather this than the high squeak, which might be forthcoming, considering the dryness of my throat. Oh, for a Dr Pepper. She nods.

"Feel it."

I move one small step toward her. I stretch out my hand, but I cannot quite reach her ankle. She pulls me toward her. The awkwardness of my position causes me to drop the wrench and tumble onto the bed. She slowly runs my hand against her injured ankle and up toward her thigh.

I abruptly draw my hand away and lean backward. In so doing, I lose my balance and topple heavily onto the floor. Ow! I have fallen onto the open jaws of the wrench. I spring up, fumble my way toward the door. I shout at it. "Radiator's shut off."

I slam the door behind me and stumble down the murky corridor. In the Mazda brightness of the staircase, I gently massage my wretched buttock.

In any case, I have retained my Parsifalian purity, but my wound, my wound, the indelicate imprint of the monkey wrench remains. The grail that Parsifal could not find is on my left buttock.

That night, I notice a wild strawberry, a flaming red, to which I apply an ointment. It lasts about a week, as scarlet as the letter *she* deserves. To think that poor, gentle Hester Prynne had sinned so little and suffered so much. Would Hester have enticed an innocent sixteen-year-old boy onto her bed or under the elm? A boy so burdened with the troubles of the world? Yet, why do *I* bear the mark, and in so unlikely a place, rather than this wanton daughter of Eve? God is so perverse at times. Which side is he really on?

My wrestling with angel and devil is doing little good for my cribbage game and less for my sleep. If I did the right thing, why am I not sleeping the sleep of the righteous? The puritan in me is having a hard time of it. For that matter, so is the pimp in me. And so is the Cherubino. As I struggle for peace of mind, the truth appears out of the blue.

It is Glenn Stauffer whom I've done it for. That's it, of course.
Our hotel is his home. It is his castle. Man's castle is not a steer's
barn. If Glenn Stauffer is to wear horns, let it be elsewhere. Oh, joy,
I am liberated.

On a Saturday afternoon, two large men lumber up the stairs.
They wear fedoras. One is silent. The other speaks in a flat voice.
"Let's see the register, son."

I hesitate. The spokesman flashes an open wallet at me. I see a police badge.

"We're from headquarters."

I push the long black book across the counter. The man shoves a
yellow sheet of paper at me. "Came over the wire last night."

I read it: "George Simmons, using the alias Glenn Stauffer. Bank
robbery. Kansas City. With woman. Brunette. Information leads us
to believe Chicago. Near North. May be armed. Caution advised."

"Anyone here by that name?" I nod.

"Is he in?"

Again, I nod. I had seen him go upstairs about half an hour earlier, with the Saturday *Three-Star* tucked under his arm. After paying his rent, he'd made a brief comment on the weather. Yes, she is
upstairs too. The brunette.

"Got a key?"

"Yes, sir."

"Lead the way, son."

I take the ring of keys off the hook. The men are close behind
me as I mount the stairs and walk down the corridor toward the
room. I am fingering the passkey. We pause in front of the door. We
have arrived soundlessly. I hear a faint conversation inside. The
crackle of a fresh newspaper being turned. Sounds of domesticity.
Man's castle.

Shall I knock? My knuckles are poised. One of the men shakes
his head, his fingers to his lips. He points to the keys in my hand.
Very carefully, very slowly, soundlessly, I insert the key in the lock,
turn the knob, and let the door float open. The men rush in.

Glenn Stauffer is reclining comfortably on the bed. He is in his polka-dot shorts. The *Three-Star* is spread out about him. The comics section is still in his hands as he is lifted off the bed by one of the men. He is held high, as a baby hoisted by a father. Like those of a frightened child, Glenn Stauffer's lips pucker, as though he is about to cry. How tiny and helpless he looks. The other man quickly frisks the bed, flipping away the punched-in pillow and turning over the mattress. Betty Stauffer, against the wall, covers her face.

Glenn Stauffer, in stocking feet and polka-dot shorts, is shoved against the bedstead by the other, who towers over him.

"You George Simmons?"

"My name is Glenn Stauffer."

His voice quavers. The other speaks softly now.

"Make it easy on yourself, George. Get dressed."

She rushes toward him. She is sobbing. He gently embraces her. The three of us look on—the three of us, for I am one of *them*. They are blubbering incoherently at one another. Betty is half a head taller than Glenn when he is fully dressed. Now, they both appear to be lost little orphans. He is blurting out brokenly.

"She don't know nothin' about this, honest. I picked her up—we met in a taxi dance hall. K. C. I been workin' here in the auto plant, Ford. Honest. You can check with my boss." He looks toward me. He is in tears. "Have I given you any trouble?"

I shake my head. I feel funny. A hard knot in my stomach. A cramp. My throat hurts. Do I have a fever? I'm in a cold sweat.

She is mumbling at him, "I love you, I love you, I love you." Her wet cheek is pressed hard against his. One of the others gently suggests she let him get dressed.

I ask if I might be excused. There is nobody downstairs minding the place.

"Sure," says one of the men. "Thanks, son. You're good. You opened the door so quick, you almost caught *us* with our pants down." He chuckles appreciatively. Obviously, I've done well. I race down the stairs, hang the keys back on the hook, and rush blindly toward the toilet. I make sure the door is bolted. I try to throw up. I am unsuccessful.

I am back in the clerk's cage. Too soon. The two men and Glenn Stauffer or George Simmons are at the landing. He waves at me. So-long. I wave back. We are both embarrassed. I mumble something about good luck, but he doesn't hear me.

It being Saturday, the lobby is busy. Cards played; racing forms studied; politics and religion argued; women discussed, pro and con. All is silence as I enter. They have an idea. Horace Bane is staring out the window. I look toward him. He doesn't see me. I study the calendar hanging crookedly on the wall. Its artwork: *September Morn*. It doesn't matter.

If a man's home is his castle—and surely that was the raison d'être of my behavior in the Stauffer affair, or so I convinced myself—why didn't I knock? There was that moment of uncertainty, outside the door. Why did I pause, with my knuckles poised, instead of doing the most natural thing: knocking on the door of a guest? Of course, the detective would say, Shhh, don't know. That's his job. But I am not a detective. I am not a cop. I'm a hotelier. And as I have told myself, not once but thousands of times, a man's home is his castle. Oh, boy. In that moment, at the age of sweet sixteen, I had behaved as a precocious advocate of the no-knock law.

George Simmons, alias Glenn Stauffer, was a bank robber. Perhaps he had a gun. Perhaps. The hard fact is: I knew Glenn Stauffer, not George Simmons. When I heard the *Three-Star*'s crackle outside his door, I envisioned Glenn on the bed, for I could tell from whence the sound came. I envisioned him in his shorts, for on past occasions I had seen him thus. The hard fact is: *I wasn't worried about any violence on his part.* I was thinking of pleasing the detectives. Quite obviously, I succeeded.

Because of my righteous behavior, I still see a small man in polka-dot shorts, in the presence of his sweetheart, hoisted high, an absurd and helpless baby. In his home that is his castle. Talk about humiliation. I can't speak for Glenn Stauffer. I can only speak for myself.

That was 1928. I was the Good Citizen and I still feel guilty. Perhaps that mark on my buttock should have remained.

Part II

8

Seeking Work

I was twenty-two when I graduated from law school, and like most students during the Depression, I was worried about getting work. We all looked in the *Civil Service News* to find available civil service jobs. Though it was 1934, the panic of '29 had taken hold and the country was still in shock.

The Civil Service entrance examination, modeled after British Career Service exams, lasted three or four days and asked about history, arithmetic, current events, everything. I was among those who passed, and I applied for a job as fingerprint classifier for the FBI. I didn't give much thought to the FBI aspect of it. I was thinking "fingerprint classifier," I was thinking about the *job*—the FBI had the most openings.

My first test was to appear before the bureau chief in Chicago, Melvin Purvis. Hoover attacked Purvis because he'd become nationally known for setting up the killing of Public Enemy Number One, John Dillinger, and Hoover was feeling eclipsed. Purvis was a Southerner, soft-spoken and polite when he interviewed me. Mostly, he wanted to know what books I read. I remember mentioning Thomas Wolfe's *Look Homeward, Angel* and Ring Lardner's *You Know Me, Al*. He passed me.

I discovered this years later, after requesting my FBI dossier, in which I found a memorandum from Hoover to his comptroller:

"Put Louis Terkel on the payroll at $1420 a year as fingerprint clas-sifier." I was in. It was a University of Chicago professor, his name blacked out, who said: "I remember him. Slovenly, didn't care much, a low-class Jew. He is not one of our type of boys." The next note is another from Hoover to his comptroller: "Take Louis Terkel off the payroll." I was out. Today I wonder how I was not "one of our type of boys." (Here's a fantasy: Mr. Hoover re-hires me for rea-sons I cannot fathom. It may be the end of Public Enemy Number One, Dillinger, at the hands of Melvin Purvis and he wants credit for capturing the New Public Enemy Number One. This is by far more dangerous. Nobody knows who he looks like, nobody has ever seen his face. He is absolutely elusive. I was hired as a finger-print classifier, which called for precision; but I become my other self: Inspector Clouseau, the hapless, fumbling detective, Pete Sell-ers' film creation. He has been my role model—or have I been his? In any event, my unique approach has come through. I have found my man. Only I have seen his face. My immediate supervisors are elated. They call a national conference—all radio and TV stations are alerted. As multi-millions hold their breath, I slowly, ever so carefully peel off the seal and there is the face and name—*posilutely* and *absotively*—of John Edgar Hoover.)

I wasn't despairing because there was still an open-territory feel-ing. The whole country was in a strange, unsettled state. Soon after, another job came along: Roosevelt had created the FERA, the Fed-eral Emergency Relief Administration. They hired me for a project that involved understanding the nature of unemployment at the time. In what industry was unemployment highest? Where? San Francisco, unemployed longshoremen; Pittsburgh, steelworkers; Akron, rubber workers. We had to find out who the unemployed were and why they lost their jobs.

Each city was assigned a table, and each table had a guy and five girls—the guy got more money, he was in charge. I was the guy in charge of Omaha. What's in Omaha? Stockyards. This was a good period for me: The job wasn't civil service, but it paid, I didn't have to put up an attorney's shingle, and the girls were good company.

In 1935, a horse named Omaha was running in the Kentucky Derby. I'm saying to the girls, "Omaha! I'm going to bet a half a dollar on him." Below the Wells-Grand was a cigar store that was run by a bookie. The girls had never placed a bet in their lives, but I got them excited about Omaha, so each one gave me a quarter. The Derby is Saturday afternoon, and I'm with my friend and we're going to see a movie. I figure we'll go to the movie and I'll place the bet—my half-a-dollar and the girls' money—later. We see *Bolero*, with George Raft and Carole Lombard, at the Castle Theater, right next to the Boston Store where my brother worked as a shoe dog on the fifth floor. We leave the movie, and go outside, and what is the headline? OMAHA WINS DERBY, PAYS 8 TO 1. Oh my God. I can imagine they'll be jumping up and down on Monday when I come in. I can't tell the girls I didn't place the bet. So it's $3.50 times five girls. I had to borrow about $18 to pay them because I had picked the winner. What happens Monday? The girls *are* jumping up and down, kissing me. They'd heard about it on the radio, and oh, were they happy. Just my luck: picking a winner who costs me twenty-eight bucks. And George Raft can't even act.

I'd have stuck out the Depression in Chicago, but for reasons of personal safety, I felt the need to decamp for other pastures. An event from my shady past had caught up with me.

College kids would often pick up an extra ten bucks or so working as poll watchers on Election Day. Moler's was a college barbershop where barbers trained and gave free or ten-cent haircuts—a favorite spot for the guys on skid row. The barbershop was closed that day so it could be a polling place, and many of the skid-rowers came in to vote, early and often, as the Chicago saying goes. A guy named Berghoff was my poll-watching partner. The city election officials would hire five guys: Three were judges and the other two were clerks. They'd get paid $7.50 a day. These were guys like some who stayed at the Wells-Grand Hotel—doddering old men, unsure and frail. These old guys were simply officials of the city, whereas the precinct captains, the guys who arranged for them to serve, were Republicans and Democrats. The Democratic precinct captain's name was Gordon and the Republican's was Romano, which happened to be the name of a Chicago family involved in various quasi-legal activities.

My righteous colleague, Berghoff, sat at the table by the judges, scribbling notes. I sat in the barber chair and watched. When Berghoff wasn't writing, he was glaring at me because I wasn't taking any notes. Some guys came in to vote three, four times. Money changed hands outside the barbershop; bottles of muscatel in paper bags, too; precinct captains kindly accompanied certain voters right into the booth. This went on all day. At one point, Gordon stuck a five-dollar bill in my shirt pocket. "Buy yourself a hat."

I said, "I don't wear hats," and handed back the five-dollar bill. Anything wrong going on?

Sure enough, this particular precinct was investigated. There's a trial, and Berghoff and I are subpoenaed. Who's on trial? The trembling old guys, the judges and clerks. The prosecutor is a light-skinned black guy named Cashin; the judge is named Jarecki.

Berghoff, good-looking, a law student, one of these upstanding law-and-order guys, is the first to testify. "Do you recognize these five defendants?" The five guys stand up and they're called by name. I'm thinking they'll probably get six months in prison, probably die there. Of course, the names of the two precinct captains are never mentioned!

It's my turn. Now what do I do? I could be Berghoff and say exactly what happened. Instead I say, "I don't remember."

Cashin says, "You don't remember? You just heard your colleague, Mr. Berghoff."

"Yeah, well, I don't remember." I don't think I knew I was going to lie until the moment I did.

I was like Huck Finn on the raft. When did Huck decide? Remember Jim, the runaway slave, and his companion, Huck, on the raft. The slave chasers, the bounty hunters say, "Is that guy on the raft white or black?" And in that one moment: "He's *white*." Oh my God. Well, here am I saying, "I don't remember."

"You don't *remember*?" You see the guys, shaky, about to fall down. So very much like guys I know from the hotel. That's when I decided, and at that moment I committed something close to perjury. The old guys were let off because of the split testimony. The gumless one, the gimpy one, the old rummy, the shaky one—Civilization, Teddy Tils . . .

Berghoff looked at me and I looked at him, and we hated each other's guts. I obviously violated a law, yet why did I feel good? As Huck put it: "If I go to hell, I go to hell."

Time passes and the court decides to call on the precinct captains, Gordon and Romano.

Prince Arthur Quinn was our precinct captain (later to become our state senator).* Young Prince Arthur knew my brother Benny, because Benny used to play the horses and gamble at a joint called Johnson's, a big booking palace on Clark Street two blocks away from the hotel. Prince Arthur was known to stop in at Johnson's now and then.

One day he comes in and says, "Hey, Ben, you got a kid brother. You like your kid brother?"

"Oh, I love my kid brother."

"Louis, is that his name?"

"Yeah."

"You want him to live, don'tcha?"

"Yeah."

"You know, he may get shot."

Artie explained: "I just wanted you to know that your kid brother is going to be called up as a witness against Romano. The Romano your brother remembers weighed about two hundred

* His father was known as Hot Stove Jimmy Quinn, back in the days of Hinky Dink and Bathhouse John early in the century. His father, sitting at the hot stove, named guys he thought should be mayor.

and sixty pounds. He's lost about a hundred pounds, he wears glasses, has a mustache. Your brother won't recognize him, he won't know who he is. But at the same time, I know his relatives, these wops, they're gonna knock him off if he fingers Romano. All Louis has to say is, 'I don't know the guy.' "

Benny says, "Oh, my brother, he'll play along."

So Benny tells all this to me. I think, holy Christ, I can't get called in front of Jarecki again. I can't tell the judge I don't remember Gordon and Romano. What am I gonna do? Then I thought of New York. I was in good standing with the FERA guys who ran the project because I did a decent job. I told them my aunt was very ill in New York and asked if they had any openings there. They did. They said they'd see if they could work something out. It so happened they could.

I went to New York for about six months and worked on the same unemployment project. And I kept seeing plays. Saturday, you could always pick up a single ticket for a matinee. That season I saw *Winterset*, about the Sacco and Vanzetti case, with Burgess Meredith. And *Porgy and Bess*. I saw Nazimova as Mrs. Alving in *Ghosts*, and Ruth Gordon and Pauline Lord in *Ethan Frome*. I was hooked on theater.

While I'm in New York living with my grandmother, I get a wire. The examination I'd taken for the fingerprint job had led to a different offer: counting Baby Bonds for the treasury department. It was an addition to the bonus FDR gave shortly after he was elected. A couple of thousand of us who hadn't made fingerprint classifier were called to Washington. Roosevelt had finally come through for the veterans of World War I. Remember? In 1932, thousands of veterans and family members, suffering from the Depression, campaigned and demonstrated in Washington, demanding the cash payout Herbert Hoover had vetoed in that failed attempt. The great marine hero Smedley Butler spoke on behalf of the soldiers, but to no avail.

An aside: Butler was "a pint-sized Marine for all seasons," in the words of his colleague General Douglas MacArthur, who once described him for *Smithsonian* magazine. "He was small, round-shouldered. He weighed barely 140 pounds dripping wet, and even when he was dry his uniforms seemed to hang off him like an over-size bathing suit. Yet this unlikely model for a recruiting poster was one of the really great generals in American history."

It was somewhat astonishing, a pivot punch from nowhere, to read how this hero described himself in *Common Sense* magazine, November, 1935:

> I spent 33 years and 4 months in active as a member of our country's most agile military force—the Marine Corps. I served in all commissioned ranks from a second lieutenant to Major-General. And during that period, I spent most of my time being a high-class muscle man for Big Business, for Wall Street and for the bankers. In short, I was a racketeer for capitalism . . . Thus I helped make Mexico and especially Tampico safe for American oil interests in 1914. I helped make Haiti and Cuba a decent place for the National City bank boys to collect revenues in. I helped in the raping of half a dozen Central American republics for the benefit of Wall Street . . . I helped purify Nicaragua for the International Banking House of Brown Brothers in 1909–12.

When the World War I veterans refused to leave, Hoover ordered the police to remove them. The D.C. chief of police, Captain Pelham Glassford, refused to take part in assaulting the veterans, in effect saying: I will not tear-gas my buddies. So Hoover instead enlisted Douglas MacArthur, with George Patton and Dwight Eisenhower as aides, to smoke the veterans out with tear gas and scare them off with bayonets.

It was a disaster—people were injured, some died. But now Roosevelt is president and finally a bonus is passed. Then came a move by congress to give the veterans an extra bonus—that was called the Baby Bonus. Say a guy named Joe Miller in Provo, Utah, is going to get an extra fifty bucks. I count out two $25 bonds. That's what we did all day. That's *all* we did all day. It drove me crazy.

I ended up sharing an apartment with a colleague, Monroe Campbell Jr., a very funny Southerner. He was gay, which I didn't realize until we started living together. He kept it quiet so he wouldn't get fired. Monroe found a nice Georgetown apartment up above a tearoom. Fifty bucks a month in Georgetown! Monroe liked to throw parties, and naturally, I was his co-host—mostly his friends, gay, wonderful people. All of Monroe's women friends looked like Dorothy Parker or Louise Brooks: bobbed helmet hair, only gray instead of black.

We used to go to the Deck, a gay bar with a nautical theme. The bouncers were women, very butch, some tough. But they all liked me. They knew I was hetero and the word they used for me was "jam." It's not a term used today, but apparently back then it applied to someone they could trust—a straight guy, wholly innocent, not overly hip, but someone you could bank on. Monroe was the first gay person with whom I became good friends.

We had a number of homosexuals who lived at the hotel, but I did not know them. Unlike the happenings in the Book of Luke, there was always room at the inn. Even for gay people.★ Even for couples without luggage.

I wasn't in Washington, D.C., for long, less than a year, but if it hadn't been for my friends and acting, I'd have lost my mind counting those endless Baby Bonds.

I had heard about the Washington Civic Theater Group and their plan to stage Sinclair Lewis's *It Can't Happen Here*, a play about fascism coming to America. Remember, there were several Ameri-

---

★ In DC, I was the one heterosexual that was accepted at the Deck. And since then? Better than any of the grandest of prizes, I'm in the Lesbian and Gay Hall of Fame of writers—one of the few heterosexuals, perhaps the only one. I also may be the only white in the Hall of Fame of Black Writers. There was a gathering of black writers, and Haki Madhubuti mentioned my name. They all looked up, "Studs?! But he's not African American, he's white." Haki said, "He's white genetically, but he's ours spiritually." I made those two halls of fame, which ain't half bad.

can fascist groups, among them the Silver Shirts. Gerald L.K. Smith, Brinkley, the monkey-gland quack, the founder of the America First Party, et al. I auditioned for the director, Day Tuttle, and won the role of a George Wallace–type figure named Shad LeDue. We performed at the Wardman Park Hotel Theatre, which seated four or five hundred people. I received a glowing write-up from a reviewer at the Washington *Star*.★

Shad LeDue is a handyman working for a man named Doremus Jessup, an old-world liberal editor of the paper. Jessup is basically a nice person, but he looks down on LeDue as crude, as a nothing. LeDue belongs to a group called the Corpos that take over the community, and he becomes a sort of gauleiter, a petty tyrant of the town, strutting around in a special Corpos uniform. What hit me most about playing LeDue was the question: Who are the guys who join these kinds of groups? Who are the guys who become like him? Who are the ones who fix the lock on the door, who put the bulb in?

You're the professor and the janitor hates your guts because he thinks you look down upon him or barely even recognize his presence. There are millions who, deep, deep down, feel disdained (which is exactly how the Reagan Democrats came into being). I remember years later C.P. Ellis telling me of how he became a Klansman and how the Klan used him, feeding on his feelings of being a nobody. Because if you're *nobody*, you can't endure it unless there's somebody below you.

I have never forgotten performing the role of Shad and the feeling I had standing on the stage in front of that large audience, the feeling of power in wearing that uniform. If ever there were a contemporary (2007) challenge to our sense of self, it is this one; especially, fundamentalism in either its spiritual or its secular form.

★ The same reviewer who said of Margaret Truman's celebrated vocal engagement, "Better she remain a vice president's daughter," to which Harry Truman replied, "I'm going to punch him in the nose."

9

The Actor

People have asked what might I have been had I not become what I am. Well, I would not have been a lawyer because it just wasn't there for me—I passed the bar, but it was more Sullivan and Cromwell than Clarence Darrow.

I have been an eclectic disk jockey; a radio soap opera gangster; a sports and political commentator; a jazz critic; a pioneer in TV, Chicago style; an oral historian and a gadfly.

How come I did not became a lawyer? I had attended the University of Chicago law school and received my degree.

It is difficult to explain; allow me. I did so in a response to the registrar of the University of Chicago law school asking certain alumni of their experiences. It was several years after I had covered the waterfront and had became something of a minor celebrity. Chicago was my home of course.

My three years at the U of C law school (class of '34) were the most bleak yet fascinating of my life. It was not the fault of the good professors; they did the best they could with me. Mine was a hopeless case. I was shamefully inattentive; my mind and heart were elsewhere.

During those years when I should have kept my gimlet eye on the Grail—Winston, Strawn and Shaw, or Mayer, Meyer, Austrian and Platt, and such home-and-hearths as Lake Forest, Kenilworth and Glencoe—I was lost in a world of daydream and fantasy. I had become a movie and theatre aficionado, and, most passionately, a lover of the blues.

I saw in Judge Hinton who taught procedure a bespectacled Lionel Barrymore. I saw in Professor Kent, who taught contracts, the portly Edward Arnold, who in movies best portrayed tycoons. And years later, whenever I saw the Brit actor, Alan Bates, I saw Charles Oscar Gregory who taught torts.

It was Sheldon Tefft, teaching Equity, who most impressed me. What I remember is not anything that he said, since, sadly, nothing memorable was said in torts, contracts and procedure. It was his voice that overawed me. His was a *basso profundo*, one octave lower than Feodor Chaliapin's. It was not Mussorgsky's Boris I envisioned in him; more of a *basso buffo*.

One day he called on me. (It was the only time I was ever called on during my three-year tenure, nor did I ever volunteer—perish the thought. I had successfully concealed myself behind a tall student until I heard Tefft's sepulchral voice call out my name.)

I hadn't the foggiest idea what the case was about, something in re a spite fence. I didn't like the smell of the decision, though I had no idea why. I said, "This is no court of equity, it's a court of iniquity." There may have been a nervous snicker from two or three of the class. (There were about two hundred of us males, three women.) I shall never forget the Dickensian touch in Tefft's righteous retort: "Not very amusing. Zero, of course." Of course, he was right.

What is so singular about my attachment to my alma mater is that the jewels in the crown among its present faculty, those most publicly profiled, are of a slightly more conservative bent than I, somewhat Scalian in nature. (I imagine it was something of an honor to have had Mr. Justice Scalia on our faculty at one time. It was years after I had departed. I imagine myself in his class, fantasizing again; seeing him as Puccini's Scarpia, Rome's fearsome police chief. What a rogue and peasant slave am I, to think such dark thoughts.

True, there are malcontents and congenital naysayers who look upon the U of C law school as an adjunct to our Nobel-wreathed school of economics, an institution that has succeeded admirably in proselytizing our new religion: Free Marketry. Yet, I realize the intemperance and unfairness of this note, because there are faculty members, past and present, and fellow alumni, whom I have come to respect and in some instances revere.

Those I know and especially remember with admiration and affection are Leon Despres, one of our city's finest public servants; Malcolm Sharp (I was in his very first class, Corporations); Abner Mikva, who has held to the highest standards; and, of course, the most beloved of all our law school teachers, Harry Kalven, gallant and learned advocate of the First Amendment.

Oh, yeah, I flunked the first bar exam held in June '34. They were yes-or-no questions. I had neglected to take the Baker or Evans quiz courses designed for the occasion. It wouldn't have helped anyway. I did pass the bar exam held in November. They were yes-but-on-the-other-hand essay questions. I was good at that.

Despite all of the above misadventures, I love the U of C law school and treasure those three years of attendance. Allow me to explain.

Never having driven an automobile, I was a streetcar student, traveling from the Near North Side to Hyde Park. It involved three trolleys. One point of transfer was in the black belt, known as Bronzeville. It was there while waiting that I heard recorded music—blues songs—blaring out of the gallimaufry stores; everything secondhand was for sale. Even used phonograph records. I fell deeply in love and bought them by the score, a nickel or a dime each. It may explain why I was so often late for class.

So it was that I came to listen to and learn from some of my most memorable mentors: Big Bill Broonzy; Memphis Slim; Tampa Red; Memphis Minnie; Roosevelt Sykes, the Honey Dripper; Duke Ellington's scratchy "Black and Tan Fantasy," Louis's "West End Blues" in which his horn and his mouth are fused, and even from Peatie Wheatstraw, the Devil's Son-in-Law.

Were it not for the U of C law school, where would I have been? What would have become of me? Those three years altered my life for the better. I think. And for that reason, I am deeply grateful.

INSTEAD OF LAW, I might have found myself doing something involving hotels. Deep down my dream might have been to become a theater critic—I did review a couple of plays for *Friday*, a short-lived liberal magazine. Remember, I started seeing plays when I was very young because of the posters put up at the hotel by the press agents.

Nobody at the hotel attended plays, but the press agents came to town a couple of weeks ahead of any play and they'd put up posters in the big hotels around the Loop. Since the Wells-Grand was in the vicinity, what the hell, they put up a sign: *In Abraham's Bosom*, by Paul Green, with Rose McClendon, a great black actress; or *Burlesque*, with Hal Skelly and Barbara Stanwyck. *Burlesque* is about an old hoofer and his faithful partner, a theme that's been done a million times. Skelly plays the old-time hoofer whose girl sticks with him even though a very rich guy, a good guy, wants to take her away. Toward the end, the old hoofer says, "You had this good guy and instead you're with me. Why are you doing that?" They're doing a soft-shoe as the curtain is descending.

She says, "Well, I married you for better or for worse."

He says, "Yeah. Better for me and worse for you." That's how it closes. I remember those last lines.

The Theatre Guild was an important group in American theatre. They traveled around, but they were based in New York. Lunt and Fontanne were members of the Guild, and they would do Lunt and Fontanne plays, such as George Bernard Shaw's *Arms and the Man* and *Pygmalion*. The Theatre Guild was a great theater company.

I remember seeing a play by the two Czech brothers, the Capeks.

It was called *RUR*, *Rossum's Universal Robots*. It's about a robotic revolution. Here's this factory that's spreading the idea of robots all over the world. The human beings are being served, but the robots revolt and take over and the human beings are out. The play is about a young couple of robots who have something called heart. These two robots, like Ferdinand and Miranda in *The Tempest*, discover each other. She's the one who says, "What something perfect this human being is." She'd never seen one before. They see each other. And that's how it ends, on a note of hope that the human being might come back. Never has *RUR* been as apropos as it is today.

FORTUNATELY, during my aimless search for a career, I met a man named Charlie DeSheim, who was also working for FERA. As a result of that meeting, I became an actor . . . entirely by accident. Charlie DeSheim was brilliant, quite a good actor, and a director.

After I met him, I'd get two tickets and see plays with Charlie, and all the time we'd talk theater. Charlie had a labor theater group and one day he said, "Don't be such a dilettante, why don't you come down and see us at work?" So I did. Today in Chicago we've got terrific acting, with many groups at work. But then it was very unusual; this was the only theater outfit of its kind. The group was originally called the Workers' Theater; eventually it became the Chicago Repertory Group. Those ten years, during the thirties and forties, when I was involved with the Rep Group, may have been the turning point of my life.

We were a farm club of the Group Theater—we used the same technique. Read the same book, *An Actor Prepares* by Konstantin Stanislavski. We'd work from a painting, say, *The Poker Players* by Monet, two guys playing poker. You know which one's the winner and which the loser. You take off from that picture and improvise the scene.

My first roles were small and offstage. In *Waiting for Lefty*, the theater is a union hall—the idea is that the people in the audience are union members. Actors were planted throughout the house and would say their lines from the audience. One of those turns out to be a phony, a fink. I lay into him and he starts running through the auditorium. This was during the time of a taxicab drivers' strike in Chicago, and we were performing at a strike meeting with cab-drivers in the audience. What do you think they did when this guy started running? They started smacking him! I hollered: "It's a play! It's a play! Don't! Don't! He's an actor!" The audience finally got the idea. The guy says, "I'm not doing this role any more." So I did his role (but that was nothing like being onstage).

I was sitting there one night, as a spectator, waiting for *Waiting for Lefty* to start. A guy gets sick and doesn't show up for a big part, so I pinch-hit. Joe. Right up on the stage, never been on stage before in my life. This is opening night at the Civic Opera House. I'd had no dress rehearsal for technical matters, lights, nothing. The lights go on, and I get up and start talking. In the play, I return home and the lights dim. I never had lights dim. Charlie told me in advance, "Keep talking. Even though the lights dim, they're not going out."

I remember I got a funny sort of feeling, but I kept on talking. I come home, and the place is empty. And then the woman playing my wife appears and I say: "Where's all the furniture, honey?"

"They took it away. No installment paid."

"When?"

"Today."

"They can't do that."

"They can't? They did." That's how my life as an actor began. That experience, doing that role, being in that theater group, *altered* my life.

Suddenly I had a way to earn a little money. Soap operas in Chicago! Charlie said, "There are loads of soap operas. You've got a rough talking voice; why don't you try out?" I became a sporadic soap-opera villain.

It was a catch-as-catch can existence. I'd appear as someone named Pete or Bugs or Bullets or The Chicago Kid. At times, my well-deserved end came in more bloody fashion. I was run off the cliff by some local constable; I was shot by a companion; in all instances, I was disappeared. In despair, I once asked the director if I couldn't play a good guy for a change, the hero perhaps. Ruefully, he explained, heroes had pear-shaped tones; mine were apricot-shaped.★

★ *Talking to Myself* (The New Press, 1995, p. 150).

10

Observer to Activist

The Chicago Rep Group was a center.* Its audience was made up of teachers and social workers and cabdrivers. It was the Great Depression and this was the theater of then: *Waiting for Lefty*, *Cradle Will Rock*. We'd perform street theater at picket lines and soup kitchens; we regularly appeared before unions, performing *Waiting for Lefty* as various strikes were being organized—performing in Union halls, Finnish halls, Polish halls, Czech halls. Chicago was full of vitality. High, low . . . roller coaster. This was the world I was engaged with and it was exciting.

When the Newspaper Guild was being organized in 1937, we did a special sketch for the occasion: COMPANY UNION SUITS HEARST in the soup kitchen. No one had ever thought of organizing newspapermen. Newspaper guys thought: Union? We're not blue collar . . . The guy who got them thinking otherwise was Heywood Broun. The big memory of 1937 is the steelworkers' strike and the Memorial Day Massacre. Though I wasn't present at the event, I was there the day after.

---

* When the war came along, everyone split up and went different places. Some to the West Coast, others to the East. Charlie DeSheim went to New York and became a member of the Group Theater. He was Nick the bartender in William Saroyan's *The Time of Your Life*. Charlie was big—he had an Orson Welles–type contract to go to Hollywood, but he caught phlebitis and died. William Saroyan spoke at his services.

The steelworkers were being organized, it was succeeding, and the big steel companies recognized the union—Carnegie, US Steel, and Bethlehem all had agreements. But one holdout in Chicago was the Republic Steel Company. The virulently anti-union head of the board, Tom Girdler, hired Chicago policemen, led by Captain Mooney, to protect the scabs and keep the union guys out during a strike at the plant. The strike was on, but this was not a strike day, it was Memorial Day.   ·

The workers and their families decided to have a picnic on the grounds: chicken and potato salad, and baseball. They were playing games, making speeches, and in the afternoon, a spontaneous parade took form. Someone threw a rock at someone else, next thing you know Captain Mooney orders: Shoot! The cops shot ten guys *in the back.*

The next day, I and a few other Rep Group members took a streetcar to Sam's Place, which was a bar where the union guys all met. This was a scene out of Matthew Brady's photo just after Gettysburg. Guys with wounds, bandages, beaten and bloody. Harry Harper, as handsome as David Niven, was shot in the eye. He wore a black patch and resembled the Hathaway shirt man in the celebrated ad.

About a week later there's a huge rally at the Opera House, *overflowing* with steelworkers. This was a bitterness rally after the Memorial Day Massacre. (My wife later told me that the Chinese had gatherings called bitterness meetings, in protest of wrongs.) I'm way up in the balcony next to a steelworker, and Carl Sandburg is taking a year-and-a-half to get a sentence out. Sandburg was a ham, and when he talked it took forever just for him to introduce a guy. "And, ah, they say . . ." and you're waiting, going crazy, ". . . there was a riot. And they say . . ." And you sigh. ". . . the strikers used sticks . . . and stones . . ." and the steelworker next to me says, "Come *on!*" Finally, "Now may I introduce the pres-i-dent of the brother-hood of . . . sleep-ing car porters . . . A. Phillip Randolph."

The chairman of the rally, Robert Morse Lovett, a beloved teacher of American Studies at the U of C, gets up and says, "Mooney is a killer, Mooney is a killer, we've got to stop these killers!"

The next day, Robert Maynard Hutchins, the brand-new young chancellor of the U of C, is in his office. All kinds of calls are coming in, members of the board are saying, "Fire Lovett. We've lost five million in funds!" •

Just then a popular old professor appears, James Webber Linn. The old professor says to the young new chancellor, "If you fire Bob Lovett, you'll have on your desk the resignations, signed and sealed, of twenty tenured college professors."

Hutchins says, "No, *I* won't. My successor will." That was the spirit of the times.

11

A Bouquet from the Colonel

After I returned to Chicago from Washington, I kept up with the Rep Group and again acted as a gangster in Chicago soap operas. By this time the Works Progress Administration (WPA) had begun. There was hammer-and-shovel work—millions repairing and building roads, construction of low-income housing and public buildings. There were the arts projects: painting, dance, music, theater. Out of the Federal Theater Project came a new style called the Living Newspaper. It was an invention of the columnist Heywood Broun, founder of the Newspaper Guild.

Living Newspaper was multimedia theater: It might be a piece of newsreel, a narrator, a dramatic scene, a bit of music. It always involved the social issues of the day. There's a bit of that in *Citizen Kane*—at the beginning you have *The March of Time*. Roosevelt's second inaugural address had a core phrase: "I see one third of a nation ill-fed, ill-clothed, ill-housed." *One Third of a Nation* was a Living Newspaper about the lack of housing. New York had a production, but Chicago had its own adaptation, about wooden two-flats rather than tall tenements. I played Angus K. Buttoncooper, the "little man" narrator.

Meanwhile, I had applied to the WPA Writer's Project, submitting something in longhand about Tecumseh, the Indian chief, and his eloquence as a speaker. A new endeavor came out of the Writer's

Project—the Radio Division. There were six writers; Barry Farnol was our chief. We did a series in collaboration with the Art Institute. We'd consult their curators—I spoke with the French curator for a script on Daumier; the American curator for one on Albert Pinkham Ryder; the Dutch curator for one about van Gogh.

The scripts aired on WGN, with a director and professional actors. WGN Radio (along with the Chicago *Tribune*) was owned by Colonel Robert McCormick, known to all Chicago as "the Colonel."

One day Barry Farnol comes in and says, "Would you believe what I've got? This letter went to the head of our project, Curtis McDougall: 'I have just listened to your fine program about great artists on my station and it was wonderful. I'm so proud to have you with us, and I want to thank you for enriching Chicago's culture.' " Signed "Colonel Robert M. McCormick."

I'm convinced that the Colonel fell asleep long before the program ended, and certainly before the credits came on. The credits? "Written by: [say] Studs Terkel [or Arnie Freeman, or Richard Durham], under the auspices of the Works Progress Administration, Harry Hopkins, Director." And if there was one person the Colonel hated more than Franklin Delano Roosevelt, it was Harry Hopkins. He had to have been sound asleep when those credits hit the airwaves.

The Colonel had something called the *Saturday Evening Symphony Hour* on WGN, heard throughout the country. Win Stracke was a member of the chorus. His friend Fran Coughlin produced the show and said to Win: "I've got a problem. The Colonel has to speak at one time or another in the show—five minutes about his adventures, and knowledge of the war, and the military. My problem: The Colonel has potatoes in his mouth. People automatically turn him off. The audience gets cut to a *third*. I gotta figure out how to do this. I won't have him on at a certain time, I'll keep changing it around so people can never be certain."

Win witnessed one especially memorable performance. The

theater seats about five hundred people, the Colonel sits fifth row center so he can more easily come up to the stage to speak. Aisle seat, naturally. This day, four beings enter and parade down the aisle: The Colonel, his Great Dane, Governor Dwight Green (the handsomest governor Illinois ever had) with his red silk kerchief, and finally the Colonel's wife. That was the order: the Colonel, the dog, the governor, the wife.

The Colonel takes the stage: "In the battle of Ontario . . ." and the audience is immediately getting the glazed look. Fran Coughlin has his hands clasped in prayer, "Oh, God, I hope this will be over fast." Just then the dog starts snuffling. The snuffle was *tremendous.* Heard all over America. Mrs. McCormick did the only logical thing: She reached over to the governor, took out his silk handkerchief, reached across the governor to wipe the dog's nose with the handkerchief, the dog snuffled into it, and then she put the handkerchief back in the governor's pocket, and the Colonel went on talking. Win said it was quite a wonderful moment.

A MAN NAMED ED GOURFAIN was my first benefactor. Eddie was an advertising agency guy, a fan of the Chicago Repertory group. He's the guy who got me started on the air as *myself*, while I was still working as a gangster in soap operas. Eddie liked my style, so during the 1940s, he put me on his show as a commentator—I was the only pro-Roosevelt commentator in Chicago at the time.

Ed happened to know a guy named Louie Greenberg, who was an accountant for the Mob in Chicago. Ed sent me to a meeting with Greenberg. Eddie said, "Greenberg's going to give you a watch, it's not going to work. He's going to give you something else, that's not going to work. But you have to remember that he gave you stuff."

By this time Ed's agency had hired Paul Harvey and he was a sensation. He would outdraw me a thousand to one. No comparison. Louie Greenberg says to me, "Can you open a brewery for me?

Paul Harvey did." In fairness to Paul, he had no idea who his sponsors were. I did. Harvey was always hail-fellow-well-met.

At the end of the meeting, Greenberg says, "Here, I want you to have this," and it's a watch that doesn't work, and some perfume for my wife. Then Louie says he wants to show me something. "See this little book I got here? Some guys have books with the names of horses they want to play, names of girls they want to see. I have names of guys I'm going to get even with. They're all in my book."

Except for one thing . . . one of those guys had Louie's name in *his* book, and one day Louie and his wife are found dead—a head job—outside a famous Emerald Avenue restaurant on the South Side where he'd taken us for our meeting. I felt bad that I hadn't come through for him.

THE FIRST SPONSOR Ed got for the show was Erie Clothing Company, Hyman Blumberg, proprietor. I had a sort of liberal, pro-FDR audience, and Erie Clothing was doing well. Blumberg himself had never heard my show; he took Ed's word that it was OK. Then I goofed up, in perverse fashion as it turned out.

The poet Archibald MacLeish had written a book called *You Have Seen Their Faces*, Margaret Bourke-White did the photography. I loved MacLeish's writing; it was powerful. The Colonel was socking everybody who had anything to do with the New Deal. First time he had color cartoons on the front page of the *Tribune*, all anti–New Deal, by John McCutcheon. They showed: "crazy professors" carrying a red flag; guys leaning on shovels, lazy no-good "boondoggling" bums. And one was an attack on Archibald MacLeish, whom Roosevelt had appointed Librarian of Congress.

One day, I read the Colonel's piece against Archibald MacLeish. I quoted some of Archibald MacLeish's poetry on the air. I said, "This is the man Colonel McCormick calls traitorous." Then I blasted the Colonel. It had never happened before. The Colonel was *never* blasted.

Next day, Eddie Gourfain calls me: "We're in trouble. Hyman Blumberg is about to bounce you from Erie Clothing."

"Bounced for what?"

"Because of your Archibald MacLeish thing."

"You mean he didn't like the MacLeish thing?"

"*No*, no! You're about to be bounced because of the *reaction* to it."

"What *was* the reaction?"

Ed does a takeoff on Blumberg, accent and all. "What happened? A couple comes in from Rockford, they drive all the way in: Protestant people, very rich, aristocratic, a man with a gray moustache and his wife. They come in and buy a thousand dollars' worth of clothes." A thousand dollars was a lot of money back then. Blumberg is flying: "They buy all the clothes and they say, 'Can we see the manager?'

"I come out, they say: 'I want to congratulate you, Mr. Blumberg, you're the first one with enough guts to criticize Colonel McCormick. My wife and I have been waiting all our lives for this! We don't need these clothes, but we had to support you.' "

And all Blumberg knows is: "I criticized Colonel McCormick? I, Hyman Blumberg?"

Eddie says, "But they bought a thousand dollars' worth of clothes!" The response?

"Me, Hyman Blumberg, criticizing Colonel McCormick?! *Get Toikel off the air!*"

So I lost my sponsor.

Another sponsor lost was a furrier, William Lewis. "Mr. Gourfain, you gotta do something about that Terkel. I depend upon the Polacks and the Schvartzers. I depend on them, don't I, for credits? Instead, after Terkel is on the air I got all kinds of phone calls about how great he is, and they buy stuff for *cash*. These schoolteachers and goddamn social workers, and library people, these intellectuals, they buy the stuff and they're paying cash. *Do something!* Get rid of him!"

You could say that was the beginning of my following.

12

Ida

The first time I saw Ida, I remember she was wearing a little maroon smock. She was working for FERA, same as Charlie DeSheim and myself. She was a graduate of the University of Chicago School of Social Service Administration, which was like all seven sisters rolled into one, *the* school for social workers. Sophonisba Breckinridge was the head of the SSA, along with the celebrated sisters Grace and Edith Abbott, and Ida studied with them, she had the best of credentials.

A funny story: when she was twenty-two, twenty-three, a young social worker, she was assigned to someone at Mecca Flats, a huge complex, mostly African American. This was before public housing. She went to see a client, a middle-aged black woman, who answered the door: "Little girl," she said, "I thought you was a settled lady, instead, you ain't nothin' but pig meat," because she was so little and young. "Pig meat" was a phrase used affectionately about someone innocent and cute.

Working for the FERA, at times I'd go from agency to agency, and Ida was working at a West Side agency I visited. That first time we met, someone who did volunteer work for the Rep Group was also there and told me Ida was sympathetic to the kinds of causes we supported. The woman said, "See her, maybe she'll buy some tickets."

I looked at Ida; she looked pretty good. I noticed that not only was she pretty, beautiful, really, but that people were drawn to her. It seemed like there was always somebody at her table; if not a client, her co-workers would be sitting there. Someone might be crying about something, or just talking intently. I liked something about her, liked that people opened up to her.

That first day she bought a couple of tickets, and that's how we started to get acquainted. She liked the plays, and then I guess she got caught up in the idea of a theater group. She would have been perfect as Mattie Silver in *Ethan Frome*, but she wasn't an actress. They needed someone to help sell tickets and that's what she ended up doing.

When we met, I was also working in radio soap operas, and I think Ida saw me as a sort of gangster. I wore my fedora down at a raffish tilt, and talked a certain way, with just a touch of the hooligan. I was Jimmy Cagney.★

Our first real date was when I took her to see *Club de Femmes,* a very advanced French movie that touched on lesbianism; it starred Danielle Darrieux, who later became a collaborationist. Ida was impressed. Afterward, we went to dinner. The bar served peach brandy, a *horrible* drink. It came in a huge glass, which made it worse. We had peach brandy that night. Awful. But she agreed to go out with me again. I took her to see a lot of foreign films, French, Italian, Russian films. *Alexander Nevsky*, Prokofiev music, *The Baker's Wife*, with the great Raimu. She'd never seen films like that before.

Ida had several different roommates, and one was named Stern, a rather elfin and playful girl. One night Ida dreamt she'd gone outside, naked, and Stern shut the door on her. In the dream, she's standing outside naked and just then a man passes by and Ida says,

★ Ida always called me Louis, never Studs. The nickname came about during my first appearance in *Waiting for Lefty*. Two other guys in the cast were named Louis, which made for some confusion. At the time, I was entranced by the writings of James T. Farrell and his Studs Lonigan trilogy. Everyone started calling me Studs.

"I'm not at my best, Mr. Smith." She did have a certain humor. I liked that about her, too.

Once we started getting serious, it was an easy, very delightful courtship, though visiting my mother was always an adventure. I was still living with Annie at the time. When Ida was first going to meet my mother, I warned her, "Well, she's a little on the nervous side." An understatement, you might say.

First thing, Annie says, "So you're it, you're a college girl. Hmm . . ." Then the topper: "You should kiss my hands and feet for giving you such a man!"

Ida said, "Oh, all right, sure." And she bent down . . .

"Oh, *stop!*" Annie brushed her off. Ida had her number and my mother knew she had it. Annie treated Ida differently than the others. Sophie and Mary, Meyer and Benny's wives, were simple, hard-working women, stenographers, typists, who didn't go to college, and my mother was scornful. She wanted a certain kind of recognition and success, and to her, Sophie and Mary in no way met the standard.

When my Aunt Fanny, my father's sister, and her husband knew I was going with Ida, they wanted to meet her, and so did my cousin Charlie. He was also one of my closest friends, and he hung around with real killers. He had by this time become a soldier in the Mob and had married a semi-hooker who was also there for the introduction. We went to a club to eat with them. Now, here's sweet Ida from Wisconsin. Her parents, hardworking people, good people, owned a wearing apparel store. There were eight kids in the family—one shy of a baseball team: five boys, three girls. So we're at this gathering to meet my family.

Ida said: "My introduction to your aunt was a rather interesting one. The first thing Fanny said to me, she took me by the arm, and kissed me on the cheek, and she said, 'I want to tell you something. See that woman there? She killed my brother.' " She was pointing at my mother. That was Ida's introduction to the Terkel family. "She killed my brother."

∙ ∙ ∙

WE DATED FOR ABOUT A YEAR, and then we got hitched. One day, I said, "Let's get married." Like that.

She said, "Great."

Ida's brother-in-law worked for a steel company and was doing pretty well, so the wedding was at her sister's house in Highland Park. Annie was a certain kind of woman who, shall we say, was hard to make happy, but even my brother Ben was a little shocked at the festivities. There was no booze.

My mother said, "Where's the pastrami sandwiches?" Well, you know she's going to complain anyway. What they had was coffee and cake.

Ida said, "It was my idea."

"Your idea? Coffee and a piece of cake?!"

Benny wanted a little shot of whiskey so he thought the whole thing was rather outrageous. "No drinks?! Unbelievable."

Ida said, "This is the way I'd like it. I asked for this."

But my mother, of course, that's all she needed. "No corned beef sandwich? What is this?" So that was the wedding. 1939.

OUR LIVELIEST GUEST was always Ida's younger sister, Minsa. She was a character—very pretty and very, very eccentric. She'd studied dance with Martha Graham and ended up marrying a renowned Italian painter, Alberto Burri.

Earlier on, during one visit, Minsa made three dates in the same day: with a young dentist, a young lawyer, and a young doctor. My job was to entertain each guy as she went for a walk with the previous one.

Ida said to her, "You know, you really can't do that. Three dates. That's a lot. And see, Studs is stuck here now." And I *was* stuck.

I said, "Maybe I'll get these guys drunk or something." But each one waited patiently and she got rid of the last guy without the next one knowing.

Minsa had an innocence about her, and yet she was always in charge. Another visit, she has a boyfriend, Frederick something, a Viennese guy. He does nothing, sort of hangs around. Apparently, he has a gold mine somewhere, a map and all that. Minsa wants to stay in Chicago, and she wants to be at a hotel that's modest in price but not seedy. So Ida finds something called Canterbury Courts. We're there, waiting, and I decide to go out and get a bottle of J&B to celebrate, to welcome our visitors.

I walk to the corner; I see a big crowd gathering. There's a young guy with glasses, a cabdriver. There's somebody in a coolie hat, gesticulating wildly, and of course it's Minsa. She's bawling the cabdriver out. Standing to the side is Frederick, with the luggage, always lots of luggage. I'm coming closer, and Minsa calls out, "Oh, Studs, darling, see what he did? He deliberately says he's out of gas. Now where is it we have to walk?"

I say, "You're only half a block away." This poor guy says, "I *am* out of gas."

She says, "I'm going to call and report you. What's your license number?"

I say, "No, you're not." I say to the guy, "Don't worry, it's OK."

"You're sure?"

"It's OK."

So now we come with the bottle of booze and the two of them, upstairs, and there's Ida waiting in the hotel room. Minsa says, "What have you got here? This is a junkyard. What in the world?" And now they have a dispute.

Ida says, "Minsa, you wanted something modest-priced, this is modest in price!"

"No, I'm not going to have it!" She goes out and finds another hotel, and the next thing you know a young bellhop is carrying all her luggage. Whatever she wants. She has a way. I went to tip him a fin, and she says, "Oh, no, no." And the *bellhop* says, "No, no, no . . ." She did something to people.

Ida and Minsa were close, despite everything. Ida was closest to all of them. She's the one the family all came to, the one they all called.

Ida was a far better person than I, that's the reality of it. People wouldn't exactly come to me for advice. They would for an idea or to put my name on a letter, but for personal advice, they'd come to her, men and women both. She had a certain empathy I lack. And she was more politically active than I.

She had several black friends, also social workers, and was part of a group of three or four that went into a restaurant to break the color line. Things were thrown at them. Ida was gentle, but she was no pushover. When there were gatherings, she was there to demonstrate. As Garry Wills put it, "Studs was envious of her because her dossier was bigger than his." She was arrested along with Garry during an anti-Vietnam protest.

One of my favorite stories about her: She's picketing a church, and an old priest comes out and says, "Get away from my sidewalk!"

She says, "Oh, Father, I thought the sidewalk belonged to the people who walk on it."

"Get away, this is my church."

"Father, I thought the church was that of your parish."

"What is your name?" he demands.

"Ida Terkel, Father, what's yours?" And then he rushes back inside furious.

A young priest at the top of the stairs looks at Ida, this rather attractive, lithe woman, and he winks. A big wink! A wink that Ida says was definitely everything. But mostly it was a wink to show he agreed with her reasons for being there. So that was her manner. Easygoing. But on occasion . . .

Once Mike Royko was off on a tear, talking about ragheads. Ida interrupted: "Mike."

He says, "What?"

She says, "Fuck off."

"Did you hear what she said?" She hardly ever used foul language. Everybody there was astonished. Mike could never get mad at her. He was just stunned 'cause he thinks, sweet little Ida. "Did you hear what she said to me? She told me to fuck off!" And then he says, "What a bod!" He'd always say that of her.

She looked like a dancer, and she was a fantastic dancer, light as a feather. Guys loved to dance with her. I'm a lousy dancer. She finally gave up trying to get me on the dance floor. I did dance with her one time. She said, "Now, you've just got to relax." She's leading me, trying to.

"I can't do it, I can't do anything."

"Sit down." By this time, a couple of guys had come over anyway. Like, "Look, we want to dance with Ida. Do you mind?"

"Nah, go ahead." It made her happy to dance.

AFTER IDA DIED, so many letters were sent to me, and to our son, Dan. There was one from this big girl, beautiful girl, about six feet tall. A lovely Amazon. When Ida was sick, she'd worked for us for a couple of weeks. She was a bit of a country girl, unsophisticated. She wrote: "I was only with you for a couple of weeks, and I knew your wife only a short time, but it changed my life." She said they were shopping at Treasure Island, an upscale supermarket, and they were overcharged, it was a big mistake.

Ida said, "Don't worry about it."

The girl said Ida went over to tell the cashier of the error. "I saw the way she spoke to the cashier, and she didn't want to hurt this woman who was just working there. She did it in such a kind way. I was so affected by that. And I never forgot her."

Little things like that . . . Did she play a tremendous role in my life? Yeah, you could say so.

13

Reveille

I didn't think the country could lose World War II. Somehow the feeling was so strong here; there was a unity, a tremendous solidarity. We were all a little too gung-ho. The phrase "gung-ho" was at first a Communist saying. It was used by Mao and brought here by Major Colonel Evans Carlson. "Gung-ho" meant "working together." Isn't that funny?

I was going along with the people in the Chicago Repertory Theater Group. Remember, this was after the Spanish Civil War and the Anti-Fascist Refugee Committee—for those who'd been fighting for the Republican Army in Spain. Woody Guthrie used to tease lefties about their change from being antiwar to pro–ending Fascism.

I was drafted, but I would have gone anyway. Oh, I was absolutely patriotic. I wanted to join; I was against Hitler. I was doing broadcasts at the time, pro-Roosevelt broadcasts in favor of a short ballot so soldiers overseas could vote. They were overwhelmingly for Roosevelt.

Ida was for my going, though she didn't care for war. She's the one who insisted I use quotes in the title of *"The Good War."* Before being inducted, I had been raising money for the Soviet American Friendship Committee and the Anti-Fascist Committee. She'd write to me in the Air Force telling me I'd been missed at this or that event. But these were private letters, they were love letters, and I later found out FBI guys were reading them. The Air Force was spying on me and I didn't know.

September of 1942 is when I went into the Air Force. By this time, I was fairly well known; I'd been on the air doing pro-FDR commentaries and all that. The Chicago Repertory Theatre Group used to have parties that were *the* parties of the year. They'd put on sketches and skits from various plays. All our parties were for causes, and I'd been the emcee of a number of events. The theater group threw a big party in honor of my going into the Air Force, but the cause may have been for a guy about to be lynched, or for the Anti-Fascist Refugee Committee. It was a big jam, a midnight party, and Billie Holiday came over from a nearby nightclub to sing. A couple of guys in the band were friends of the rep group.

Billie said to me, "What would you like to hear, baby?" She sang "Strange Fruit" and "Fine and Mellow."

So I go in the Air Force, LS—Limited Service—because of a perforated eardrum. We were in three different barracks, BTC, Basic Training Centers. Being in the Air Force changed me in certain ways. Until then, I'd never smoked, never used swear words. I was older than most of the kids, but I liked the camaraderie.

First we were sent to Jefferson Barracks in Missouri for regular barracks stuff, basic training. We were all LS guys. Nothing unusual happened, except seeing this country kid taking a bunch of East Coast sharpies for a ride in dice. He looked just like a goofy, freckled, perfect rube, an easy mark, a Toby. His humor was pulling his eyelids back so his eyes would pop out. Toby humor. (Toby was a tent-show hero for rural people, and Toby always gets the better of the big-city wise guy.)

These hotshots from New York and Philadelphia played dice and poker and he'd wipe them out every night. They didn't know what hit 'em. I got a great kick out of that.

In basic training, you learn the use of a gun. I never understood how that all worked. Being LS, I wasn't going to be sent overseas to fight, so it didn't matter. We'd do our calisthenics and one exercise was leaping over a fence. Everybody could leap over a fence except me. I wrote to Ida: "All I say is, 'Stalingrad!' " Stalingrad was a big turning point of the war where the Soviet Army held off the German troops. So I'd holler "Stalingrad!" and bump into the fence. I'd holler "Stalingrad!" and fall on my ass. I tried and tried. Couldn't make it. They finally took me off it as hopeless.

Then we went to learn typing at Camp Foley, in Logan, Colorado. I didn't learn typing at all. I couldn't learn; I wasn't very good mechanically. The big thing at Camp Foley was Mike U. and me. He was this crooked bailiff from New Orleans, the only guy older than me. I was thirty-one, the other guys were eighteen, nineteen— all away from home for the first time and scared stiff—and Mike was about forty. He knew the First Sergeant and got us out of doing all kinds of stuff. Mike had wonderful stories and these kids would listen to him. He and I were avuncular with the younger guys.

I remember a frigid winter morning, outside of Denver, in the Rockies, cold as hell. Calisthenics. Six o'clock in the morning. *Freezing.* Mike says, "Where you going?"

"I'm going out."

"Are you *crazy*? Come with me!"

"No, I gotta go."

He says, "Come with me!" We go to the PX, it's open, and we get two nickel cigars, Red Dot cigars. We go down into the men's room of the PX in the basement, and it's *warm*, and it's wonderful. The windows are barred and we're puffing away at the cigars. We look at the kids out there and they're so *cold*, and they're doing all the exercises *trembling*.

"Toikel, Toikel . . ."—certain Deep Southerners have a New York accent. "Toikel! Look at those boys. Ain't you proud of them?"

I said, "I am very proud of them."

"Look at those wonderful young warriors. They're defending us. They're *terrific*." Puffing a cigar like General MacArthur.

Mike was outrageous. He was great, but he'd never allow me to do anything. "You're thirty-one! Are ya crazy? Let's get a couple of cigars and be proud of our men."

After Camp Foley, we went to Miami for a short stint. Our job there was to see that the windows and shades were kept clean. Since I'd worked at the Wells-Grand, they had me listed as a hotel clerk. The First Sergeant, a tough German guy named Schmidt, was always goofing off. He said, "You were the clerk of a hotel. Look, every day I have to take a nap between one and three. Be sure you wake me up." I'd wake him up at a certain hour, so he gave me privileges. I'm always getting in good with someone, it seems. (In my FBI dossier, the comments were always pro-me.)

A guy in town I knew from Chicago radio days was in charge of a local theater. He was doing radio shows, short stories, dramas, for soldiers, done by soldiers. I was an actor, I was good at radio, so he had me come in and I appeared in a good number, and that helped pass the time.

Then came Greensboro, North Carolina, it was a new camp just starting, and that's where I was made into a sergeant. That's also where I met Jack O'Keefe: redheaded, freckled, tooth missing. He was so funny. He used to write for Eddie Cantor. He had a certain way of talking, a sort of gargle. The words came out and you'd be rolling on the floor. He loved beer. Beer, beer, beer, all the time. When he wasn't around, you knew he was off somewhere drunk.

Captain Berlinrut, a very nice guy, knew I was Jack's friend. He'd tell me: "Go pick up the package." O'Keefe is the package. He says, "You know where he is?"

I say, "Yeah."

"Pick it up." So I'd go find O'Keefe. There he is, staying with this poor woman with six kids. She worked for the Levi Strauss clothing company, which was there in Greensboro, and she always had an icebox full of beer.

I say, "Jack, we gotta go."

And now he's going to take the offensive. He starts talking about the South and racism. He's warming up for the captain. He knows he's gotta face Captain Berlinrut after being gone for four days, and so he's, "Fucking racist bastards . . ." O'Keefe walks right in to Captain Berlinrut. "How are you, Sergeant O'Keefe?" "You know something, I don't have much hope for our country. There's too much racism and viciousness!" Berlinrut is trying not to laugh. He goes on: "Captain Berlinrut, we've got to do something about this."

"I know, but where were you for four days?"

"Let me tell you about what happened. On the way here, I saw an old black man going by and this other guy just shoved him out of the way. You gotta stick up—"

"Yeah, that's great, but about the four days?" That was Jack.

I worked in the special services, arranging entertainment for the soldiers. I had a radio show about what was happening in the world, anti-fascist news, events, and music. *Oklahoma!* had just come out, so we had songs from *Oklahoma!* We had a couple of singers. I found this kid, Elmer Bernstein, who played piano, and I took him out of the branch so he could play piano for groups. He went on to become a very popular movie-music composer.

The colonels all liked my program. Then I get a call from G2, which is Army Intelligence. A kid I knew had been spying on me, a Southern kid who worked for the Chicago papers. You know what he said in his report about me? "Good-natured, amiable, great company, I would trust him with anything. Absolutely American." Below, his superior writes: "All the more reason. Keep your eye on him."

By then, I knew I was being shadowed. I wasn't nervous, but it was strange. Now I'm called into G2 by this captain, a New Englander, who seems a pleasant enough guy. The first thing he says is, "I didn't ask for this job." Then he tells me about himself, how he used to work for John Winant, an enlightened Republican senator from New Hampshire who ended up killing himself. The G2 finally says, "Well, I've got a whole list of things about you, and one big factor is this little slip of paper."

It was a yellow sheet of paper that said: BILLIE HOLIDAY WILL AP-
PEAR AT FAREWELL FOR STUDS. It said she'd be appearing with J.C.
Higginbottom the trombonist. The fact that Billie Holiday sang for
me was held against me because the FBI hated her. As soon as she
began performing "Strange Fruit" and singing at benefits for politically progressive causes, the FBI started tailing her.

I went into the Air Force in September, 1942, and was released in
August, 1943. The kids with me were going overseas, and because
of my eardrums I couldn't go with them. I felt bad; I wanted to go
overseas, because of the avuncular feeling for these kids and that
feeling of camaraderie. Hell, yes, I was close to some of them. Don't
know what happened to them once we parted.

After I got out of the Air Force, I wanted to join the Red Cross,
so I wrote, sent my record. They said, "Fantastic, come see us." I go
see them and they're unfriendly, completely cold: "No, we have no
position for you." They're all wearing rimless glasses, look the same,
icy stares, will not even shake my hand.

As I walked out I'm sure all eyes were on me. What happened? A
Chicago FBI guy was giving information to a man named Dan
Lydon who ran a neighborhood newspaper. Lydon had a column
about me: "How come Studs Terkel is still on the air?" He's a dangerous commie. Unbelievable. An FBI guy had spilled the goods! It
resembled the Valerie Plame scandal. Sometimes you gotta wonder
exactly who the patriots are. The fact remains that I was followed
for a long time.

14

Lucky Breaks I

After leaving the Army, I came back to Chicago, and through a friend got a job with the Meyerhoff agency, bang, right off the bat. P.K. Wrigley, the chewing-gum heir and Cubs baseball-team owner, offered his island, Catalina, to the Merchant Marines for the duration of the war. I went there to do scripts for a series called *We Deliver the Goods*. Many people don't realize that, as a percentage of personnel serving, the Merchant Marines lost as many men in World War II as the Army and Navy put together.

In the meantime, it is September, 1944, and the elections are coming up—Roosevelt running for his fourth term, against Tom Dewey. Leo Lerner, the owner of a neighborhood newspaper chain, was the founder of the Independent Voters of Illinois. He wanted me to be the voice of the IVI. Leo and I visit Marshall Field III and he gives us a $5,000 check to start the program. I was the voice on the air once a week, Friday nights, on WCFL. I got paid maybe fifty bucks a shot.

By this time at Meyerhoff, I'm working on the Wrigley account, under the wing of I.J. Wagner, the inventor of the singing commercial. He liked me and suggested I do a sports show, *The Atlas Prager Sports Reel*. Atlas Prager was a local beer, outfit-controlled. The show was on every night at 6:00. The announcer would say, "Atlas Prager got it, Atlas Prager *get* it!" Wagner deliberately made it irritating so you'd remember the name.

Most ballgames were in the daytime then. I'd announce the scores and give the racetrack results. Then I'd do a story of an event that fit that particular day. July 4, 1919, Jack Dempsey knocked out Jess Willard. I'd recreate the fight. Occasionally I'd have a guest. One day, Jack Kearns, Dempsey's colorful manager, happened to be in town—a great con artist, fantastic figure—so he was my guest on July 4, 1944.

Eventually, Wagner said, "I'm moving to a new agency, Oleon and Bronner, and I want you to come with me. What would you like to do?"

I said, "Records, recordings." The term "disc jockey" was just beginning to be used. I said, "Not just jazz, but *all* kinds: classical, folk, blues, opera . . ."

He said: "Buy all the records you want." I bought them at the Concord Record Shop. I remember thinking, "This is pretty expensive"; it was a big library. But they gave all of them to me. Big tax break for them.

I thought of naming my show *The Wax Museum* because wax was the basis of it, all those old records. The show started in 1945 and was on an ABC-related station in Chicago Sunday nights, sponsored by Edelweiss Beer.

My first program had a Villa-Lobos piece, "Bachianas Brasileiras #5," sung by a Brazilian soprano, and Burl Ives singing "Down in the Valley," Louis Armstrong's "West End Blues," a Lotte Lehmann *Lied*, and then a piece from an opera. I would tell the story of the opera in slang. My narrator was always Long Shot Sylvester, who was a horseplayer, a tout, who happened to love opera. He'd tell the story in his own lingo: "*Carmen* was about a tomato who loved not too wisely but too often." He'd talk about Carmen and what she does to Don José. "When Carmen abandons Don for the toreador, they're outside da bullring.

"Don says, 'What are ya doin' to me? I gave my whole life for ya.'

"Carmen says, 'Go home, your mudder wants ya.' " And that's true; his mother is dying.

"He says, 'Say that again, I'll put a knife in your chest.' "

" 'Go home, your mudder wants ya.' So he puts a knife in her chest and he kills her. And the moral is: Better a live, cold potato than a dead hot tomato." Then I'd play the "Habanera," from *Carmen* as sung in 1918 by, say, Emma Calvé, who was a celebrated Carmen of her day.

That's how *The Wax Museum* came to be. Suddenly it had a following: People who had never heard jazz before heard Louis Armstrong's "West End Blues"; people who had never heard opera before heard, say, *The Marriage of Figaro*. Mostly people responded to music that appealed to them, although sometimes until that moment, they hadn't known of it.

That's when the eclectic disc jockey was born. I was a disc jockey; only my repertoire was different from those of the other disc jockeys. It was funny when the payola scandal broke. Record companies buying off disc jockeys to plug songs. I was a guy playing records, so I'd get these calls: "What kind of car do you have?"

I said, "I don't have a car."

"We'll send you golden keys. You want a Mercedes? Cadillac?"

"I don't have a car."

"What are you talking about? You're a disc jockey!"

"Yeah, I'm a disc jockey but I don't drive cars. Why should I? The bus is there!"

WHEN I WAS DOING the disc jockey show *The Wax Museum*, what came to be known as Chicago-style television was just getting off the ground. Dave Garroway had started *Garroway at Large*, and Burr Tillstrom was in *Kukla, Fran, and Ollie*. Charlie Andrews, Garroway's writer, said to me, "I gotta get you on TV."

Charlie decided the set would be a restaurant. I was on with a gay black piano player, Fletcher Butler. Fletcher was often hired by wealthy families to play songs about their guests, and he made big dough doing that, so he soon quit the show. That's when Charlie got the idea of adding Win Stracke, whom I knew from the Rep Group. We got along well because I liked good music and opera, and Win had once sung with chamber groups and knew classical and folk music and all the hymns ever written.

At the time, I was in the play *Detective Story* with Chester Morris (earlier known as Boston Blackie in the movies). Paul Lipson was in town as one of the featured players—Lipson later had the distinction of having played Tevye in *Fiddler on the Roof* more times than Zero Mostel. We went to see the TV version of the show *Vic and Sade*. They'd added an actress, Beverly Younger. We were looking for a waitress for my show, and Lipson said to me, "She's *good*."

I said, "She's very good." Next day I say to Charlie, "We found our waitress."

Studs' Place opens with her, and in comes a wandering hobo. That's Win. He's a self-educated hobo who comes in singing, "Down in the Valley" and "Wandering." Win becomes part of the show as a handyman. We still needed an elfin figure, a pianist perhaps.

I had in mind a guy named Max Miller, who was good, but who would have destroyed the show because he was constantly angry. We wanted humor, someone with a light touch. Charlie took me to Helsing's Bar where George Gobel was the headliner, and the pianist was Chet Roble. We heard Chet play and I agreed: "He's it." The chemistry between the four of us was perfect.

Studs' Place was a revolutionary program; we were pioneers. Remember, this was 1949, and TV was a brand-new medium. The radio had brought hearing a voice into your home, but seeing someone, the visual aspect, this was brand new. Ida and I didn't have a TV set when *Studs' Place* was on—we used to go over to Win's house to watch. Working in TV at that time, it was frontier country, you could do anything—your own impulses could be expressed and nobody was there to stop it. The reverse of what TV has become today.

We had one camera, maybe two, I forget. We would do subtle

things; we never underestimated the audience. My idea was to have songs woven into the show. The music would fit the plot and there'd be one jazz piece for Chet and one folk, or even a classical piece—say, "Oh du, mein holder Abendstern" ("To an Evening Star") from *Tannhäuser*—for Win.

In one show, we had Bev's husband, the actor Les Podewell, play a deaf guy who meets a deaf girl and a romance begins between them. Win starts playing "Spanish Is the Loving Tongue," a Richard Dyer-Bennett song. They get up and they start dancing. They touch Win's guitar, and in touching the guitar, they feel the music and they dance.

Our themes were all about ordinary things, about daily life. Today some would say that's too dull, the lack of glamour. But the ordinariness is what made it unique, and people loved *Studs' Place*. The character I played was both good and bad, pointing up the frailties of human nature: I could be benevolent; I could be a faker and a phony, too.

There were all kinds of actors around Chicago, and Charlie had the idea of doing a show about a bottle of cognac and a janitor. We hired Kurt Kupfer, a real honest-to-God Belgian actor who happened to be working as a janitor. He was a war refugee. In the show, Kupfer plays a janitor whose daughter is getting married. What shall we give as a gift? On the wall of Studs' Place is a bottle of cognac, 1812 cognac, a Napoleonic brand of cognac. It's fantastic, and it's there to be *seen*. My pride as well as my ego is at stake. But Win has this idea: "How about us giving the bottle of cognac to the janitor and the daughter? And during the presentation we sip from it and toast the bride. Wouldn't that be a wonderful thing?"

I say: "Are you out of your mind? On a wall, it adds class. It's *there*. People look at it. We'll waste it!"

Win says, "Is it wasting it to give it to a battered old boy at a high moment in his life? That's *real* class."

Something happens during the show. We hear the old guy talking and I'm affected by his words. We take the bottle down off the wall, Win opens it, and Kurt Kupfer says, "Is this for me and my child?"

"Yeah," I say, "It's for you. I thought we would toast your daughter." I ask myself, rhetorically, "Now what's more important, that or keeping the wine on the wall?" At times I can be such a phony.

The show was so filled with the ordinary that people thought it took place in a real restaurant. Bev started wearing a waitress's union button out and about, and often a waitress would say, "Why are you letting Studs talk to you that way?" Years after the show ended, people would say, "Where is it? Where is Studs' Place?"

We started rehearsing on Monday for Friday's show. Tuesday we come back, it's still very rough. By Friday it's pretty well ready and we have a dress rehearsal and then go live. We never had a script. Charlie and I would do the plot, or a guy named Bob Hartman, or Red Bunning once in a while, but mostly it was Charlie and me, with Dan Petrie directing. We'd make it a simple plot, meet, and read it to the cast. Bit by bit, out of the actor would come the lines; the dialogue had to be from them, the words were the actors' own. Thus the credits read: "Dialogue by the Cast."

Bev walked out after the first rehearsal. No script. She's an *actress*. Whoever heard of no script? "Where are the lines?"

"The lines come from you, your experience."

She said, "I can't do that."

I said, "Try it." She did and she was wonderful. She'd traveled around the country doing summer stock versions of Broadway hits. Being intelligent and thoughtful, she remembered waitresses from all these small-town restaurants, women who had a mother wit about them, and she used those memories.

In Chet's case, he was familiar with guys who hung around in the half-world. Chet had phrases like, "Here comes Joe Books," an intellectual guy. "Joe Loot," rich guy. "Joe Dames," ladies man.

We did a show about quitting smoking, way back around 1950. I knew a doctor in New Orleans, one of the first MDs to speak against cigarettes. We see Chet starting to light up and we're going to fine him. "That's ten bucks."

"What are you talking about? That's not lit, it's not lit." Chet's a good bit taller than I am and he's pounding the cigarette against my forehead. "Is it lit? Is it lit? You don't *feel* lit, do ya? Is it *lit*?! What do you think I am, a Dick Smith or somethin'?" He'd make up these names. I don't know who Dick Smith was, but apparently in the underworld, they have phrases like that. "Dick Smith" might have stood for a liar and a thief, or a guy that didn't keep his word. "What am I, a Dick Smith?"

Every now and then we'd have con men in the plot. Charlie Andrews had an idea: two old con men, who are having a hard time, try to get a free meal. Of course, they have something to sell: a magic penknife. They come up to me, and in the meantime, Win, Bev, and Chet are suspicious of the two old mooches. We hired two very old actors to play the two old con men: Butler Mandeville, who was a gay guy about ninety, and Alex McQueen, a little fellow. This time, I'm being a good guy, I'm saying, "Gee, no kidding. A magic knife." I like these two old guys 'cause they're working so hard to convince me their knife is magic.

Mike Royko once wrote a column about me and Willie the Weeper, this fifteen-year-old kid who weighed about three hundred pounds and mooched on Michigan Avenue. He'd corner you and start weeping, sobbing . . . "My mother . . ." And of course, you give him a buck. "My two little brothers, my sister . . ." Another buck. "Oh-h-h, the landlord . . ."

Royko says, "Studs, you're an easy mark."

I say, "Mike, have you forgotten what a great performance he gave? Now, how much would you pay to see Laurence Olivier or Marlon Brando? Here's a kid who's fantastic!"

Same thing applies here. I know what these two old guys have is a plain old penknife. Mandeville says, "But it's not a knife, it's a remarkable thing." He's trying to pull it open, and it doesn't work. "See what it does? Even pulling it out is tough." They go into their routine.

Meanwhile, Bev and Win are saying, "Gee, why is Studs spending time on this?"

I say, "This is great. How much?"

"Well, we'll give you a bargain. We think ten dollars. This is worth a hundred."

I say, "You're right." I say, "How about a meal? We'll call Louie the chef"—Louie never appears in person on the show—"Louie, a special meal! Bean soup, steak, everything, for our two honored guests."

It was a wonderful episode. I secretly sneak them a sawbuck. At the very end, the others are bawling me out. That's when I say, "Didn't you see a great performance? Didn't you see everything they did? It was acting, good acting. Isn't that worth a meal?"

We finished the dress rehearsal and were going on live about two hours later. This was at the Studebaker Theatre on Michigan Boulevard. The show goes on in about fifteen minutes on the whole network, and suddenly the script girl is hollering, "Butler's leaving!"

"What?!"

"Butler's going into a cab!"

"Oh, my god."

Butler says, "Well, the program's over." He was approaching senility and thought he'd put on the makeup and powder, done the show once, and that was that. We were lucky to grab him; we could have been in a hell of a jam. Live TV was a very different animal from what it is today.

For a time we were kept going by a local sponsor, Manor House Coffee. Each week one of the cast took a turn. Flossie Murdoch of the Earl Ludgin agency would write a special commercial to fit each character, Win would sing a folksong, Chet would play a blues. I always signed off with, "We came to you from Chicago."

So it's Chet's turn, and Chet was impish, and in rehearsals he'd goof around and say, "Maxwell House Coffee"—which happened to be the name of Manor House's big rival. We'd say, "Chet, don't horse around."

"Nah, don't worry. Maxwell House Coffee . . ."

So the show is live, the commercial is in the middle of the show, and here comes the commercial. Chet's playing and then he says, "So I give you . . ." We see him freeze, we die. He desperately blurts out "Maxwell House Coffee . . ."

He finishes, and there's a hush, and he turns pale. Now we have to pick up the show where we left off. Me and Bev and Win have one thing in mind: to keep Chet from jumping out the window— we were up on the fortieth floor. All we know is: Finish the show and grab Chet.

Monte Kinney, who represents the sponsor, is on the set. The show ends, Chet runs out, we run after him, and Monte runs after all of us: "Chet, it's OK, it's not the end of the world."

We try to grab Chet, he runs into the elevator, we jump in the next elevator and chase him. That was something. Imagine those last fifteen minutes. Somehow, we finished on time!

One of the mysteries of the show was how we did manage to finish on time. To this day we still can't figure that out. We talked about it for years afterward. How did we do it? We don't know. It was free-flowing; a word or two might be changed as we went along. We got everything in and somehow it always finished on time.

STUDS' PLACE was finally dropped in 1951. The audience didn't know why. It was a very popular show and I was being courted in New York, same as Mike Wallace. All of a sudden, we heard we were in trouble. NBC sent a New York public relations man in to see me. He said: "We're in trouble because of you. There are all these petitions and your name is right near the top." These were petitions for the Anti-Fascist Refugee Committee, the Committee for Civil Rights, things of that nature.

I said: "Yeah."

He said: "Don't you know that Communists are behind these petitions?"

I couldn't help myself, I said: "Suppose Communists come out against cancer? Do we have to automatically come out for cancer?"

He said: "That's not very funny." And then he says, "These days you have to stand up and be counted." Well, another moment when the imp of the perverse, as Poe calls it, took over. I stood up. He said: "That's not funny either."

We stopped being in trouble: They decided to drop the program.

When we were finally knocked off the air, we did one last episode. In it, we lose our lease, and we're saying good-bye to the joint. The show ends with Grace hanging up her apron, Chet closing the piano lid, Win hanging the guitar on the wall, and me just looking over the joint. That was it.

Part III

15

American Dreamer

I felt hopeful with the New Deal. During the Great Depression there was a feeling of despair. The people we had chosen to lead us out, Franklin Delano Roosevelt, and Eleanor, and the colleagues they chose, advocated governmental intervention as the free market fell on its ass. That gave me hope.

I remember the day Roosevelt died. April 12, 1945. The Cold War was beginning and I was having trouble getting radio sponsors. This progressive guy from New York was sponsoring me and there was a gathering at the hotel. The word came, "The president is dead." I left that party at the Palmer House. Everyone in the streets was crying, including me, leaning against a lamppost.

Here's the funny thing: Kennedy gets shot twenty-some years later, and this kid I know is visiting from my Air Force days. I'm about to take him out to eat and we get the word Kennedy's dead. He starts crying, but not me. I felt bad, but I wasn't crying. With Roosevelt a father died, you see. Someone who represented what you felt was hopeful. Someone you could lean on.

When I interviewed Gardiner Means, an economist active in the New Deal, he said, "You have no idea how Washington changed almost overnight those first hundred days." It was a slow, shuffling, fat city of the South, that's all it was. Suddenly it became the center of an attempt to save a society. People came from places such as New

York and Chicago, people who were never allowed in Washington before. The sons of rabbis, of priests, of ministers, of old professors arrived. Instead of approaching the country as though it were a Norman Rockwell painting, you saw a new approach of recognizing history and the needs of the people.

Remember, Roosevelt was elected four times, and he died the second year of his last term. When we speak of the New Deal, for me, its brightest moment is FDR's second term, 1936–1940, when tremendous revolutions occurred; when the federal agencies he'd created in the first term began to pay off by giving jobs and spirit to the American people.

During the first term, 1932–1936, Roosevelt eliminated Prohibition right off the bat. With millions unemployed, he created the Civilian Conservation Corps, primarily for young guys, to help out their families, to provide unemployment relief. They planted trees, built roads, and sent most of the money home. Nineteen thirty-five was a big year: Social Security was enacted; the Works Progress Administration (WPA) came into being, run by Harry Hopkins, alongside the Farm Security Administration (FSA) and the Resettlement Administration (RA), headed by Rex Tugwell.

It's not that FDR himself was so brilliant, but he surrounded himself with people of vision: Hopkins, Tugwell, Frances Perkins as Secretary of Labor, Harold Ickes, who said of Thomas Dewey, "He looks like a bridegroom on a wedding cake," and Henry Wallace.

For the first two terms, Wallace was Secretary of Agriculture. He came from a family of longtime Republicans who had a populist sensibility. Wallace was a farmer and a brilliant agronomist who invented hybrid corn. That made him wealthy, but that didn't change him. When he had lunch he'd ask, "You got any rat cheese?"

Roosevelt appointed Wallace as his vice president in 1940. While Wallace was vice president he traveled around the world. When most vice presidents travel, they visit the mayor, the big shots and industrialists. Wallace was likely to go to the public library to look something up. So he's somewhere in Bolivia or Argentina, gets off the train, no bodyguard, and has a look around. He sees a field, pulls up some of the wheat or corn and feels it, smells it. He speaks Spanish, and he says to the farmer, "This is good. Where did you get this? How do you do that?"

He leaves and the farmer says, "Who is that guy? He sounds like a very good farmer."

"Oh, that's the vice president of the United States." That was Henry Wallace.

Wallace was a key figure in the New Deal because he had all these ideas about improving farming methods and equipment. Having traveled, he'd picked up a thing or two and had some understanding of the rest of the world.

It was Wallace who created the RA, under the Department of Agriculture, and along with the WPA set up these camps for the migrant workers. The camps were in particular parts of the country. In fact, there was a black camp. John Beecher, a progressive Southern poet and a descendent of Harriet Beecher Stowe, was in charge of a camp that had only black sharecroppers. They ran it and ran it beautifully.

In the novel *The Grapes of Wrath*, Tom and Ma Joad, like thousands of other Okies, make the long trip to California hoping to get jobs picking crops of some sort. On the road they're humiliated and beaten up by vigilantes, by the growers, by the Legionnaires. Suddenly they come to a camp. They think it's just another jungle camp, but it isn't, a sign says: RESETTLEMENT ADMINISTRATION, HENRY WALLACE, SECRETARY OF AGRICULTURE. An actor made up to look like FDR, wearing a pince-nez, says, "This is your camp."

Tom and his mother look at each other: "What do you mean, our camp?"

"You and your colleagues who have come here are going to run this place. You people choose your committees. If someone is drunk, you kick him out. There are showers and ladies' auxiliaries, and we try to find you jobs. But mostly you decide what's going on."

Tom says, "Why aren't there more places like this?"

The guy says, "I wish I could tell you."

A man I call Paul Edwards in *Hard Times* describes how, as young men, he and his brother rode the freight trains going east, looking for work. They once found themselves on a fruit train, and because they were starving, they ate oranges until they couldn't open their mouths anymore. Now and then there was a kindly railroad bull, but in the main the bulls just beat them and kicked them off. One day the train stops, the bulls come and say, "Everybody off!" Paul thinks, "Oh, God, here we go again, to the jail for vagrancy." And instead, these are social workers, working for the federal government.

The men are taken to this big camp and there are clean cots and clean linens and towels and soap and breakfast waiting—cereal, coffee, scrambled eggs. And Paul's little brother, who was about sixteen, says, "Where are we?"

Paul says, "We're in heaven." They find out this is part of the New Deal, the National Youth Administration (NYA). (Every state had one; in Texas, the head of it was a young guy named Lyndon Baines Johnson.) They realize then that something new is going on: a government that cares. All this was happening under Henry Wallace.

The RA is the group, in addition to the WPA, that set up these camps. Margaret Bourke-White, Dorothea Lange, Gordon Parks, Ben Shahn, and Walker Evans, among the best of our photographers, were all part of the RA, and of what it later became, the Farm Security Administration (FSA). When we see the portraits made by Dorothea Lange, that famous shot of the mother and two kids, and the work of the others, all this came out of the New Deal.

John Steinbeck might not have written *The Grapes of Wrath* were it not for the government. Steinbeck went to C.B. Baldwin of the RA and said, "I need somebody to be my guide, someone who can tell me how they lived, what they thought, the pea pickers, the fruit pickers." And so a man named Tom Collins was assigned to him.

Beanie Baldwin said, "What I did was probably illegal, but we helped him and Tom Collins with a buck or two." Here's a case where the government helped subsidize one of America's classics.

Steinbeck dedicated the book, not only to his wife, but also to Tom Collins. Steinbeck's wife asked me to write the introduction to the fiftieth anniversary issue of *The Grapes of Wrath*. While I was working on it, Congressman Joe Kennedy, Bobby Kennedy's son, called me to come visit the farmers of Iowa. Here it is the 1980s, and you've got farmers who are starving. You saw the Depression in the Iowa countryside: the topsoil worn out, dust, towns with FOR SALE signs everywhere. You'd see a mangy little dog running around, the only inhabitant of twenty or thirty streets.

I ran into a farmer named Carroll Nearmyer, who could have been Pa Joad, his despair was so deep. He had a revolver at his side. He was prepared to kill himself. The circumstance was a replay of the Great Depression. But never once did you hear the word "Reaganville" in the eighties as you heard "Hooverville" in the thirties.

HENRY WALLACE was the heart and soul of the New Deal. He said of the twentieth century, "Let this be the century of the common man." He fought for Social Security, for the right to organize in plants. The big shots hated him because he was giving people a sense of their own power.

The New Deal really ended when the war began, when Roosevelt said to the two wonder boys of the Democratic Party, Tommy Corcoran and Ben Cohen: "Boys, Dr. New Deal is over, Dr. Win-the-War is in." From then on there were all kinds of compromises to cooperate with the big boys, the industrialists.

Roosevelt appointed Wallace as his vice president in his third term, indicating that he might want Wallace to succeed him as president. But by the end of his third term Roosevelt was already very ill, and it was at the 1944 convention that Wallace was robbed of the vice presidency. That's when a group of political bosses went into action—Ed Kelly of Chicago, David Lawrence of Pennsylvania,

Frank Hague of New Jersey, and Bob Hannegan, chairman of the National Democratic Committee.

By this time, Henry Wallace had become known as being too soft on the Soviet Union. Also, he was anti-agribusiness, although that word wasn't used then. The bosses were out to get him. They hated him because he represented the radical idea of people having a stake in things, having ownership. They called him a dupe of the Communists.

The '44 convention was in Chicago, and, thousands of people had come into the convention hall. All the galleries and most delegates were for Henry Wallace. All that had to happen was for someone to say, "Henry Wallace for VP," and the place would have gone up for grabs. And Henry Wallace would have been president when Roosevelt died.

What happened? Claude Pepper, a senator from Florida, very progressive, was about to go to the podium to nominate Henry Wallace. As he came toward the podium, two political thugs took him by the arms and marched him away, led him off the stand. He couldn't make the speech. The chairman bangs the gavel. Roosevelt was on his way to Pearl Harbor during the convention and Bob Hannegan, the Democratic chief, had gotten something in writing from Roosevelt, a weary, worn out, dying man, saying he'd accept either Supreme Court Justice William O. Douglas, or Harry Truman, an unknown little hack from Missouri, as his vice president. Truman it was.

The Cold War came into being in 1944–45, when our former ally, the Soviet Union, began to be regarded as our enemy. Truman was talking bellicose, belligerent talk. Not that Stalin was any bargain. That's when those most committed to the New Deal decided to back Henry Wallace as the Progressive Party candidate for president in 1948. It was a populist party, and of course, we were all tarred with a red brush; the newspapers and radio were absolutely brutal. It's true there were Communists connected with the party. But they didn't determine Wallace's thoughts and speeches and policies. In spite of the Cold War, most Democrats wanted Wallace as their next presidential candidate, according to a Gallup poll in early 1946.

Pete Seeger was part of the Henry Wallace entourage that traveled to the South. Beanie Baldwin went along, as did Palmer Weber, a wonderful Southerner, who made all kinds of dough on the stock market and gave it to the Progressive Party. So here's this group traveling down South and they would play only at integrated events. Oh, it was dangerous. Aubrey Williams was driven out of town, hit with rocks. The vice-presidential candidate, Glen Taylor, the senator from Idaho, got the hell beaten out of him. But that group broke the color line. The Henry Wallace Southern campaign is the first group ever that did not play before a segregated audience, the first since the Reconstruction.

I was rather deeply involved in this scene. I became an emcee of many Progressive Party events here in Chicago. Zero Mostel was at one of the big gatherings and did a routine called, "Who's going to investigate the man who investigates the man who investigates me?" It was a takeoff on J. Edgar Hoover.

At the 1940 convention, a Chicago politician had put a microphone in the cellar and all over the hall you'd hear, "We want Roosevelt!" I stole that and used it in the 1948 Progressive Party Convention in Chicago. "We want Wallace!"

The war ended, there was Hiroshima, and then came the 1948 election. The pundits expected Dewey to win. Henry Wallace ran as a third-party candidate for peace; he wanted to work for peace all over the world. Strom Thurmond ran on an outright racist ticket. Truman had been thinking about resigning after his political boss in Kansas City, Missouri, was indicted for corruption: "They just indicted my boss, Tom Prendergast."

Senator Burton K. Wheeler said, "Don't you dare resign." Truman stayed in the race.

So, here's Harry Truman with a nothing campaign. One of his advisors, a lawyer and Washington operator named Clark Clifford, as brilliant as he was crooked, suggested that Truman follow Wallace's platform on the matter of minimum wage, the right of labor to organize, Social Security. In other words, Clifford suggested that Truman steal Wallace's domestic platform, and he did. Truman made several good speeches about labor, and that's how the phrase, "Give 'em hell, Harry!" came into being. 'Cause here he was hitting the big shots he'd never even touched before. So Wallace really helped elect Truman. Harry Truman did not win despite Wallace, as has been the received wisdom of the day. He won *because* of Wallace.

In the last week of the campaign, when Tom Dewey still looks like a cinch, the networks allow the top three candidates air time. Dewey, the Republican candidate, is very confident. He makes a speech for about fifteen minutes on NBC election night. Most of the big actors of the time were for Truman, who appeared on CBS. The emcee was Melvyn Douglas, and among the stars of the show were Frederic March and Florence Eldridge and Humphrey Bogart and Lauren Bacall, there to sing Harry's praises. The exceptions were Katharine Hepburn and Orson Welles. There was another Wallace voter, not in the film industry but in his own way celebrated. Albert Einstein.

My friend Lew Frank, who was one of Wallace's aides, asked the musicologist Alan Lomax and me to produce Wallace's program for ABC. The stars of the show were Henry Wallace and Paul Robeson. Woody Guthrie was due to be on, but he was sick with Huntington's by that time. Instead, we had a couple of white circuit riders singing hymns.★

I'll never forget going into that building, where many of the radio studios were. It was a busy studio, and there were hundreds of people milling around, actors waiting to audition. We walked in as a group—Henry Wallace, Paul Robeson, Lew Frank, Alan Lomax, me. As soon as the crowd saw Robeson, they dispersed as though

---

★ Circuit riders were traveling preachers in the mountain country. They'd stop wherever there was a church, white or black. Their interpretation of the Bible was as a working-man's book.

the Red Sea had parted. I was reminded of the spiritual, " 'Gyptian army got drownded."

The program was in the main these two guys: the white Midwesterner, representing rural America and the hope of little farmers; and the son of a Baptist preacher whose grandfather was a slave, who had become an athlete, an actor, a singer. I remember Paul Robeson coming up to us saying, "Boys, do you mind if I change one of the songs? Instead of 'Didn't My Lord Deliver Daniel,' I'll do 'Scandalize My Name.' " It was a funny parlor song. He wanted to show his humor.

At that time his name was poison. You know about the Peekskill Riots, the overturning of cars, the rock throwing? It was in upper New York State, near Poughkeepsie. Paul Robeson was there singing; that was enough to raise the blood pressure of every professional patriot. People going there, performers, others, had their cars smashed. The police watched and had a good time either doing nothing or taking part in the hooliganism.

So, here's Robeson wanting to sing "Scandalize My Name." "You call that a brother? No, sir! You call that a sister? No, sir! Scandalizin' my name!"

Henry Wallace had an easy way of talking, but he was used to addressing crowds. I went up to Wallace, who was sitting down at the mike. I squatted down, and I said, "Mr. Vice President, make believe you're addressing one person: that old farmer having a hard time, or that lost young family in a big city who don't know where to turn. Be very intimate. The way President Roosevelt sounded during his fireside chats." I remember saying that.

Wallace did the best he could. It was arranged so there was a dialogue and then individual soliloquies of white and black America. It needed no narrator. Robeson spoke of his beginnings and his father, and then recited that soliloquy from *Othello*. It worked out just right. Unfortunately, there's no script of it available, nothing. I think there was a recording, but no one knows where it went. It was a wonderful program, a memorable one.

On that last night, obviously, millions of voters for Wallace, whatever, two, three million, switched and voted for Harry Truman—"Give 'em hell, Harry."

Truman had been attacking Wallace as a Communist sympathizer, an agent of Russia. Wallace wanted peace in the world, and there couldn't be peace unless there was peace between the two superpowers. Stalin was a butcher and a bastard. You can't defend that, of course.

But had Wallace won, there might have been no Cold War, might have been no McCarthyism. It would have been a different world, a whole change in temperament—things like universal health care, labor rights to organize. Perhaps even peace in the world. Perhaps. My hope was factor to my mad prophecy—the dream of a Wallace presidency.

16

Are You Now or Have You Ever Been . . .

If ever there was an experience that altered my life, not simply in a political way, but in every aspect, it was the Great American Depression. I was there watching what hard times did to decent people. The great discovery is how they behaved during a specific issue, not what they were labeled. It was easy to call somebody a Commie, or a Red, or a Fascist for that matter. It's how that person behaved at a certain moment that counted.

I remember the generosity practiced by those with little. A guy would leave to get on the streetcar and he'd pass another guy a cigarette, or, getting off, would hand someone else his transfer. There were these little things. There's the innate decency of human beings. But when your livelihood is at stake, it's you *or* the other guy, not you *and* the other guy.

In *The Grapes of Wrath,* sharecropper Muley Graves is being forced off his land; a young man in goggles seated on a Caterpillar tractor is about to knock down his house. Muley, in a gesture of resistance, raises his rifle toward the tractor.

"You touch my house with that Cat and I'll blow you to kingdom come."

The man raises his goggles and declares, "You ain't gonna blow nobody nowhere. In the first place, they'll hang you and you know it. Next day they'll send someone to take my place."

Then Muley recognizes him. "Why you're Joe Davis' boy. How can you do this to your own people?"

The man on the tractor says, "I got a wife and kids to feed. Everybody else, they can look after their own selves. . . . Now go on, get out of the way!"

When, fifty years later, I visited that fourth-generation Iowa farmer and his wife facing the same foreclosure troubles, Muley's words echoed. With the bankers breathing down their necks, Mrs. Nearmyer, fretting over the effect of the times on her small daughter, asked the same question that Muley Graves does. "Whenever the deputy came to take our stuff away from us, I asked him, 'How can you go home and face your family?' I happen to know he has an eight-year-old girl too. I said, 'How can you sleep tonight, knowing that someday this could be you? You don't have to be a farmer. This is not just a farm crisis.'

"He said, 'If I don't do it, somebody else would be here. To me, it's just a job.' "*

I SHALL NEVER FORGET an assemblage known as the Workers' Alliance, sometimes called the Unemployed Council. Always labeled as Commies and Reds. These groups were in certain of the big cities, among them Chicago and New York.

The bailiffs were very busy evicting people, sometimes three or so families a day. For the most part, the bailiffs weren't bad guys and hated their work dispossessing others. They'd arrive during the day to take the furniture out of the homes of people being evicted— removing bedsteads and kitchen tables and even the toilet seats, everything but the kitchen sink. They'd take out the furniture and shut off the electricity and the plumbing. This happened more often in the deeply poverty-stricken neighborhoods, but I read of it in the papers every day.

---

* *The Great Divide: Second Thoughts on the American Dream* (Pantheon, 1988, p. 106).

When the bailiffs were done evicting people, the sidewalks would be full of furniture and clothes and pots and pans. At the end of the day, as soon as the bailiffs quit, a group of guys would come along.

It is true that the Communist Party formed the basis of the Workers' Alliance. They were full of unemployed craftsmen; among them were electricians, carpenters, plumbers, and gas men. They would put the furniture back in and restore all of the utilities. They'd keep doing that until the bailiffs finally got tired, and in many cases, the bailiffs got *so* tired, they quit.

That was how some of the people acted at that time. If one tried to be doctrinaire and impose his Communist philosophy on another, that was something else. You weren't needed. Out. No other matters counted at that moment but that the people needing help were helped.

Hundreds of miles away, in Montgomery, Alabama, Virginia Durr suffered a similar discovery as a member of an organization known as the Southern Conference for Human Welfare. This relatively small group was composed of people fighting segregation, most of them white.★

Civil rights activists were always accused by certain forces of being Communist. During the 1940s, there was a witch hunt, and Virginia was called to testify as an unfriendly witness before the Eastland Committee. Senator Jim Eastland, an avowed racist and the boss of Sunflower County, Mississippi, had set up his own Un-American Activities Committee.

I remember seeing Durr's name, and a picture, in the newspapers: The headline: SOUTHERN REBEL DEFIES EASTLAND. Picture Eastland, all three hundred furious pounds of him: "Are you or have you ever been . . ." In the wonderful photograph, Virginia sits in

★ Also in the group: the great educator Myles Horton, head of Highlander Folk School; Aubrey Williams, an inspiring Southerner, head of the National Youth Administration; and a preacher by the name of Claude Williams, who brought a real Christ of flesh and blood, an organizer, to churches when he organized the tobacco workers—he was tarred and feathered at times, too.

what is obviously a witness chair, legs crossed, powdering her nose. She will not satisfy her interrogator with a response. Senator Eastland is going crazy and finally orders her off the stand. The reporters surround her; they're entertained by her actions. One asks, "What impelled you to defy this powerful man?"

She says, "Oh, I think that man is as common as pig tracks." Then she sighs, "Oh, I guess I'm just an old-fashioned Southern snob." That's the way she talked, and oh, she was a powerful presence.

She made it clear to the senator that it didn't matter what a person was labeled; all that mattered was what that person did under specific circumstances. In this case, the battle of the Southern liberals was to eliminate the poll tax that deprived so many African Americans of the right to vote. Among the members of her little group might have been one or two Reds. But that's not what mattered to Virginia. How did a person behave on the issue of the poll tax? It was analogous to the work of the Unemployed Council.

Her friend and fellow Southern Conference member, Joe Gelders, was a Communist who fought harder than anyone to eliminate the poll tax. In fact, he was tarred and feathered several times and regularly bruised for his efforts. He, much like the Unemployed Council people, acted on behalf of his fellow man.

I first heard Virginia Durr speak at Orchestra Hall at a program against segregation during the forties, when it was not remotely fashionable to speak out on behalf of integration. The headline speaker was Dr. Mary McLeod Bethune, a celebrated African American and a close friend of Eleanor Roosevelt. We'd all heard of Mary McLeod Bethune, but it was Virginia Durr who set everybody's heart afire that day. She was dynamite—in her forties, lanky, Southern, colorful. I went backstage to shake her hand. "Thank you, dear, thank you," she said, and put a hundred leaflets in my hand. "Now dear, you better hurry outside, pass those out quickly because Dr. Bethune and I will be at the African Episcopal church in two hours."

I am about two years old, standing on the stool. My two brothers hold my hands.

My family. *Seated:* father Sam and mother Annie; *standing:* Ben, me, and Meyer.

Me and my brother Ben.

Ida and me.

Ida and me enjoying spaghetti in a Chicago restaurant.

Chester Morris, Paul Lipson, and me in the play *Detective Story.*

Examining "The Briefcase." The program was a "poor man's omnibus." (Inside the briefcase may have been a scene from Tennessee Williams's *Summer and Smoke.*)

Mahalia Jackson and me in rehearsal.

I COME FOR TO SING: One of the earliest folk song groups:
me, Win Stracke, Big Bill Broonzy, and Larry Lane. (Photograph
by Stephen Deutsch. Courtesy of the Chicago History Museum.)

Paul Lipson, me,
and Fletcher Butler.

Leo Durocher arguing with
members of *Studs' Place:* Chet
Roble, me, Beverly Younger,
and Win Stracke.

Nelson Algren at a party for me.

Accepting the Prix Italia Award in Verona, Italy.

Mme. Eugenie Leontovich and me. She created the role of the dancer Grusinskaya, which Greta Garbo played in the 1932 film *Grand Hotel*.

Win Stracke and me, slightly oiled, singing out the Scottish drinking song "a wee drappie 'ot."

Ida, me, and Florence Scala (who led the fight to save the Hull House area) at Florence's Restaurant.

Kurt Vonnegut and me at a gathering of the American Academy of Arts and Letters.

My son Dan and Tim Black, school teacher and observer.

Mike Royko and me at a bar.

Receiving an honorary degree from
Northwestern University. Garry Wills,
NU's writer-in-residence, greets me.

Me and André Schiffrin, my publisher
and editor for over forty years, working
on the manuscript of *Race*.

I dedicated my book *Hope Dies Last* to Clifford and Virginia Durr. Clifford Durr was a Birmingham, Alabama, lawyer, very soft-spoken, gentle, but strong and well known for defending political activists. At one time he was the head counsel for the Federal Communications Commission. Clifford was responsible for bringing in the Blue Book, which ensured that public-service programs would be aired.

During the New Deal, Virginia was the hostess who greeted all the young wives of representatives new to the capitol. Lady Bird Johnson loved Virginia Durr; Virginia was Lady Bird's mentor when LBJ first came to Washington as a young congressman from Texas. During the Cold War and the McCarthy days, Clifford lost a number of different jobs and they were often down on their luck. When they were under attack, LBJ tried whatever he could to smooth things over.

The Durrs were definitely not Communists, but they were not opposed to people who were Communists being in any organization of which they were a part. When Virginia ran for U.S. senator in Alabama on the Henry Wallace ticket, she said, "We're for any-body who fights for civil rights. We don't care what he's called. If he's a Communist, it's OK, provided he doesn't try to impinge his views on us."

Virgina wrote a book called *Outside the Magic Circle*. In the pref-ace, I described the three ways she could have lived her life. She was the daughter of a preacher who lost his faith: He couldn't believe that Jonah set up light housekeeping in the belly of the whale. I said that since she was part of a white, upper-middle-class society, she could have led an easy life, been a member of a garden or book club, and behaved kindly toward the colored help. Two, if she had imagi-nation and was stuck in this nice, easy world, she could go crazy, as did her schoolmate Zelda Sayre, later the wife of F. Scott Fitzgerald. The third is the one she took: She became the rebel girl and basi-cally said, "The whole system is lousy and I'm going to fight it." That's stepping outside the magic circle.

The Durrs were highly respected citizens of Montgomery until the fight to break segregation. They were friends of Myles Horton, who established Highlander Folk School, the first integrated school in the South since the Reconstruction, in Monteagle, Tennessee. It was primarily a school for adults who were organizers of labor and civil rights—white and black together. Myles was a Southerner who had studied theology at Vanderbilt and was brilliant as a teacher of adults. One of his influences was Paolo Freire, a great Brazilian educator who revolutionized the use of language. Certain words are key, words that arouse emotions because they resonate with peoples' lives: Hunger. Cold. Equality. Justice.

Highlander was burned down by the Klan, but it was reestablished in New Market, Tennessee, where it still exists. Martin Luther King Jr. went to Highlander. I was at Highlander once, very briefly. Pete Seeger went there a lot. Rosa Parks went there, too. For a time, she was the seamstress for Virginia Durr, and she often talked with her about the battle for equality. Virginia is the one who urged Rosa Parks to attend Highlander, after which she became secretary to E.D. Nixon, a former Pullman car porter who became the head of the NAACP in Montgomery.

All this played a role when Rosa Parks sat down and refused to get up on that bus. It was Virginia Durr who bailed Rosa Parks out of jail. It was Clifford Durr who represented Rosa Parks in Federal court after the Montgomery Bus Boycott—arguing that the Montgomery ordinance segregating passengers on city buses was unconstitutional.

The night the Selma-to-Montgomery march ended at George Wallace's mansion, he was furious. Wallace underwent a change after he was shot, but back then he appeared on TV naming the subversives responsible for all the troubles. Half of them were sitting in the Durr living room watching the news. History has shown these people to have been visionaries; they've been referred to as the prescient or prophetic minority. Virginia Durr fit that description especially well.

17

Blacklist

S everal years after the Wallace campaign, the subject of Commu-
nism resurfaced. When *Studs' Place* ended, it was a crisis. We
knew it was going to happen. We just knew. I wasn't scared, but I
certainly wasn't looking forward to it . . . well, the truth is, I was a
little scared, sure.

By this time McCarthy was in full flower and the Cold War was
at its most frigid; this was the time of the Hollywood Ten. But I'm
like a rubber ball. Nelson Algren called me the India Rubber Man.
Years ago there was a fighter named Johnny Risko, knocked down
but never knocked out—he'd be knocked down and bounce up
again, like an India rubber ball. That's me. Bill Coffin once said of
me in a letter to a friend: "How is the perdurable Studs?" Isn't that
a great word? Would that it had been so; I was fading fast.

During the blacklist, you're not working for a time, you start
thinking maybe you ain't got something you thought you had. I
knew my work troubles were for political reasons, but the situation
seemed somewhat hopeless. There's something that's interesting
psychologically, moments when you feel self-doubt: that is, was
your talent there to begin with? Maybe you're not that good.

Win Stracke and I talked about those doubts because *Studs' Place*
wasn't the only Chicago TV show dropped. Win had a popular
children's show called *Uncle Win's Animal Playtime*. It was set in a pet

store; he'd make up words to the tunes of old folk songs and sing to the animals. Dean's Milk was the sponsor. The show was doing beautifully. The fans and the sponsor were delighted. Then one day they dropped it, just boom.

Win got it from all directions. He'd been singing at fourth Presbyterian Church, the classiest of them all. He was their pride; he knew every hymn of John Wesley's, German *Lieder*, you name it. One day, Win is picketing a certain firm during a strike. He gets a call from the pastor: "Win, we're so proud of you, but we're going to have to let you go. I suggest you go to another city, change your name, and start over again."

"What is it I did?"

"You were picketing that petroleum company."

"Yeah, well, what about it?"

"The head of it is one of our biggest contributors." Win and I took to calling ourselves the Chicago Two.

When *Studs' Place* was dropped it *was* a tough time. We weren't in poverty, but there was a lot of anxiety. Luckily Ida was working and brought in more dough than I did. She was a social worker for the Chase House, an integrated Episcopalian childcare center, and became friends with many of the people there; they all liked her.

One time she was going to a big convention in Milwaukee. The driver was a retired cop, and along for the ride were two other women and Ida, the only white person in the car. The car was stopped. The retired cop showed his ex-policeman papers and the cop said, "OK, go ahead."

Ida said, "I wonder why they stopped us. You weren't speeding."

They looked at her and chuckled: "Oh, sweet Ida." Suddenly it hit her.

Ida kept us afloat, and while it was not the most delightful period in the world it didn't affect my personal life in Chicago; I was still this guy who was known. I'd pick up a buck here and there at women's clubs, speaking about jazz and folk music. Ed Clamage, a local florist and Legionnaire, would follow me around and send letters warning the women's clubs against having me speak. They all ignored him.

I was getting a hundred bucks a lecture, and one woman, very old and very elegant, was so furious at Clamage that she said, "I will pay you two hundred."

I wrote him a note, sent him a check for ten dollars. "Do you realize you've made me an extra hundred bucks? You're my agent, so here's your cut." Never did hear back.

Some years later, a woman named Elsie Clamage called to offer me a hundred bucks to emcee and read a poem at an event honoring her aunt. I said, "Are you related to Ed?"

"Yes, I am, Studs. But please do not connect me with him."

"Will he be there?"

"He'll probably be there, but he doesn't know you're on the program."

So it's at the Palmer House or the Hilton Ballroom, and there are two stages: one where the speakers sit, the other where the band sits. Some people are facing the band stage and can't really see our table. I say to Elsie, "Which is Ed?"

"He's at that table over there. A guy with a fat neck." I saw a fat neck holding up a very bald head. So Elsie gets up and says, "And now we give you one of Chicago's favorites, you remember *Studs' Place*? Here's the legendary Studs Terkel." I'll never forget the back of Ed's neck. There was a twitch and then it was rigid the rest of the time. He didn't move one bit for the whole hour, just sat stone still as though catatonic.

I spent a lot of time at home during the blacklist period, reading, listening to music. The FBI would come by once in a while to see me. They always came in pairs. Of course, I'd put on this big act, invite them in for a drink, while sweet Ida suddenly wasn't so sweet . . .

THE OCCASIONAL FBI VISITS to my house were not always pleasant. With a sense of some shame, I say this. My wife, usually the most gracious of hostesses, was for some reason, inhospitable. There were at least two occasions I recall when she peremptorily showed them to the door. She always let in small boys who sold magazine subscriptions for the benefit of the nation's halt, lame, and blind; as well as to make points that would enable them to attend Harvard. But to the FBI, she manifested—how can I say it?—contempt. I was, of course, terribly embarrassed.

I myself was hospitable at all times. I seated them. I offered them choices of Scotch or bourbon. I had triple shots in mind. Invariably, they refused. Once, I suggested vodka, making it quite clear it was domestic. I thought I was quite amusing. At no time did our visitors laugh. Nor did my wife. I felt bad. I did so want to make them feel at home. I never succeeded.

They had questions in mind. They frequently consulted small notebooks. They hardly had the chance to ask any of their questions. It wasn't that I was rude. On the contrary; I simply felt what I had to tell them was far more interesting than what they had to ask me.

I read Thoreau to them; his sermon on John Brown. Passages out of Walden. Paine. I told them these are times that try men's souls. And so on. We hold these truths, I even tried out on them. Nothing doing. Their attention wandered. They were like small restless boys in the classroom, wiggling in their seats. At times, I showed them where the bathroom was and asked if they wanted any reading matter. No, they didn't. I have done some of my most exploratory reading there, I told them. No response.

After several such visits, with a notable lack of response on their part, my patience, I must admit, did wear thin. On one occasion, a visitor took out his notebook and studied it. Our son, five years old at the time, peered over his shoulder. The guest abruptly shut the book. The boy was startled.

"Why did you do that?" I asked.

"He was peeking in my book."

"He's five years old."

"This is government information."

"Is it pornographic?"

"I don't know what you're talking about."

"Isn't it fit for a child to see?

"This is serious."

"Does it have dirty words or dirty pictures?"

"What??"

"Does it? Come on, be a sport, lemme see. I won't show it to the kid."

With the determined step of an FBI man, he stalked toward the door. He had trouble with the lock. I opened it. "One for the road?" I was determinedly hospitable. He walked out without so much as a thank-you. His colleague followed suit, step by step.

The last time I heard from the FBI was a good twenty-five years ago. It was a telephone call. I was not in the best of moods. In sorting through my records, preparing for my disc jockey program, I had dropped a 78 rpm. It smashed into a million pieces. It was a collector's item: "Joe Louis Blues." Lyrics by Richard Wright. Vocal by Paul Robeson. Accompaniment, Count Basie and his band. I was furious as I answered the phone.

"Are you Louis Terkel, known as Studs?"

"Yeah!" Damn my clumsiness.

"This is Martin Shea, FBI." It was a rich, stentorian bass. Strong, firmly American.

"Cut the shit. Who is it? Eddie?" I was in no mood for badinage.

"Shea of the FBI." A note of uncertainty. An octave higher than before. A baritone.

"Fer Chrissake, don't fuck around! Jimmy, ya sonofabitch!"

"I'm Shea of the FBI." An intimation of tremolo. A tenor.

"Look, you cocksucker! I'm not in the mood. I just broke a valuable record. Understand?"

"I'm Shea of the FBI!" Another octave up. A mezzo-soprano. I was quite certain it was he. My fury, though, was uncontrollable. All the more so because it was he.

"Look, fucko. Keep this up and I'll kick the shit out of ya!"

Really! I'm so flabby I can't swat a mosquito.

The voice was higher now. It was a countertenor. No, it was a despairing falsetto. A castrato, that was it.

"I'm Shea of the FBI!"

"You prick . . ."

A click. He had hung up. From Feodor Chaliapin to Alfred Deller. It was a remarkable piece of virtuosity, surpassing even Yma Sumac. That was the last I heard from the FBI. Oh well.★

MEANTIME, I was trying my hand at writing soap operas for Erna Phillips, the queen of the soaps. I started to write material that she liked, and then one day she called up and said: "I didn't know that you were on the attorney general's list, that you were blacklisted. Why didn't you tell me? I'm in trouble."

Apparently she'd mentioned me at a dinner with professional colleagues, and this one guy said, "You can't hire him." So she paid me what I had coming in cash. She didn't want her name associated with me even that much.

At the same time, I was doing *Wax Museum* and writing a Sunday column about jazz for the Chicago *Sun-Times*. The column was called *The Hot Plate*: I reviewed new jazz, blues, and show-tunes records. I've read the columns again—an old friend who goes to the Chicago public library found them in the microfilms and sent them to me. They were pretty awful; slick and facile.

One day, the Sunday editor called me in for a meeting. He announced that they were dropping the column. Why? Lack of space. The next week a new column appeared by Howard Miller, an ultra-right-wing guy who Mike Royko used to go after in print. They gave him three columns in place of my one. Fired me because they had no room . . . for me, that is. So there it was. My journalist

★ *Talking to Myself* (The New Press, 1995, pp. 127–129).

friend Herman Kogan was furious. So was the Sunday editor. He
was a good guy, Irish, drunk. But he'd been told I had to go. I went
back to being a radio guy, but the troubles were not over.

I hate meetings, and like Groucho Marx, wouldn't want to be-
long to any club that would have me, but now and again, exceptions
must be made. I confess, I was a member of the St. Louis Browns'
Fan's Club. A small but select group: Bill Leonard, Frank Holzfeind,
and Freddie Townsend.

Bill Leonard was the drama critic of the *Journal of Commerce* and
the nightclub critic of the Chicago *Tribune*. Frank Holzfeind ran
the Blue Note, a noted jazz club. Freddie Townsend was a public-
relations man who was genially drunk all the time. Every day he'd
welcome you, "Merry Christmas!" Every day was Christmas. They
were all old baseball fans, fond of imbibing a few, and had formed
the St. Louis Browns' Fan's Club after attending the St. Louis
Browns' final game: a post-existence fan club.

That column attacking me appeared in one of the West Side
neighborhood papers; several columns, as a matter of fact—the
work of Dan Lydon. How come I'm not knocked off the air? And
he prints all kinds of information about me in the columns—the
Red Cross rejection included.

Freddie Townsend, who was doing publicity for the Palmer
House, cancels all the ads to Lydon's paper. Lydon is outraged:
"What are you doing?!"

Freddie says: "Well, you knocked out Studs Terkel. I'm with-
drawing all the ads from your paper."

Lydon says: "Yeah, but he's a Commie. I got a wife and kids."

Freddie says, "So does Studs," and hangs up on him.

In the main, the Chicago public didn't know about me being
blacklisted because so many newspaper guys were friends of mine. I
was blacklisted in the trade. Outside the trade, they didn't know.

New York was different. I went to New York after *Studs' Place*
was knocked off the air in 1951. There I met with Henry Jaffe, an
agent who also was the lawyer for the American Federation of

Television and Radio Artists (AFTRA). He says, "How about *Studs' Place*? This was a big show, got rave reviews. Let me call up the vice president of NBC."

I'm sitting there while Jaffe makes the call: "What about this *Studs' Place*, the Chicago program? Studs is with me now." A pause, then he says, "It was knocked off. How come? What's it all about?" A long pause, and then he looks at me. "Oh, you can't talk about it on the phone. Well, you've told me what it is, thank you." Then to me, "Well, it looks like you're in political trouble."

The next day the headline in *PM* is that his own wife, the actress Jean Muir, who had a role on a TV show, has been blacklisted. So there it was. New York didn't work out.

There was one point when I thought I might be called to testify before the House Un-American Activities Committee, but I wasn't. Today we honor Dalton Trumbo, who went through everything. I suppose I'd have gone with him; at least I like to think so. Others did otherwise. Think of Larry Parks, pathetic, on his knees. "Please don't make me . . ."

Parks named names, and then he apologized. But his life was never the same and he died shortly thereafter. So did Lee J. Cobb. John Garfield was about to name names and then he died from a heart attack. Mady Christian created the role of Mama in *I Remember Mama*. She was named, humiliated, and eventually she killed herself. Likewise Albert Decker, a villain in movies, a dapper man.

Lionel Stander, the comic, was one of the heroes. He arrived at the hearings with a blonde on each arm. He takes the stand: "Are you now or have you ever been . . ."

Stander replies: "You want me to name names of un-Americans? You bet, yessir."

"Well name them."

"*You*, sir. Senator Dies, you are Number One un-American. Senator Thomas, you're Number Two un-American . . ." Everyone was going crazy.

"Get off the stand."

"Let me finish. Every member of this committee is un-American." It was fantastic.

A number of people stood up to their inquisitors. Ring Lardner Jr. among them: "Of course I could name names. But, Senator, I just would not like myself in the morning."

Being called, it was all so haphazard; it was just chance that I wasn't. Luck played a big role and the big luck was being in Chicago! Had I been on the Coast or New York, I might have been dead meat.

Through all this, I was never quite in despair, never really lacking confidence. But it was just the situation, would the situation ever change? Then things popped a little: Along came WFMT radio, and the books.

18

Lucky Breaks II

During the blacklist, I was often at home listening to the radio, not in the best temper. I just happened upon WFMT while turning the dial. I distinctly remember hearing Carl Orff's *Carmina Burana*. I like a station that plays music of that sort.

I started listening to it regularly and noticed that they had actors on, kids from the Compass Players. They were performing excerpts from *The Catcher in the Rye*, which was controversial at the time. They had Herman Kogan on as a guest commentator debating another literary critic on the value of *The Catcher in the Rye*.

Hey, this is a very good station, I think. I call them up. They knew me immediately, because of the *Wax Museum* and *Studs' Place*. Bernie and Rita Jacobs ran the station; Rita was also an announcer and happened to pick up the phone the day I called. I said, "This station sounds pretty good. How about my working for you?"

She said, "That's wonderful, except for one thing: we're flat broke, we haven't any money."

I said, "I haven't any either, so we're even." I started out working for nothing.

At first, Bernie and Rita and Norm Pellegrini were the entire full-time staff; Mike Nichols worked as a part-time announcer while attending the University of Chicago. Norm was the announcer and the program director; he chose the records.

I began working there in 1952, when they had the second floor of the Hotel Guyon, a once somewhat fashionable, but by then seedy hotel. Bernie had little education and wanted very much to be recognized as a man of culture. When I started, he said, "As far as the program is concerned, anything goes. You can read short stories, interview anyone you want, play records." Anything! My hour.

The following year, along came Ray Nordstrand with all his zest. Ray and Norm always had a slight . . . not hostility, but a tendency toward competition. They were wholly different. Ray was about *selling*; Norm was a man of the arts. Ray's father had worked hard as a janitor, and Ray worked like a dog. He was a lot like Bernie Jacobs, now that I think about it: Both wanted to be accepted as cultured. Choosing the music was perfect for Norm. He was good to me. He might have bawled me out once in a while about some political comment, but otherwise, he left me alone to do whatever I wanted.

Then Jimmy Unrath came along as an announcer and engineer. (The place was so small that its announcers had to be engineers, too.) Finally Lois Baum was hired. She was sort of a glamorous figure, classy. I got a kick out of her immediately because she was always correcting me, telling me off. She'd leave me notes, signed "Miss Grundy." She did have a sense of humor about herself.

It was a good group of people, and then, bit by bit, it grew. For a long time it had a real family feeling. My career has always had a roller-coaster touch, but WFMT was a high point in my life. Forty-five years of it.

When I was first starting out on WFMT, unpaid, and only on one day a week, I also had a jazz program on WAIT. I was on in the afternoon, between two black disc jockeys, Daddy O'Daley and Freddy Williams. One day I was in a cab, and the driver, a black kid, hears my voice and says, "You're white! I'll be damned." I took that as a great compliment. The show was mostly records, though now and then I had someone on—Billie Holiday once, though sadly the show was never taped.

At that time, a man named Vince Garrity had his own special program, *Sounds of the City*. It went this way: "This is for Joe Slezak, a wonderful guy in the Fifth Ward. Terrific guy." The whole program was naming names. Mike Royko loved it—every day, Vince Garrity naming those names. Red Quinlin, head of a Chicago radio station, got the craziest idea in the world: a show with the unusual combination of Vincent DePaul Garrity and me.

Sounds of the City aired from 11 P.M. to 1 A.M. What goes on in the city in those dark night hours? The original idea was for Vince to go out and get the tape, and for me to talk about it on the air.

Vince and I had nothing in common; we were the last guys you'd think of together. Vince was Vince: short, squat, glasses—ex-office boy of Mayor Kelly, ex–bat boy for the Cubs, acquainted with every cop on the beat. Somehow the combination of the two of us was so crazy and right that it worked.

We did things no one else was doing: two guys, five days a week, capturing the life of the city. Sometimes I was in the studio getting material from the newspapers with Vince wandering out in the world; sometimes I went with him.

The editors of the Hearst paper *The American* would call me up about an item; we'd follow up on it. One of the great episodes was an interview with a currency exchange clerk, a hero who was going to make the front page the next day—he had pushed an alarm button and stopped a robber from getting away with $100,000. I said, "You're a hero."

He said: "I'm an ass, are you kidding?"

"But you just saved a hundred thousand dollars. Wouldn't you do it again?"

"Hell, no! I must've been nuts. I saved this guy a hundred grand! I could've been shot. Hero, hell. I'm an idiot." Then I slipped in a piece of music, probably a comic song from *The Marriage of Figaro*.

A good clothing company was robbed, the owner says with pride, "Oh-h-h, do they have good taste."

"Who has good taste?"

"The robbers, they took the best."

Then Vince starts advertising for the guy: "Kuppenheimer's . . . Let me tell you more about what they took. These robbers have excellent taste."

That program, the city at night, was exciting. We captured all kinds of events. It was one of the first times I'd interviewed a variety of people—the family celebration for a Mexican kid coming home from Korea, a guy in the park whose shirt had just been stolen. We were even at the birth of a child born in a black ghetto.

Our engineer, Hansen, and I traveled to the home of a woman with grown kids who was giving birth to a new baby. We came in with a nurse and a young intern. The family was playing the record, "Move On Up a Little Higher," Mahalia Jackson's hit song. Of course you wanted to move the baby up, too. The intern says: "Tincture of thyme will take care of it."

I remember holding the mike up when out comes the baby, a girl, and I say: "What's the name?" I held the mike, not too close, and said: "Welcome to the world!" And then there was a yowl.

I remember interviewing Battling Nelson. He was the lightweight champion way back. We're talking about 1906, during the San Francisco earthquake—he was there giving money to earthquake victims. A guy tips me off he's in Chicago, and where to find him.

Battling Nelson is in a seedy, forty-watt-bulb, Ontario Hotel room. I went with Hansen the engineer. Nelson's wife is cackling as the old boy tries to remember certain events in his life, glory moments. Old Bat has a tremendous sheaf of papers and a ton of scrapbooks, photos, Nelson, the Durable Dane and the King of Denmark, et cetera. He opens it up and there are headlines, and he talks, and there's his voice. Remember, he's from 1908, 1910, the kind of guy Hemingway wrote about.

After Red Quinlin left, the new head dumped me. He did say, "These tapes are yours if you want them." I didn't take them.

Should have. Who the hell else would have Battling Nelson's voice today?

IN THE MIDST of my eclectic career wanderings, I had another shot at TV. Sometime in the early fifties, Charlie Carnegie, the sales manager of the Leader Cleaners dry-cleaning chain, put me on a TV show called *The Briefcase*, ten o'clock at night. I'd come out with a briefcase and pull papers out of it: "Tonight, the guest will be Geraldine Page." Or, "Here's music, the Fine Arts Quartet," or . . . "Pete Seeger."

It was an Omnibus-type show. There's a play in town, I'd have the actor of the play in a dramatic or funny skit with me. I acted in almost all the shows. William Marshall, a pretty good Othello, came on and he and I did a scene from *Othello*, but a good Iago I was not. I did do a decent salesman in the last scene of *Summer and Smoke* with Geraldine Page. We'd do things like that, and because *The Briefcase* was live, it was exhilarating.

The show lasted close to a year, and we had a total audience of about twenty-seven people—certain fans remembered me from *Wax Museum* and *Studs' Place*. It appeared I could do anything and get away with it.

This is the show where I turned down Mike Nichols, Elaine May, and Shelly Berman. Mike and Elaine were just becoming known, and Mike called asking to be on my show. I knew them from the *Compass Players*. I said, "No, I can't." Isn't that crazy? You could call that a blooper, one among many.

Many years later, Oprah Winfrey, just starting out in Chicago, calls asking me to be on her new Chicago talk program. She said she was an admirer of mine and wanted me on as one of her early Chicago guests. I was in the middle of dicey negotiations, distracted. My head in a topsy-turvy state. "No, I'm sorry, I can't right now." The truth is, I had the interests of WFMT on my mind.

My instincts are not always on the money. There was Bruce

Springsteen. Either a representative of his or of *Entertainment Tonight* called: "Bruce Springsteen admires you and your writings."

I said, "I admire him."

"He'd like to be on with you on . . ." and then I heard the words *"Entertainment Tonight."*

I said, "No, not that. Neither of us will be good on that." That's before I realized that entertainment and news had become the same thing.

ORIGINALLY I was on WFMT on Sunday mornings. I hosted the first meeting of Big Bill Broonzy and Pete Seeger. Mo Asch put that out on a record. Then there was a whole series I did called *This Is Our Story*, modeled after Alan Lomax's book *Listen to Our Story*. It's songs of certain periods and times and circumstances: minstrel songs, labor songs, railroad songs. "Hear That Lonesome Whistle Blow." Did a show with Sonny Terry and Brownie McGhee, who were in Chicago with Tennessee Williams—they played a bluesy score in the background of *Cat on a Hot Tin Roof*.

Mine, for its own kind of show, was getting an audience. Bernie said, "Let's do this daily." So we went to five days a week. But I couldn't do *Wax Museum* five days a week; I planned each hour so carefully, I couldn't make the pace. That's when I started interviewing guests. I had talked about people like John Jacob Niles, Richard Dyer-Bennett, Burl Ives, Pete Seeger, and Jimmy and Marian McPartland on *Wax Museum*. I'd talked about various writers and read short stories on the air. When they came to town, or if locally based, had an upcoming engagement, I talked *with* them.

My first guest was the dapper tenor saxophonist Bud Freeman. Always dressed just so. He'd say, "I happen to be an anglophile." When Jack Teagarden, the great trombonist, saw Bud, he'd call out, "There's Barrymore!"

I knew Bud because his brother Arnie had been a member of the Chicago Repertory Group. Arnie played a little Frenchman in commercials for a French drink called Byrrh. He became so famous that people would stop him on the street. Remember, TV was still very new. There was a show called *T-Men in Action*, Treasury Men in Action. Arnie had a slight mustache and often played a gangster— not the leader, but the smooth guy, usually Italian. He was on *T-Men* a lot.

One day, Arnie's watching a double feature in a Forty-second Street movie house: two British films, *Tight Little Island* and *The Importance of Being Earnest*. Suddenly a woman hollers, "Help, help, this man stole my purse!" She's pointing at Arnie.

He says, "What are you talking about?" The house detective takes Arnie outside, and then the cops come. "What is this? I don't know what she's talking about." Suddenly it occurs to him: "Lady, do you watch television?"

She says, "That's where I saw you! *T-Men in Action*!"

Those cops were so impressed they couldn't get over it: "Where do you live? We'll take you home. Can we have an autograph?" You could see the power of TV and celebrity from the very first.

In my hour, I could do anything, and I included music in almost every program. I'm a good reader and I started reading short stories. Say, Flannery O'Connor's "Parker's Back." Parker's back is tattooed with the Seven Stations of the Cross; he's smitten with this bony, Jesus-possessed woman and wants to impress her. I'd read that and play a certain hymn. For Chekhov's "Darling," I'd slip in bits of Russian music here and there. Music has *always* been a part of my show, even of the talk programs.

Norm Pellegrini was my first engineer, followed by Frank Tuller, and then various others. I must pay tribute to Jim Unrath, whose big contribution was to work with me on documentaries that won all sorts of awards and public honors. Without Jimmy, none of that would have happened.

For years, he was the morning announcer at WFMT, but way back he volunteered to work with me. Jimmy gets a kick out of me. He calls me "Boy Fellini" because I don't fully say things; it's all in my *head*. But Jimmy has a sense; he's the one who *gets* what I'm imagining better than anybody.

Early on, WFMT was not an all-night station the way it is now, it would shut down at midnight. The place would be empty during the night and that's when we worked on the documentaries. We'd work 'til three in the morning and Jimmy would come home with me and sleep on the couch for a few hours before going back to work the morning shift.

The first thing Jimmy and I did together was an hour documentary about the work of Nelson Algren. We used a short story of his called "Come in at the Door" as the basis and the name for the program. The story is a page or so but we connected it with other Algren pieces. We used a couple of actors, as well as Nelson's and my voices. That piece, you might say, was the essence of Algren.

The story involves a hooker who's in bad shape and a pimp who's occupying the room she's paid for. He won't let her in unless she throws a twenty-dollar bill over the transom to show that she's earned her keep. The hooker says, "I ain't got it, honey."

Says the pimp, "When you do it next time and you have enough money you can come in at the door." In that story she gets sent up for drugs.

"Twenty months and a day," says the justice, "to keep America strong and mighty."

She says, "I got out after twenty months and a day, and you know what? The country was still strong and mighty."

We made a number of documentaries, fifteen or twenty of them. One was very funny, on the unveiling of Picasso's statue in Chicago. Picasso's gift to Chicago was bewildering to the great many people gathering at the plaza. Mayor Daley the elder had made it a point to fill the plaza with citizens. It was jammed. I asked various people their aesthetic opinions of the statue. They merely said, as though with one voice, "If it's good enough for Mayor Daley, it's good enough for me." That made it official. Mayor Daley had become our arbiter of culture as well.

We did a series entitled *Joy Street*. Later we did digests of some of my books, especially *Hard Times*. We did a documentary called *This Train* about the 1963 March on Washington. Ida was the one who heard about the train going from Chicago to Washington, D.C., and said, "Let's go on that train."

During the severe snowstorm of 1967, when all the cars were stuck, Ida was the one saying, "Go outside, you gotta go outside!" She was excited because no one could drive and everywhere people were walking and talking to one another. She wanted me to get out there with my tape recorder. I'll never forget how an old lady she met, shortly after the storm, had lifted her spirits. "I fell down in the snow twenty times and I was picked up twenty times and I was offered coffee twenty times . . ." A long pause. "You just can't beat people." Ida adopted that refrain as her own.

Before the August '63 March on Washington, someone from the NAACP had the idea of sending a train to Washington. Think of Abraham Lincoln, the funeral train from Washington to Springfield, and the meaning of trains in the lives of black people. "This train don't carry no gamblers, this train . . ." Throughout the documentary, that was the theme: This train is bound for glory. Big Bill Broonzy singing sometimes, but other versions as well.

The train has always been the mecca for Deep South sharecroppers, African Americans overwhelmingly. Ever since the "underground railway" of Harriet Tubman, it has had special meaning.

My wife and I took the memorable over-ground train trip to Washington, D.C. Two hundred thousand others joined us at the Lincoln Memorial Pool to hear Martin Luther King Jr. commemorate his dream.

On the train I talked with people off and on throughout the whole trip. Timuel Black, the captain of the train, said the only other time he'd ever felt this exhilarated was when he entered Paris with the Quartermaster Corps (the first American soldiers in Paris after General Leclerc and his troops liberated the city from German occupation).

For a long stretch, I found myself sitting next to the singer and performer Etta Moten Barnett. Etta, then in her sixties, lived to be 103, and was quite beautiful. "What do I think of a train?" she said, and then hummed softly, "This train is bound for glory, this train." She said, "Even those Jim Crow trains had something special. Little babies running back and forth, their mother so careful to wrap up that fried chicken in certain kind of paper and put it in certain kind of boxes. They came to you offering their boxes with the chicken." She described the powerful camaraderie that existed within adversity.

We went through Pennsylvania, then Ohio, passing what seemed like miles of empty yards. She said, "Where are the jobs?"

Sitting with us much of that time was a white minister, Howard Schomer. He was head of the United Church of Christ Seminary at the University of Chicago, and eloquent. He said, "Forty acres and a mule was the promise. It's a check that bounced, and now we've come to redeem that check."

Lawrence Landry, whom I knew, was sort of the co-captain of the train. I sat in the washroom while he spoke of his father the Pullman-car porter, and of what that job had meant. Landry talked about the beginnings of the porters and the union, and the importance of Pullman-car porters in being messengers, spreading the news. The porters would drop the Chicago *Defender*, a newspaper for African Americans, off at the railroad stations. When you were a Pullman-car porter, you'd come to town with that white stripe down your blue pants and walk into the pool hall or the barbershop. "There he is! What's the latest from Chicago?" People would sit and listen to the porter giving them the news.

I wandered up and down the train, and at nighttime if people were only half asleep, even just a little awake, I'd join them. That was an incredible trip, being on that train, being part of something big.

Said one elderly black woman, "I'm not gonna get any good out of it, I'm doing it for my grandchild."

And a man named Simpson: "My wife and my grandchildren,

they say, 'Why you going? You can see it on the television.' " He said, "I don't want to see it, I wants to be *in* it."

I remember that phrase: "I wants to be in it." He wanted to be in that moment, he wanted to count, to be a part of history. That was the thing I remember most strongly, the voices of people wanting to make a difference.

ONE OF THE ASPECTS that amuses me is when certain people complain about my oral history work as "writing with a tape recorder." They become very indignant indeed. "What sort of writing is that?"

They'd be even more furious were they to know the truth: I'm technologically impaired, wholly undeveloped when it comes to equipment. After all, the typewriter is a machine of communication, like a telephone or a telegraph. The funny thing is, I am as inept with the tape recorder as I am with the automobile, or the bicycle. This is the age of the computer, and I haven't the faintest idea how one works; I've barely mastered the electric typewriter. I can't explain why that is; I imagine it's just the way my brain works. Or doesn't work.

An example of my ineptitude: My work with Jimmy on one particular program based on a long, radio-style prose poem by Norman Corwin. The name "Norman Corwin" has no meaning whatsoever to the young today, which gives you an idea about the gap that exists in our culture. His was the writing that elevated radio scribbling to an art form. Corwin was the best, considered the bard of all radio writers. He produced a series that CBS ran; the most notable program, *On a Note of Triumph*, aired the day Germany surrendered toward the end of World War II. Subsequently, Corwin had written a script, printed in a slim book, *Overkill and Megalove*—his response to Hiroshima, a remarkable piece.

I wanted to do a documentary on it and called him up for permission, and he said "Go ahead." Jimmy is going to be the engineer on this. Jimmy is a tall man, and *huge*. At one time he looked just like Steve Allen, but due to glands or appetite, at this point he weighed about 350 pounds, in contrast to a rather short me. So visually, this was a goofy combination, but it was the reverse of the guys in *Of Mice and Men*. In Steinbeck's book, the big dumb guy was Lenny and the little one with the brains was George. In this case, I am Lenny.

Overkill and Megalove is about the madness of war that leads to the obliteration of the human species. A bomb falls and the two major powers keep fighting until everybody else is dead except for the two leaders. The two guys left in the world say, "Let's sign a peace pact." I found a Japanese actor to be the voice of one leader, and I did the voice for the other, who is also the narrator.

At the end, the program called for a remarkable sound that was almost impossible to get. As the leaders are talking, the narrator is dying and his speech becomes more and more difficult, until finally, he expires. In the meantime, his number-one enemy, the only other person left on earth, has just died.

I wanted the last sound of the last man on earth.

That's how Corwin has it in his script, but it's a sound that he can't describe. Because of all the technology involved in the war, I figured I had to find a sound that was electrified as well as natural; I wanted a sound that was of this earth and yet something beyond, signifying the emptiness of all beings.

Jimmy has an idea for the sound but he can't do it alone because it involves three turntables. Jimmy knows I'm mechanically hopeless. He's using all ten of his fingers and he's almost got it covered, but he needs just one more element, another digit to start a third tape recorder. It's hardly complicated, just a button or two. This is George talking to Lenny in *Of Mice and Men*.

JIM (firmly): "Now, what I want you to do is very simple. Do you hear me?"

ME (the good student): "I follow ya, Jim. I can do it."

JIM: "I'm going to be busy. I haven't got eleven fingers; I've only got ten. Now, I can't get that other machine going, but if you press this button you can. You press that button on only one occasion. When I give you the nod. When I nod at you like this." (He nods.) "Do you follow me?"

Finally we're ready to roll. After considerable effort Jimmy's got everything working and he's looking at me and he nods at me and I look at him and I say, "Now?"

Jimmy clutches his hand to his forehead and says, "No, no, let's start again. Didn't I tell you that when I nod my head you press the button?" (Jimmy demonstrates, nods yes.) "Did I tell you to say 'now'?"

"No, you didn't."

"Then why did you say 'now'?" Jimmy sighs.

"I was silent for a few seconds."

"You lost two seconds on that, one second, one tenth of a second. It's gone! Now, what do I want you to do?"

"You want me to press the button when you nod your head."

"OK, you got it now? Don't say 'now.' Don't . . . say . . . *anything*."

I say, "I got it."

"Oh-*kay*," and he's looking at me. "Here we go!" Jimmy does the same fantastically intricate maneuverings. How he does it I don't know, but he nods at me and I look back and nod, meaning "Now?" I don't say anything. I just nod back, and watch as Jimmy drops the earphones . . . And then he adopts Rodin's *Thinker* pose. By and by he says, "What did I tell you? Not to say anything."

I say, "Well, it's true I didn't say anything, did I?"

"No, you didn't say anything, it's true. All right, one last try and then I go home, that's it, forget it. One last try. Will you remember to say *nothing*? And don't pause. And do nothing except press the button when I nod my head."

"I got it."

"Now repeat it."

It's Lenny and George, there's no doubt about it. I repeat it. "Good boy." And so now he does it again and finally I get it right. And the sound was *perfect*. It's a certain kind of sound that we could not have gotten on tape without me pushing that button.

That's an example of how I worked with Jimmy. And how I work with machines. As you can see, I'm not the fastest gun in the West.

By that time, we'd already made the documentary *Born to Live*. Rita Jacobs was the one who suggested we submit a program to the Prix Italia contest. We submitted under the radio documentary category. UNESCO sponsored the contest that year; for the first time, they awarded a special three-thousand-dollar prize. We won that prize.

Rita had come in one day saying, "Here's a wire from Prix Italia inviting you to submit," and of course, Jimmy volunteered to be my engineer.

Just a week earlier, I'd interviewed a young woman, a *hibakusha*—a survivor of Hiroshima. She had been brought to see me by a Quaker woman whose husband had been on the ship *Golden Rule*, the first vessel ever to try disrupting a nuclear test in protest against the nuclear arms race. The Quaker and the *hibakusha* spoke in Japanese, and we brought an interpreter in to translate. We used that in the beginning of *Born to Live*, which is about life suddenly wiped out.

Dennis Mitchell, the dean of British TV documentaries taught me there's no need for a narrator when you do a documentary, as he showed in his great classic *Morning in the Streets*. *Born to Live* opens cold: the girl speaking Japanese. She says,

And we saw the plane, Sunday morning, beautiful. I was eleven, and all of a sudden something dropped and all of a sudden there was horror. People died on the spot. It just went bang. And I'm looking for my mother and she's nowhere. Everywhere I went looking for my mother. And then I sang that song she used to sing.

And she sang it. Throughout the piece, we had this song, a haunting song.

I had other songs connecting the sequences; one with a social worker I knew, Perry Miranda. He had interviewed a seventeen-year-old kid whose body was covered with tattoos. On his finger was etched D-E-A-T-H. The boy says, "I got that on my hand because we're going to die."

"Well, don't you believe there's anything," says Perry, "between the time you're born and the time you die?"

"I guess you're born to die, born to die."

"How about being born to live?"

It went on to other voices, among them: Miriam Makeba, Jimmy Baldwin, and the Reverend William Sloane Coffin. Finally this old woman says, "Oh, I work all my life and when's it gonna end? And my sweat comes down my neck like a big bouquet . . ." Finally, she says, "But I don't care what it is. Wind's blowing and howling, I'm still outside. The wind got no home. All I know is I'm on my way." And you hear the voice of Mahalia Jackson singing, "I'm on my way to Canaanland . . ."

How are you gonna beat that? That crazy program is good even now. If anything, it is more apropos now than it was then.

19

A Casual Conversation

How I became an oral historian is a matter of a chance encounter. WFMT had a little program booklet named *The WFMT Guide*, later called *Perspective*. Transcribed interviews of mine began to appear in *Perspective*. Some were with celebrated people I may have visited, such as Bertrand Russell and C.P. Snow; others, with those visiting Chicago, such as Marlon Brando. But the magazine also featured so-called ordinary people I'd interviewed on my program—politically, culturally, civically engaged people.

Now comes a fortuitous series of events. One year, Chicago's best-known comedy group, Second City, traveled to London as part of an exchange—the British comedy group The Establishment came to Chicago.

The British comedienne Eleanor Bron happened to hear my program on *WFMT* while she was in Chicago. Eleanor, one of the first women to go to Cambridge University, remained friends with a former schoolmate of hers, Elena de la Iglesia, who had married André Schiffrin, a publisher in New York. Eleanor mentioned my interviews to André, who was at that time the editor of Pantheon Books, part of the umbrella group called Random House. Although André was born in Paris, he attended Cambridge and spent a great deal of time in England. One day the phone rings, and a soft voice with a slight British accent is at the other end. André.

Pantheon had just put out an American edition of *Report from a Chinese Village* by Jan Myrdal.★ The book tells the story of a village in North China after the Mao Communist takeover, of how that revolution affected people in a small town in ways both good and bad.

This was 1965, and the situation here in the United States was being described as a triple revolution: the growth of the civil rights movement, the development of automation and the computer, and the advancing ability to wipe out the planet eight ways from Sunday.

André suggested I do a book about an American village and how the revolution we were then experiencing affected it . . . an American village called Chicago. My first words: "Are you out of your mind? How can you compare a small village in China with the huge metropolis of Chicago?" Nonetheless, I did it: *Division Street: America.* There is a Division Street in Chicago, but I meant the title as metaphorical—the Division Street on which the country was finding itself.

Division Street was well received by critics, as well as by readers. André called again a few months later and said, "Our sense of history is so impaired. Young people don't know about the great American Depression of the thirties. There's been no book about how ordinary people were affected by the Depression."

I said: "Are you out of your mind?" I did *Hard Times*, the title stolen from Dickens, the subtitle, *An Oral History of the Great American Depression.* I wanted to call it *Hard Times* because of a thirteen-year-old kid from Appalachia.† This young boy said: "I don't know the word depression, I don't know what means. I know a per-

---

★ Jan was the son of the Swedish economist Gunnar Myrdal, who wrote *An American Dilemma: The Negro Problem and Modern Democracy* and whose later books were being published by André Schiffrin at Pantheon.

† Chicago has many Appalachians, mountain people, poor whites, as well as a tremendous number of Southern blacks—the inner migration.

son who feels low down is depressed. But you talked about people not working. We called that hard times."

And that book went over rather well, critically and in readership.

Several months later, again a call from André: "How about a book about the jobs people do?"

"The what?" (My hearing, even then, faulty.)

"*Jobs*. A book about how people feel about their work. It could be a waitress, a manager, a garage mechanic, a stone mason." So the book *Working* came into being, a surprising bestseller.★

Later on I had the idea of doing *Talking to Myself*, which is more my own style. I talked about twenty tapes' worth, and that became the basis of an oral memoir. Then, "*The Good War*," again André's idea. He set things in motion, and that's more or less how the disc jockey became known as an oral historian.

We think of historians as scholars who research in great scope and detail. What I do in great scope and detail is converse; the phrase "oral historian," when it refers to me, carries a somewhat whimsical connotation. People say, "Oh, he's so friendly, he makes conversation with anyone. He gets people to talk, he gets things out of people others miss." They attribute that to my generosity of spirit and my open-mindedness when the truth is very simple: I like to hear conversation, which gives *me* an excuse to talk as well.

My years at the Wells-Grand Hotel were a factor, those formative years during the Depression. Being in the lobby, hearing all kinds of conversation, goofy as well as reasoned talk. These guys weren't all intellectuals; some were barbaric in their thoughts, arguing back and forth, foolishly in many instances. But it's simply my nature to be curious, to find out what's going on—how those men felt about the jobs lost, about fighting over nothing because they felt they were nothing. I never did get to ask *them*. I never thought of writing then, it never occurred to me. I was just part of the scene there in the hotel.

★ *Working* has now sold over a million copies in various editions. (Ed.)

There's no real science to finding people who can articulate their feelings, the non-celebrated among us. I keep my ears open and I have all kinds of sources, people I know who are out and about in the world.

Years ago, Gloria Steinem said she liked the strong women in my books. In the early books, some of the most exciting women came from Ida's tips and observations. I was busy doing the radio programs, but Ida was involved with social workers, their unions, and one activist group or another. She was close to Saul Alinsky's wife, Helene, the first president of the Social Workers' Union.* Ida knew people like Della Reuther, who belonged to a left-wing group. Della was a wonderful, huge Lithuanian woman. In *Division Street*, I called her Eva Barnes.

> Most that disturbs me today is when I talk to some of my neighbors, none of them, they don't like this Vietnam going on, but here's where they say: "What's the use? Who are we? We can't say nothing. We have no word. We got the president. We elected him. We got congressmen in there. They're responsible. Let them worry. Why should I worry about it?" It's already pounded into them, you're just a little guy, you vote and you're through, it won't do no good anyhow.
>
> I think different. I think, like they say, that if I'm a voter, I should have a say-so in this. In everything . . . but anything good for the people is never given easy. Never given easy.†

THE WORK OF FLANNERY O'CONNOR has played a role in my life, despite my being agnostic, what I call a cowardly atheist. O'Connor was a devout Catholic, the endings of many of her stories apocalyptic: In her short story "The River," the big thing is to count.

The story is about a Tennessee Williams–type couple, decadent

---

* Helene, a good swimmer, drowned trying to save some children in Lake Michigan.
† From *Division Street: America* (The New Press, 2006, p. 71).

and drunk and goofy. Their little boy has a babysitter: a strait-laced, rough, fundamentalist woman. The little kid goes with the babysitter to evangelical meetings and baptisms by the river. He sees a guy or a girl's head shoved into the water by a charismatic young minister who says: "Now you count."

One day the kid, who feels he is nothing to his parents, walks out into the river . . . to count. When people feel they don't count, they are lost. What's left? Get as much as you can for yourself and forget the rest.

Eva Barnes, again, could be speaking of the moment:

> The answer is selfishness and greed and jealousy . . . but it's deeper than this, the more I think about it. It's this fear, fear of everything. Fear of the war in Vietnam, fear of Communism, fear of atomic bombs. There's a fear there.★

As is true for so many I've met through the years, the antidote for despair and hopelessness is in joining with others. After a distinguished Chicago physician had been cited for contempt by the House Committee on Un-American Activities, Eva Barnes joined a demonstration.

> I don't know him personally, but I know what I read about him, what a good doctor he is, what a humble man he is. And so I said, "Well, I gotta go defend that man. I gotta be one of the people to be counted." I can't set home.†

My friend Virginia Durr said about the Depression:

> People started to blame themselves. The preacher was saying, "You shouldn't have bought that second radio. You shouldn't have bought that secondhand car." People started thinking, "this is America; if I were good, *I'd* be behind that mahogany desk. I'm

★ From *Division Street: America* (The New Press, 2006, p. 63).
† From *Division Street: America* (The New Press, 2006, p. 69).

not smart enough, I'm not tough enough, I'm not strong enough, I'm not energetic enough. Therefore, I hold my hat in my hand with my head slightly bowed."

Which feeds the belief that *you don't count.*

The journalist Nick Von Hoffman worked with Saul Alinsky for a while and said: "Once a person joins a group, a demonstration or a union, they're a different person." That particular fight may have succeeded or failed, but you realize there's someone who thinks as you do, and so you become stronger as a result, no matter what the outcome. You count!

WHEN I LOOK FOR PEOPLE, I'm not looking only for those who share my views; I'm looking for those who have grown to think a certain way, who have changed their views. A number of conservative people are in my books; not as many as more progressive thinkers, but that's not the point of my books at all. I'm looking for those who can talk about how they see their lives and the world around them. Who can explain how and why they became one way or another.

While I was interviewing for the first book, a street worker introduced me to Hal Malden, who was once a neo-Nazi. Hal was a big heavyset man who had always felt like an outsider.

I always felt that I was somehow awkward or clumsy or something, that I was inept. I really don't know why. I don't think I am now, any more than anyone else is. And if I am, so what? At the time, I was very, very sensitive about it.★

When we spoke, he was in jail, sentenced to one year, fined $700. The charge: defamation of character. The victim: a celebrated Negro performer, Sammy Davis Jr. Malden, at the time of the misdemeanor, was a member of the American Nazi party. "I wanted to

★ From *Division Street: America* (The New Press, 2006, p. 326).

be an individualist: a person who feels he does what he should or wants to do. I'm in jail as a result of doing what I thought was right—at the time."★

The ability to question what surrounded him, whether in jail or in a neo-Nazi meeting, gave him the insight of a sociologist, and in fact, he eventually became a social worker, esteemed by colleagues for his compassion.

> There were no really happy people in this whole thing. . . . They have this enemy called "they." You ask one of them who "they" is, they'll say "Well, the Jews."
>
> You say, "Who?"
>
> "Well, you know."
>
> If you say, "No, I don't know, tell me," they become very frustrated; they get agitated and they say. "Hell, you wouldn't believe it if I told you." "They"—the Negro, the Communist . . . "They" is someone who is keeping them from their rightful place in society.†

He may have been wholly in opposition to Eva Barnes politically, but he came to feel as she about the beauty of the world.

> I don't want anything to be perfect. I like the one little flaw. It's said they never make a perfect Oriental rug and they leave a little flaw in 'em. Beauty is something that gives you pleasure. Blues like Big Bill's . . . It's the opposite of the order I was lookin' for. It's the human touch. I don't feel the world could ever be perfect, because if it were, it wouldn't be human. It would be nothing at all.‡

PEOPLE SAY I must have great empathy to work as I do. What I elicit from those interviewed, they see as proof of my emotional connec-

★ From *Division Street: America* (The New Press, 2006, p. 325).
† From *Division Street: America* (The New Press, 2006, p. 327).
‡ From *Division Street: America* (The New Press, 2006, p. 330).

tion. The truth is, I don't see it that way. When people suggest I have a deep feeling for others, I ask: Do they mean am I so deeply moved that it's difficult to go on? The answer is no.

Feeling is specific but it's also abstract. How do you feel? You're not the bush-league kid on TV, standing at the edge of the winner's circle. You're not the so-called interviewer lying in wait as a woman carries her dead child from the burning wreckage of a bombed building. "How do you feel?" You want to choke that person. The great actress Eleonora Duse would have hit them with the dead child.

You can also be a phony feeler. "I can't tell you," says this person on TV to the audience, "how deeply moved I was by that." It's a story. Don't say you're deeply moved. That's what was so questionable about Arthur Miller's *Death of a Salesman*: when the wife is crying at the epilogue, she shouldn't cry; you, in the audience, should.

Then there's the opposite, the idiots wedded to their notepads of written questions. "What happened when your child died? Now, what time of day was that?" You want to hit that person with two kids.

What I bring to the interview is respect. The person recognizes that you respect them because you're listening. Because you're listening, they feel good about talking to you. When someone tells me a thing that happened, what do I feel inside? I want to get the story out. It's for the person who reads it to have the feeling. In *The Grapes of Wrath*, when Ma Joad says, "How will I know, Tom?" the reader is moved. "You'll know it, Ma." Remember, it's Ma Joad who says, "We're not the kissing kind." I like that. In most cases, the person I encounter is not a celebrity; rather the ordinary person. "Ordinary" is a word I loathe. It has a patronizing air. I have come across ordinary people who have done extraordinary things.

How do I get people to say things they keep from others and even from themselves? Simple. It is my ineptitude, my slovenliness. The other, the ordinary person feels not only as good a being as I am; rather he feels somewhat superior. I have not come from *60*

Minutes or *Today*. I have come, a hapless retardee in matters me-
chanical. I make it clear to the person that now and then I screw
things up. I say I can't drive a car. I punch the wrong button. I goof
up. The other points out to me: Look, the reel isn't moving, or the
cassette seems to be stuck. Of course. At that moment, the other
feels needed, by me.

The feeling of being needed may be the most important to any
human, and especially to one who is regarded as no more than ordinary. In that way, there is empathy.

It's a funny thing, this particular ambivalence I have toward the
tape recorder, and my ineptitude with it, as with all things mechan-
ical. The tape recorder has been my right arm; has enabled me to
get the word, and thus the telling detail that otherwise might be
forgotten.

It's not simply the use of a tape recorder. I ask the person tran-
scribing to listen carefully and type everything: pauses, horns beep-
ing, clocks ticking, everything. What I want is to capture the full
conversation. I want to recreate in my mind exactly what it was like
to be with that person, to get as much as possible of what was in that
person's mind at that particular moment.

Logorrhea, I think, is one of my interview secrets—the inability
to stop talking. However, I do know, way in the back of my head,
when I'm saying something irrelevant just to hear the sound of my
voice. While I have able assistance from transcribers, and editors, I
happen to be a pretty good editor, too. That is, I'm engaged in conversation so much, I'm able to discern what is vamping 'til ready.
The editing is key.

I take my questions out as often as I can in order to create something of a soliloquy. What I like is to relate seemingly unrelated
things, to illuminate from the unexpected quarter. If it's a whimsical
or wry, humorous exchange, or maybe a transition moment that
needs a key question to lead someplace else, I leave the question in.

But the question always has to serve a purpose. Why did the person stop talking at a certain moment, or change his or her mind? Why was there a pause?

As you're crafting each individual interview, you keep in mind the span of the entire book. What first comes out of an interview are tons of ore; you have to get that gold dust in your hands. That's just the beginning. Now, how does it become a necklace or a ring or a gold watch? You have to get the form; you have to mold the gold dust. First you're the prospector, now you become the sculptor. Next, you find a gallery, and the book is the gallery. This is shorthand, almost simple-minded, and yet in a sense that's what is involved.

THIS STORY MIGHT EXPLAIN something about how I work. I have to get into the book whatever I think the book needs, no matter what the obstacle might be, as long as it doesn't hurt anybody. Sometimes I call on people I know, if they happen to fit the bill. Ida was one I called upon, spontaneously.

I was working on the book about the Great Depression, doing a section on Jim, a friend of mine from the Writers' Project. Jim had once upon a time been the editor of a newspaper, well known in his mid-size town in Ohio, but he'd lost his job during the Depression. He's flat broke and leaves his wife and kids at her mother's house and comes to Chicago to find work. No luck. Unemployed, no money to send home, he's staying with a friend. He has nothing. He goes to a social worker and she says, "Where do you stay?"

"With friends."

"Friends? What sort of friends are they?"

He's already feeling down, he starts to get very emotional. "What sort of friends? Friends! Do you know what the word 'friend' means?" He's almost crying at the humiliation, but furious as well. So I have a chapter, "Honor and Humiliation," about him.

But are all social workers this way? I say, no, this is wrong. There are two kinds of social workers, just as there are two kinds of people. So I ask Ida, the former social worker: "Who of your friends would be good to talk with?"

She starts naming: "Charlotte would be very good."

"Not quite." She names a few other people. I look at Ida: "Wait a minute. Didn't you tell me a story once about you and an elderly guy who was a client?"

Ida was very private and absolutely hated publicity. She says, "Oh no, you're not going to do that."

"I am going to do that. I'll change your name!"★

She says, "No, I don't want to."

"Change your name. I gotta do it. It's gotta be in. Because we've got this other social worker, this bitch, and I want someone good. It has to be you, I'm sorry. I need that incident you told me about."

So she says, "Well . . ."

I'm sitting on the divan with her, and I've got the mike. Ida tells the story, and as she tells it, her voice has a slight tremor.

I remember him, tall, gray-haired, living with his little grandchild. The place was bare, but he was a dignified man.

One day, Mrs. Falls, the superintendent, says, "From now on in, we have to look in the closet. If they say they need clothes, you have to *see* that they do."

I told her, "But I can't do that."

"What do you mean you can't?"

"I can't look in a person's closet. He's so poor."

"Well, if you don't, it's your job. Simple as that."

So Ida goes to his place and there's this guy . . . now her voice is starting to waver as she tells the story. Meanwhile I'm mumbling, "This is pretty good."

She's looking at me, not quite glaring, and she goes on . . .

★ Ida is named Eileen Barth in *Hard Times*.

And there he was. And I said, "I hope you'll forgive me but I have orders to look into your closet."

He says, 'Look into my closet? Well, sure. Go ahead." I looked in and it was empty, of course. And he . . ."

On my tape, there's a pause and you hear her softly suppressing a sob. "He was so humiliated . . ." And then comes the kicker. ". . . and I was, too." And she lets go.

That's when I jumped up and said, "This is *fantastic*."

And she sobs, "You bastard."

I had to get that in the book. She was wiping her eyes and I was chuckling, delighted. "Now, we'll have a drink."

20

The Feeling Tone

There are so many "ordinary" woman heroes I've encountered on my adventures. Florence Scala, who tried to save the soul of our city. She and Jessie Binford formed an unbreakable bond. They lost the fight to save the Hull House community, yet they won the wondrous respect and admiration of our city's scholars.

There is Marylou Wolff, who said, "If I can learn a truth of power and corruption and how to fight it, anybody can."

There is Jean Gump, of a middle-class suburb, who headed the Parent Teachers Association and the Council of Catholic Women. She celebrated Good Friday by breaking through the barbed wire along the highway and "damaging" the missile sites. She poured her blood on them, and held up a sign that was seen by millions of car drivers: BEAT YOUR SWORDS INTO PLOWSHARES AND STUDY WAR NO MORE.

And there is Nancy Jefferson, who was raised on a small Tennessee farm. At mealtimes, or in times of trouble, she was taught to ring a bell.

You used to pull this rope. Sometimes if it was especially cold, you'd keep pullin' and keep pullin' the bell. Maybe by the time your hands got raw almost, you'd hear a little tinklin' of the bell. That's the way I visualize the community. We all keep pullin' at the rope and our hands are getting' raw, but you do hear a little tin-klin'. We gotta keep pullin' and I believe the bell will ring.★

There are such heroes in the most astonishing places. My choice of these four was arbitrary. These four could have been any of hundreds who dream of Canaanland.

"The Feeling Tone" was a phrase used by Lucille Dickerson. It was a tone of Rose Rigsby, a natural-born street poet.

Peggy Terry was the mountain woman of Chicago, who brought together whites and blacks and whose speech was always lyrical.

How can I describe the wondrous gallant lawyer, Pearl Hart? She, defending all those who dissented, challenged corrupt Authority. She was attacked herself, but that never stopped her. Whenever she won, her victory was ours.

ONE DAY, Florence Scala, still in the fight to save the Hull House community, invited me to visit her friend, Nancy Dickerson.†

Nancy was an African American hospital aide at a classy North Side hospital. Always, she had a book in her hand, one paperback or another. It might be Langston Hughes, his poetry and his humor. Or William Faulkner's *The Sound and the Fury*. "I carried my books openly. I was always reading. Young white doctors and nurses would look at me eyes wide open, and whisper, "Faulkner?"

" 'Yeah, don't you read Faulkner?' I always did this."

Nancy's feisty sense of independence, despite her many burdens, says all about the human spirit. She was her own breed of sociologist. "I have learned that a Negro woman can do anything she wants to do if she's got enough nerve. So can a white man. But a white woman and a Negro man are slaves until this day."‡

The hope and joy of her life was her grandson, Marvin Jackson.

★ *Talking to Myself* (The New Press, 1995, p. 336).
† She is called Lucy Jefferson in *Hard Times*.
‡ *Division Street: America* (The New Press, 1993, p. 14).

She fought hard to get him out of their abysmal public school and into St. Ignatius, a highly regarded Catholic school. He continued through Stanford and became a neurologist, despite dispiriting comments from veteran doctors that the field might prove too difficult for him. She died before he became the chief of Washington University Hospital's neurology department. Said Dr. Marvin Jackson, "It was my grandmother who educated me to become the professional I am and to do the work I love."★

Nancy's words have stayed with me. "Let's face it. What counts is knowledge. And feeling. You see, there is such a thing as a feeling tone. One is friendly and one is hostile. And if you don't have this, baby, you've had it."

I wish she'd had the chance to meet a different neurologist, Dr. Oliver Sacks, who delighted at seeing those words. The good doctor said: "Goethe spoke of seeing with a feeling eye and feeling with a seeing hand. Henry Head,† the British neurologist, always looked for something he called "the feeling tone." I got very excited when I came across Lucille Jefferson's phrase. Nothing is more wonderful or to be celebrated than something that will unlock a person's capacities allowing him to grow and think."

DURING THE TUMULTUOUS SIXTIES, there emerged in Chicago a woman of the Ozarks, Peggy Terry. Of the Chicago migrants of that time, she, above all others, fused the "mountain hillbilly," as she called herself, with the Chicago African American. Especially close was the feeling tone expressed between Peggy and African Americans from small towns. It was she that formed and drum-majored many of the rallies of Chicago's have-nots at the time. She told me, "When I was reading *The Grapes of Wrath* this was just like my life. I was never so proud of poor people before, as I was after I read that book."

★ Dr. Marvin Jackson is currently Flight Surgeon, midwestern region of the FAA.
† Distinguished nineteenth-century neurologist.

Peggy's father was a Klansman, and she grew up hating black people. She happened to be living in Montgomery, Alabama, during the bus boycott and saw Dr. Martin Luther King Jr. repeatedly beaten at the jail.

> I remember one time he came out of jail in all white clothes. About five or six white men jumped him. Suddenly something says to me, "Two on one is nigger fun." That's what they always said when they saw two white kids beatin' up on a black kid. When I saw 'em beatin' up on Reverend King, something clicked.
>
> When I heard he was gonna get out of jail, me and some other white women wanted to see this smart-aleck nigger. I'm so thankful I went down there that day because I might have gone all my life just the way I was. When I saw all those people beating up on him and he didn't fight back, and didn't cuss like I would have done, and he didn't say anything, I was just turned upside down.★

After joining the Congress of Racial Equality, Peggy ended up in jail a number of times herself.

There is one moment I shall never forget. Peggy Terry speaking at Operation PUSH, Jesse Jackson's community center in 1968, four years after Martin Luther King Jr. had won the Nobel Peace Prize. Jesse Jackson introduced her. The place was overflowing, the crowd overwhelmingly black.

Peggy spoke very simply about her days on the picket lines. "When I was asked why I, a white woman, deliberately spent time in prison with 'niggers,' I said, 'Where else could a non-educated hillbilly shake hands with a Nobel Laureate?' "

I was present at the event. How could I forget the audience reaction? There was an uproar; there were cheers, laughter, and prayers, all aimed at Peggy Terry. She acknowledged the response, saying: "That's the simple truth. I never felt more important than that moment."

★ *Race: How Blacks and Whites Think and Feel About the American Obsession* (The New Press, 1992, p. 53).

Peggy was forever growing. One of her recurring refrains was, "There is so much to know that I must find out." And she did. She appeared in several of my books. Each time there was a new dimension: She had so many arrows to her bow.

I HAD JUST STARTED WORKING on the first book, *Division Street*. Father Pond, an Episcopalian priest in a white working-class area on Chicago's West Side, told me I had to talk to someone named Rose Rigsby. I said, "Who's Rose Rigsby?"

"When you meet her, you'll find out."

Rose was from a German-Irish family. They ran an appliance store, but the father and mother were in many respects like children. There were about eight kids, and Rose was pretty much head of the family, she ran things. Rose had been sickly when she was a child and her mother had taken care of her, but Rose turned out to be tough, a leader. She talked like a guy, and at first you'd think Rose was a lesbian, but no, she's Rose!

She'd formed a clan in her community. Some of the members were black, and all of them were delinquents who'd been in and out of a juvenile detention center, the Audy Home. In fact, Rose was known as the Deaconess of Audy. But Rose was also a writer. The educator John Holt thought she was fantastic. In a poem she wrote advising a friend not to be like her, Rose says: "I'm nothing but a big fat zero in the eyes of God." If that's not a poet . . .

One day I get a call, about eight in the morning, from the proprietor of a motel near O'Hare Airport. This guy says, "I hope I haven't disturbed you. By the way, is your wife listening?"

I said, "No, it's OK."

He said, "I know who you are, I like your stuff. I don't want to get you in trouble. You're sure your wife's not listening?"

"No, no, go ahead."

"Well, I run this motel, and last night these three young girls, about seventeen, eighteen, came in with these three Texans, cowboy hats and all. They take rooms and have a party and the place is a mess. It's a *shambles*. You sure your wife's not listening?"

"No, she's not."

"The reason I called, I found a piece of paper, a tissue, and written in lipstick is your name. It says 'Studs,' and your phone number is there. I just thought I'd tell you that."

"I'm glad you did, thank you very much. Don't worry about it. Thanks a lot." I knew one of those girls had to be Rose. I hung up, told Ida about the call, and went off to work.

Then Ida picked up the story. It's noon, I'm at WFMT, Ida's at home. The bell rings, she goes to the door and there they stand, three disheveled girls. Ida said: "You never saw three as bedraggled as they. In the center, of course, is Rose, she's in charge. They just look at her. I say, 'Rose, come on in.' " That was Ida. So they come in and sit on the divan.

Now what's she going to do with them? "Let me give you a nice little drink." She's got ginger ale in mind, or a glass of milk. Meanwhile, their breath is 100 proof. So they sit there sipping whatever it is.

Then Ida gets an idea. "I'll play a Billie Holiday record." She puts on a Billie Holiday slow blues. Ida used to do a wonderful takeoff on Billie Holiday. The girls had never heard of Billie Holiday. Ida tells them Billie used to wear a gardenia in her hair when she sang. They're listening, and Ida's doing Billie. Ida puts a rose in her hair and closes her eyes and sways. At the end she gives them a sawbuck and they leave.

That night Nelson Algren is visiting us, so we tell Nelson the story. He says: "Of course they were fascinated. Ida acted it out, she told them a story. These kids have never been told a story in their lives."

Meantime, there's trouble. Rose meets a woman named Shirley Garzutti, a hippie before her time, Italian, married to a Puerto Rican guy who works at the Congress Hotel. They've got about four kids. Garzutti writes, too—she even won a Jerzy Kosinski prize—but she's busy with her husband and kids and has no time for Rose. But Rose wants attention, Garzutti's attention. Rose is annoyed, and she throws a rock through the Garzuttis' window, breaking it, and she does this several times. The husband goes over to Rose and punches her right in the mouth. So there's a lawsuit—Rose is to stay away from Shirley Garzutti, per a restraining order.

Burton Joseph, a *Playboy* lawyer, nice man, had met Rose and was taken with her, and agrees to represent her, pro bono. The judge is a very nice black woman, impressed because I'm a witness for Rose. The judge says, "You've got to stay away from Mrs. Garzutti or else there'll be trouble. This is Studs Terkel, very well-known in Chicago. He's your character witness, so don't you embarrass him. Do you promise you'll stay away from Shirley Garzutti?"

Rose says, "I can't promise that." I remember the woman judge looking at me: She's thinking, "What are we going do with her?" Finally we get Rose to agree.

Eventually Rose got married and had a kid. The wedding was at the Green Mill before it became a jazz place. Some time later a group is giving me an award, a liberal group, but they happen to be fighting a union. Who happens to be lead organizer of the union? Rose. Rose was learning about being a paralegal and working for an aid organization, helping inmates at the Cook County Jail and doing a great job. Every inmate, most of them black, knew of Rose.

Meantime, one of Rose's brothers is killed, another dies in a motorcycle accident. Another brother and his girlfriend were drunk and they were having a fight, and so they call on Rose to settle the fight. Rose goes there and there's a gun on the table. Something happens, no one knows what, the gun goes off and Rose gets shot and dies.

She was maybe forty, her life just starting to go well. Of the loss, the waste, Ida said: "You know it had to be."

How do the inmates of the county jail find out? There's no Rose showing up, and they keep asking, "Where is Rose?" Finally one of the guards says, "I gotta tell you guys that Rose is dead."

The weeping at the county jail, it reminded me of the inmates who wept for Eugene Debs. I spoke at Rose's service and some of the top social workers in town were there. This was Rose.

PEARL HART was someone very special to me. She was a large lesbian woman who became a lawyer and a public defender, and possibly a founder of the Daughters of Bilitis. Pearl was courageous and absolutely dauntless. During the McCarthy days she defended everybody who was called "Red." Finally she herself was attacked.

Ida remembered, during her time as a social worker, appearing with a client in court, with Pearl as the public defender. Ida's client was a girl who'd been picked off the street as a hooker. The judge was one of those loud-mouthed, ignorant, brutal bastards—a vicious hack—and he let the girl have it in the worst way. I think the girl's trick was black, which made it even worse in his eyes. The girl was shrinking and shrinking, and Ida remembers Pearl putting her hand on the girl's shoulder, and the girl's back straightening up, just like that. Ida never forgot that scene, that gentle support.

The man who loved Pearl most was Paul Robeson. When he sang at a concert, he'd always ask her to name the encore: "What do you want to hear, Pearl?" Ida was always very moved by that. Pearl would name, not a militant, Spanish Civil War song or "Joe Hill," but instead, always, "Curly-Headed Baby."

(Robeson turned fifty in 1948, when he was in hot water for being named by the House Committee on Un-American Activities. He had many fiftieth-birthday celebrations, and at the one in Chicago, I was the emcee. I remember wondering if his voice might have been slightly going; he'd cup his hand over his ear when he sang.

Lena Horne appeared on stage that night. She was in Chicago headlining at the Chez Paree, which was a fancy nightclub in Chicago, run by the Mob. As I recall, Horne had been a hatcheck girl at the Cotton Club in New York. She made it clear that she was a sex target, for white guys as well as black, and she had felt very insecure. One day Paul Robeson came in and said just a few words to her, but suddenly, she recalled, she felt, oh, so good and strong.)

Pearl had become known as un-American in some quarters, and a good many of the audience were members of the FBI. I made that very clear: "Maybe a third of you here are FBI. I'm glad you came here to contribute. There'll be a collection later on, I hope you'll put forth."

In the middle of this very crowded tribute to Pearl Hart, people are singing, lively festivities, and in comes Judge Abraham Lincoln Marovitz. The judge was about to be nominated by the elder Mayor Daley to the Federal Court. Naturally, the FBI was investigating him.

The judge says, "Studs, I have something I want to say." He walks up to the microphone. "I think Pearl Hart is a great woman. I think she's a great American. I admire her. She's defended the defenseless, those who might otherwise not be defended. I'm delighted to be here to pay her tribute."

Now, that's something, especially from one who was known as Mayor Daley's yes man and buddy.

After Pearl died in 1975, I was again the emcee, and I called on Jim Hapgood to speak. The audience was full of left-wing labor people. I said, "Jim Hapgood is the head of the Mattachine Society. In case you don't know, it's a homosexual gathering. I felt honored to be the first hetero speaker they ever had."

You should have seen that crowd. These were people of the left, the labor unions, along with others who often challenged authority. Here we were with these labor union people who are for the put-upon, for black civil liberties, fighting for everybody, but this matter of homosexuality discomfits them. I'll never forget that. Suddenly I realized that this prejudice is deeper than deep. And all these years later, we've still got a long way to go.

Part IV

21

Truth to Power

I first met Nelson Algren on the Illinois Writers' Project during the late 1930s, before the war. Others on the Project were Richard Wright (though he left for France before I had a chance to meet him), Saul Bellow, the folklorist Jack Conroy, a black man named Frank Yerby who later wrote bestsellers, and Stuart Engstrand, who wrote a book on homosexuality called *The Sling and the Arrow*, a daring book for the time. While I was working on radio scripts, they were working on the WPA guide.★

Before meeting Nelson, I'd read *Somebody in Boots*, his first book, about riding the freights and more. I later adapted two short stories from *The Neon Wilderness* for ABC Playhouse radio. One was called *A Bottle of Milk for Mother*, and it has that great line: "I knew I'd never live to be twenty-one, anyway." The story that most affected me though was *Stickman's Laughter*. (In my adaptation I call it *Banty's Laughter*.) It's about Banty Longobardi, an ex-fighter, who gambles and loses. It was a favorite of the late Kurt Vonnegut's as well.

For a time, I used to go to poker games in Algren's flat. Nelson's building on Evergreen Avenue had a wonderful stained-glass win-

★ The WPA guides of every state are the best in the country; they had the most talented writers working on them and they make for great reading. Not only were they guides to places to visit, historic sites, and the like, they included anecdotal material, folklore, and songs.

193

dow up above the door, a religious scene, I think. You go up to the third floor, and there's Nelson, with a visor on, as in the movies, and garters on his arms. He's got the table with the green felt, and several fresh decks of cards laid out. Some of the regulars were my writer friend Dave Peltz; Jess Blue, a con man Nelson knew from East St. Louis; a Bohemian barber who often used to win; and a Jewish furniture dealer who always carried a little snub of a gun, because his store was in a poor black community and his son had been shot and killed. The dull guys won all the time because they were careful; they were accountants at heart. Nelson and I lost *all* the time.

This one night Peltz is there, along with a guy named Moretti, who's with the Moretti family, but not too successful as one of the Mob boys. And Moretti's brought his buddy, a Blackhawk Indian who called himself Chief. I'm introduced as a disc jockey, and the term "disc jockey" impressed Chief—I'm the magic voice in the box, kind of a celebrity. Chief and Moretti are sitting next to each other, and they're winning every hand. Peltz writes out a check for $200 and gives it to Chief. Chief says, "How do I know it won't bounce?" I say, "It's all right, Chief, don't worry about it." Chief says, "If it's OK with the disc jockey, it's OK with me."

Meantime, it's the custom for winners to, on the way home, take someone who's lost a bit of dough out for a meal. So I'm getting a ride with Chief and Moretti, and Moretti says, "Let's stop and have breakfast at an all-night diner." I have breakfast on *them*, of course. I have the works: ham and eggs and potatoes and all. Moretti says, "That guy Nelson acted funny, didn't he? Wonder what the trouble is." I say, "Well, that's the way he is."

Next day I get a call from Peltz. "Guess what? Nelson told me to cancel the check."

"What do you mean, cancel the check?"

"The check I gave to Chief. Nelson said they were cheating."

"But, Dave," I said, "You can't prove that. You got proof?"

He says, "They were sitting next to each other."

"No, you gotta pay."

"No," says Peltz, "I'm going to follow Nelson's advice."

A couple days later Peltz gets a call. Moretti. "What happened to my check? It bounced. What are you doing to me?" Remember, this guy's a failure in the family. He had won something, and now again, humiliation.

Finally, Peltz tells him: "Nelson said no."

"Nelson said that, huh?"

A couple days later a big brick crashes though the glass window above the door. Peltz figured he'd better pay, so he goes over with $200 in cash. Moretti says, "From now on, you're staying with me."

"What do you mean?"

"You're staying with me! I'm gonna show you the best time you ever had in your life." Peltz said that night Moretti spent three times the $200. Everything! All kinds of food, girls if he'd wanted, taken to the best places, out 'til all hours of the morning. Moretti now felt a success, a good man redeemed.

A month later I say to Nelson, "What made you tell Peltz to cancel the check?"

"Because they were cheating. I could tell."

"But you know how these guys operate, and you live upstairs. You're pretty vulnerable."

"Vulnerable? I got a bat." (It was a small, cheap, Goldblatt's-department-store kind of indoor bat.) "You see this bat? They come up those stairs I'll go bang."

I said, "They could shoot you from downstairs." He really was nutty as a fruitcake.

By the time we became friends, Simone de Beauvoir had come to Chicago and was living with Nelson at Miller Beach in the Indiana dunes. She came up to ABC with him when they were doing *A Bottle of Milk for Mother*, with John Hodiak. I had adapted it for radio. Then she went back to France.

The first time I went to Paris, it was a free trip, a junket. Air France was having its initial flight, Chicago to Paris, stopping to refuel in

Montreal. I was invited on that trip along with some crooked politicians and travel agents. We're at the George V Hotel, where the bellhops speak twenty languages. Who's at the door waiting for me in a World War II jacket? Nelson. He says, "Come on."

I say, "I got luggage, let me check it."

"Forget that. Come on. Follow me." So I give my suitcase to the bellhop and I follow him. He goes through the lobby—I'm sure a house detective is watching him—and he strides through the dining room. People are dining, and he's walking through, calling out, "This way!" and they're looking up. He goes through the kitchen, and the chefs, they're looking up. He goes out a door and takes me to Les Halles, and we have some steak and *petits pois*, and he's telling me how much to tip.

Another night, we go to this four-hundred-year-old place, high elegant. de Beauvoir is known, of course. People all look: There she is with her American lover. That's news. We walk in and sit down, haute-bourgeois people staring. Nelson has a tie, and the tie has a little flashlight under it, and there's a little wire running into his pocket. Every time this certain couple looks over, he presses the button and the light goes on. Every time they look, the light shines right at them. I got a kick out of that. She got a kick out of that. "Oh, Nelson, he's so funny."

The trouble is, later on, after she wrote *The Mandarins* and he split with her, he started ridiculing her in places like *Playboy* and *Penthouse*, horrible stories, making a fool of her. Except for one thing: They're so funny you're falling on the floor laughing. That cad.

Women liked him, despite his caddishness and boorishness. Lily Harmon was the widow of the guy who funded the Hirshhorn Museum, just loaded with money, and she loved Nelson. She's so proud that she's his lady friend she throws a party in honor of Nelson, the great writer. Guess what? He doesn't show up. She, of course, is completely humiliated. Nelson says, "And you know what? I came by the next day with flowers and chocolates. She slammed the door in my face. Now why would she do a thing like that?"

As it is, she sent a wonderful letter when he died. That's the thing. They all did. Except Amanda, his wife twice, who wanted to kill him. As his second wife, Betty, said, "It's like living with a wheel on fire." *A wheel on fire*! You gotta get burned. That was one of his perverse prides; that no one could really get at him. He was a friend of mine, we were very close, and yet nobody was really close to him. No one *could* get close.

Kurt Vonnegut respected Nelson and nominated him for the Academy of Arts and Letters. Vonnegut said, "The guy never showed up at the event." He was in the building where he was being honored, but he was sitting with this girl at the bar the whole time. Never went in. He received a special medal from the Academy and I asked, "What'd you do with the medal?"

"I dunno, I threw it away or something." He deliberately did this kind of thing, imp of the perverse. Maybe he wanted to show his independence. By that time, he'd been badly hurt by the Red scare. He was one of the signatories of clemency for the Rosenbergs, and the U.S. government denied him his passport. Those bastards did a job on him. He never forgot that.

Nelson taught at Bread Loaf, a summer writing school, a couple of times. Russell Banks was at Bread Loaf as a student and drove Nelson around the place. Later Nelson wrote a piece about Bread Loaf that was devastating. It was funny as hell, but it absolutely demolished the place where he taught. That's Nelson. And yet Russell Banks says were it not for Nelson, he wouldn't have become a writer; that Nelson edited like nobody could. Ernest Hemingway said Nelson Algren was one of the two best writers in America. Hemingway said, "Watch out for this guy. He hits you with both hands."

Nelson spent time in Cuba as a guest of Hemingway. Truman Capote could never get over the fact that Nelson was such a favorite of Hemingway's. At a gathering, Capote said, "I like Nelson, but why does Hemingway always have to attack me to praise Nelson?"

Nelson wrote serious material, but he was a funny guy, a clown figure with his dry, crazy, goofy sense of humor. I had a wonderful old-time card from Nelson, but I lost it: a photograph from fifty years ago of a little kid and a woman holding a gold watch. Below was written, "Louie, did you find work yet?" signed "Sophie." It's that very goofiness that fed his work.

His essays in *Notes from a Sea Diary: Hemingway All the Way* are very humorous. In one, he's being chased with a machete some-where in Kulon. *The Atlantic Monthly* was supposed to run some of them, but it didn't print a thing because the essays were so outra-geous. In *The Last Carousel* you find a lot of humor, yet in the mid-dle was very moving material.

When people compare me and Nelson as writers, I say he's a writer; I'm not. I'm a disc jockey who happens to have written some books. I often say, I *put together* the book instead of I wrote the book. Without even thinking about it, I use that phrase. I'm nowhere near in his league. Nelson had that extra quality that made him an honest-to-God writer who I think is one of the best of our generation. Whatever writing facilities I might have were most strongly influenced by Nelson. James T. Farrell was among the first to have captured the argot of Chicago streets, South Side Irish. He caught the language, the idiom, that Chicagoesque quality. But Nelson went a step beyond; there was a lyricism to his writing, a poetic aspect. His description of Chicago captures that very essence:

Remembering nights, when the moon was a buffalo moon, that the narrow plains between the billboards were touched by an In-dian wind. Littered with tin cans and dark with smoldering rub-ble, an Indian wind yet finds, between the shadowed canyons of The Loop, patches of prairie to touch and pass.

Between the curved steel of the El and the nearest Clark Street hockshop, between the penny arcade and the shooting gallery, be-tween the basement gin-mill and the biggest juke in Bronzeville, the prairie is caught for keeps at last. Yet on nights when the blood-red neon of the tavern legends tether the arc-lamps to all the puddles left from last night's rain, somewhere between the bright carnival of the boulevards and the dark girders of the El, ever so far and ever so faintly between the still grasses and the moving waters, clear as a cat's cry on a midnight wind, the Pottawattomies mourn in the river reeds once more.

The Pottawattomies were much too square. They left nothing behind but their dirty river.

While we shall leave for remembrance, one rusty iron heart.

The city's rust heart, that holds both the hustler and the square.

Takes them both and holds them there.

For keeps and a single day.★

My FRIEND the British journalist James Cameron played a great role in my life. He was the nonpareil, the best of all British roving correspondents of the last half of the twentieth century. Most British journalists of any worth will cite him as an inspiration. Cameron had a certain way of capturing what's important in the news. He went all over the world, and wherever he landed, he'd capture the true quality of what was happening.

In North Africa, he saw Schweitzer and discovered that Schweitzer was not all that he was made out to be. Great at playing Bach, perhaps, but not great in helping to foster creative people where he was living. Cameron was the first to reveal Syngman Rhee—the great little hero of Korea, the guy we were fighting to protect—as a phony.

James Cameron's life as a British roving correspondent was what might be whimsically called a checkered one. He got in all sorts of trouble, but he was able to keep on working. The thing about British journalism, everybody sought him, even when he was in hot water. He often offended his publishers by exposing some of their

---

★ *Chicago City on the Make* (Doubleday, 1951, p. 91).

friends in high places as corrupt. But he was never really blacklisted because he was so good that the publishers all wanted him; he was always rehired.

For years, his *bête noire* was Lord Beaverbrook, the celebrated publisher and tycoon. Beaverbrook had two papers and in one of them, he was exposing Klaus Fuchs, the Soviet spy. Cameron was in Hong Kong at the time, working for the other paper, and it was a couple of days before he read the article. The headline was: KLAUS FUCHS WINS, SO DOES JOHN STRACHEY. This was shortly after the war, and Churchill had been upset by a Labor victory. Clement Atlee, the new prime minister, had chosen Strachey as undersecretary for air. Cameron considered this to be yellow journalism in the worst sense of the word, and he said so in an open letter to the *Times* of London along with the words: "I quit."

Beaverbrook, thoroughly embarrassed by Cameron's Korea articles, threatened to kill him with a whiskey bottle. Cameron always told the story matter-of-factly. "I received four or five calls from a voice saying, 'I am the butler of Lord Beaverbrook and he must see you immediately.' Naturally, I thought it was a practical joke, so I hung up. One day at the door stands a man with his derby, glasses, umbrella, and the London *Telegraph* under his arm. He says, 'I'm the butler of Lord Beaverbrook. Why did you hang up on me? Lord Beaverbrook must see you at once. There's a plane waiting for you at Heathrow airport to take you to Cannes.' "

Cameron said, "What the hell, I'll go." So there he is and there's Beaverbrook. Beaverbrook says, "Cameron, your last book wasn't very good. May I suggest another for you." Meaning a book about *himself.* "There's a little gathering here, just four of us. The other two are Aristotle Onassis and Winston Churchill." Churchill was elderly at the time and had been ill. Beaverbrook says, "Do put on a tie."

Cameron said a phone call came from his current publisher, who was very excited and said: "We know where you are, Jimmy. You're at Beaverbrook's house and Churchill is going to be there soon. Word has been passed that Churchill is close to death. Prime Minister McMillan is calling a special conference to work out the proper tribute. Do it. What a coup this will be."

As Cameron told it, he puts on a tie, and he's walking down the stairs, grieving not for Churchill but for himself. The door opens, in come four footmen carrying the seemingly inert body of the former prime minister. "Oh my God," thinks Cameron, when suddenly the body moves, and it says with Churchillian gruffness, "Let me down, let me down, let me down."

Beaverbrook seats Churchill at one end of the table, he's at the other end, and on the other two sides sit Cameron and Onassis. Cameron is watching the old man, a totemic figure, whose Romeo and Juliet cigar is about to fall into his Courvoisier. He appears asleep. Cameron very gently removes the cigar and puts it in his own pocket, thinking it may very well be Churchill's last cigar and he wants it for his son Fergus. In the meantime, this tedious conversation is going on, about money and profits, between these two dull men, Onassis and Beaverbrook. Just then Churchill looks up as though awakened, and says: "Max!" addressing Beaverbrook, who is disturbed at being disturbed.

"What is it?"

"Did you ever go to Moscow?"

"Yes, you sent me there on a mission to Stalin. I was your minister of aviation."

"But did you ever go?"

And Cameron says of that scene: "It occurred to me it was a comic version of *King Lear.*" Of course, Churchill lived on for years.

When we first met in 1967, Cameron was on a book tour for *Here Is Your Enemy,* his report from Hanoi. His sponsors put him on all kinds of American shows. They didn't realize he was going to be clobbered as a Communist because he'd described North Vietnam as a country inhabited by human beings. He appeared on my show because I asked for him.

There I was in the studio of WFMT, having just finished a program, waiting for this guy to appear. I was looking forward to it because oh, I liked the way he wrote. He came in lugging a heavy bag, shoulders slumped, so tired. As soon as he appeared, I said, "James Cameron! I'm delighted to see you. That's a hell of a book you wrote."

"You like it? You're the first one." He'd just come from a different station and someone had given him the works.

On the show I said, "This is a great book by a marvelous newspaperman," which was the opposite of everything he'd experienced in America. He'd suffered all sorts of attacks: Eric Sevareid and Morley Safer slashed him; *Time* magazine called him a conduit for the Communists. He felt good after my show, came over to the house, we had a drink, and that's how we became friends. He ended up staying with us that trip, during which he also happened to be covering the 1968 convention. I describe our adventures in Grant Park in *Talking to Myself*. From then on, every time he came to town he stayed with us.

Cameron had an incredible ability to improvise. That's the way he wrote when he was at the Hilton Hotel during the '68 convention, sitting in that pressroom with the typewriters and the telegraphs and everything. He'd write without revising, the words just flowed off of him. I didn't learn that from him—I wish I had— but observing his style played a role in developing my own. Mostly it was his attitude and his thoughts about the matter of objectivity that affected me.

I often quote from his book *Point of Departure*, a collection of dispatches from all over the world:

> I cannot remember how often I've been challenged, especially in America, for disregarding the fundamental tenet of honest journalism, which is objectivity. This argument has arisen over the years, but of course it reached a fortissimo—long years after this— when I had been to Hanoi, and returned obsessed with the notion that I had no professional justification left if I did not at least try to make the point that North Viet Nam, despite all official arguments

to the contrary, was inhabited by human beings. The Americans could insist that they were a race of dedicated card-carrying Marxist monsters, and the Chinese could insist that they were simon-pure heroes to a man; both statements were ludicrous; as I had seen them they appeared to differ in no perceptible way from anyone else, and that to destroy their country and their lives with high explosive and petroleum jelly was no way to cure them of their defects, which in any case seemed to centre on a tenacious and obstinate belief in their own right to live. This conclusion, when expressed in printed or television journalism, was generally held to be, if not downright mischievous, then certainly "non-objective", within the terms of reference of a newspaper man, on the grounds that it was proclaimed as a point of view, and one moreover that denied a great many accepted truths. To this of course there could be no answer whatever, except that objectivity in some circumstances is both meaningless and impossible. I still do not see how a reporter attempting to define a situation involving some sort of ethical conflict can do it with sufficient demonstrable neutrality to fulfill some arbitrary concept of "objectivity." It never occurred to me, in such a situation, to be other than subjective, and as obviously so as I could manage to be. I may not always have been satisfactorily balanced; I always tended to argue that objectivity was of less importance than the truth, and that the reporter whose technique was informed by no opinion lacked a very serious dimension.★

Cameron was the first Western journalist in Hanoi during the Christmas bombings. He went to visit Ho Chi Minh, whom he had previously interviewed. They spoke in French, Ho Chi Minh saying, "I hope you'll pardon my not speaking English, Mr. Cameron, I'm a little out of practice for fairly obvious reasons." Cameron brought as a gift a whole carton of Salem cigarettes because Ho Chi Minh loved Salem cigarettes. Ho Chi Minh said, "Mr. Cameron,

★ *Point of Departure* (McGraw Hill, 1969, pp. 71–72).

I've got to ask you some questions." He asked if a certain fancy French hotel still existed. "You know, I worked there. My boss was Escoffier and I was his pastry boy."

"I heard you were very good, Mr. President." Cameron left, he had the big scoop, an interview with Ho Chi Minh; no one else had even come close to it. He wanted to return to London from Beijing, but nobody would stamp his visa. He was saying, "I *have* to go back at once!" He always traveled light and China was very cold; for three days he waited in the freezing-cold airport. He went to the visa office ten times, each time the guy said no. Cameron said, "I didn't know what to do, I was going crazy. Finally I said, 'Would you *please help* me?'

" 'Help you? Well, of course I'll help you. What is it you want?'

" 'You know what I want, a visa.'

" 'Well, of course I'll help you.' "

Stamped the visa, gave it to him. Cameron was puzzled.

" 'Why did you have me wait this long?' "

" 'You Westerners, you're all the same aren't you? Even *you*, Mr. Cameron: "I *need* this, I *need* that." We are your hosts. We are here to help you. The first time you said "Will you help me?" what did I say? I said, "Yes I would." That's all. Can't you do that? Can't you Westerners say, "Will you help me?" ' "

Cameron was just loaded with fantastic stories, all told with humor but also with a certain kind of gentleness. He once stopped off in Havana to see Fidel Castro. Fidel had heard of him and said, "Of course I'll meet with you. We'll have a *long* conversation. I'll see you at ten o'clock tonight."

Fidel doesn't show up, so Cameron, who loves Bell's scotch, drinks a lot while waiting. It's twelve, Fidel doesn't show; one, Fidel doesn't show. Cameron drinks and drinks and finally falls asleep. About two in the morning, the tread of heavy footsteps, and he's being shaken: "Mr. Cameron!" It's Castro, of course.

"Mr. President." He's thinking, "Oh God, I'm too tired."

Fidel says, "You wanted to see me. You wanted to have a conversation. What's your first question?"

Cameron says, "What is the number-one obstacle you have? Start with that."

"Let me begin . . ."

Cameron later said, "And he began to talk. And he talked. And he talked." Cameron fell *sound* asleep.

Next morning, four, five hours later, Cameron wakes up. Nobody is there in the room, but he sees the imprint of two heavy buttocks on the bed and a note saying: "Cameron. It was a delightful conversation we had. Come again next time." Signed "Fidel."

I so admired Cameron's grace. He would never make fun of someone's personal attributes, and there was real ease in the way he would devastate the opposite party without humiliating that party. He had a dignified ability to demean others without ever demeaning himself. That's an art.

I think it was his kind of grace that on occasion kept me from going off half-cocked and bawling out somebody when there were other ways of making the point. When I get mad I do rash things, write angry, insulting letters. I once called someone a craven toady, and he happened to be the book editor of a major magazine. Cameron would never have done that. Quite simply, he just knew the human condition.

CONSIDER MY THIRD OLD FRIEND who spoke truth to power, Mike Royko. He was possessed by a demon. How else can I explain his almost forty years as a Chicago columnist and observer of the human race? For five days a week he put together a column on Page 3 of the Chicago *Daily News*. When that paper closed he switched to the tabloid the Chicago *Sun-Times*. The moment the *Sun-Times* was sold by Marshall Field V to Rupert Murdoch, Royko posted a fond adieu. He quit with a comment: "No self-respecting fish would want to be wrapped in a Murdoch paper."

He wound up with the Chicago *Tribune* and worked for them at least three days a week until the moment he died. Journalists from all cities, and for that matter various countries, were curious: How could he do it? Maintain this schedule and be read by more Chicagoans than any other all this time. You'd ride the bus and immediately see half the people turn to whatever page Mike was on; he was, for a time, the city's court jester.

Some years ago, a celebrated young journalist, co-author of a bestseller, passed through town on a book promotion tour. As we sat in Riccardo's, Chicago's favorite watering hole for newspaper people, he had one pressing question: "How does Royko do it? My editor suggested I try to do what he does in D.C. I tried for a couple of weeks and came near a nervous breakdown." A long pause. "How does he do it?" I simply said, "He is possessed by a demon."

How else to explain the tavern keeper's kid, in a world he never made, a world compressed into one cockeyed wonder of a city; of the haves kicking the bejeepers out of the have-nots; of Jane Addams and Al Capone; of the neighborhood heroine Florence Scala, and Richard J. Daley and Richard M., too; and of Slats Grobnik, for God's sake? Royko was the right one in the right city at the right time: to tell us in small tales what this big crazy world in the last half of the twentieth century was all about. And the devil made him do it.

My favorite Mike Royko column appeared October 25, 1972. He wrote it the day Jackie Robinson died. It is his recollection of a Sunday, May 18, 1947, the day Jackie first appeared in Cubs Park.

Hundreds of stories, scores of books have celebrated Jackie's trials and triumphs. Mike's piece was not about Jackie. It was about Jackie's people who were in the stands that day.

> In 1947, few blacks were seen in the Loop, much less upon the white North Side at a Cubs game. This day they came by the thousands, pouring off the northbound Els. . . . They had on church clothes and funeral clothes—suits, white shirts, ties, gleaming shoes and straw hats. . . . As big as it was, the crowd was orderly, almost unnaturally so. . . . The whites tried to look as if

nothing unusual was happening, while the blacks tried to look casual and dignified. . . . Robinson came up in the first inning. They applauded, long, rolling applause. A tall middle-aged black man stood next to me, a smile of almost painful joy on his face, beating his palms together so hard they must have hurt."

During Royko's vintage years, when Richard the First held court in the palatinate called Chicago, he wrote what is inarguably an urban classic, *Boss*. Jimmy Breslin, no small potatoes himself, the only big-city minstrel in the same class with Royko, called it "the best book ever written about a city of this country."

Mike's pieces seemed to flow so naturally, to read so free and easy. You'd think it was a snap, his daily chore. The laughter it evoked or the indignation or the catch in the throat did not come about by happenstance. He worked like a dog, obstinately gnawing away at the bone of truth. So it was with nailing that right word, that telling phrase. After all, they were as much the tools of his trade as the gimlet eye was to the jeweler. His obsession with detail was positively Dickensian.

I can still see him in his cubbyhole of an office. His glasses have slipped down to the tip of his sharp nose. He is listening. Some nobody is at the other end of the phone. Sometimes it is a cry for help. Sometimes it is an astonishing tip. Sometimes it is just a funny story. The human comedy has him on the hip. Most often, it's from somebody up against it. The other calls are from some fat stuff with clout whose venality Royko has exposed to the light. Not in a million years could he ever play the hero of *The Front Page*, Hildy Johnson, the Hecht-MacArthur character of the journalist who got a scoop. Scoops did not interest Royko. Speaking truth to power did.*

RIC RICCARDO appeared in one of the most popular films ever made, though you'd never know it. He was portrayed by Humphrey

---

* Adapted in part from *Talking to Myself* (The New Press, 1995, p. 239).

Bogart, as Rick, in *Casablanca*. Riccardo's spa was the favorite, naturally, of those who spoke truth to power. For that was this man's life from the beginning. He had the bearing of Don Giovanni, say, as played by Enzio Pinza, and he did very well in that respect. But more important, he was an anti-Fascist who escaped Mussolini's castor-oil treatment. It was a special sort of punishment for dissenters. (You may have seen a filming of that in Fellini's wondrous last work, *Amarcord*.) Ric escaped that fate. His very presence afforded the place an openness and ebullience that made it a natural for three such as Algren, Cameron, and Royko.

Riccardo opened the restaurant during the Depression. During those years, it was he who carried painters who were up against it on the tab. He never really asked for recompense. Once the New Deal was enacted and WPA jobs were available, he was repaid by all. Immediately after the war ended, Riccardo's was open twenty-four hours a day for three days running. Everything—chicken, spareribs, the works—was on the house.

Riccardo was a most genial host. Often he'd pass through, accompanied by an accordionist and guitarist, singing songs, not only anti-Fascist but raffish. Songs resembling those of the Moulin Rouge in nature. What a scene it was in its heyday. There's no such joint today.

The building that the restaurant was in was next-door to the Wrigley building, and Wrigley owned them both. (Eventually Ric bought the restaurant building.) P.K. Wrigley's father owned Wrigley gum, which P.K. inherited. P.K. was known because he favored daytime baseball. I liked him for that, even though the Cubs are painfully less than splendid. Why are they so bad? Royko's theory was that they were lousy because they were among the last teams to hire black players.

Remember, for years people had been coming up to Chicago from the South in the second migration. The great many moved to the South Side. Though Daley Senior always claimed there were no ghettoes in Chicago, it was long years before most black people were comfortable walking around and about the Loop. One day, perhaps fifteen years ago, a very dignified African American couple came up to me in Riccardo's. The man said, "We just want to say to you, Mr. Terkel, we come to Riccardo's every year to commemorate our wedding. We've been married for forty years. From the very first, this was the only downtown place that accepted us."

One of the only other downtown places that welcomed integration in the fifties was the Blue Note jazz club, run by Frank Holzfeind. Frank calls one day and invites Ida and me to join him and his wife for dinner at the Ambassador. He says the Duke and a companion will be coming with us—the Duke being Duke Ellington. "Fantastic."

We're about to hang up when Frank says, "It'll help a lot if you guys come."

I say, "What do you mean by that?"

"I just told you."

I said, "Even Duke Ellington?! He's got his own train, he can tell them all to go to hell."

But that was the atmosphere of the time. Even for the Duke. Even for Mahalia Jackson. One Friday night, Mahalia finished her program at CBS Studios, which coincidentally was in the Wrigley building. She was a star; I was her emcee. After we finished the show, I said, "Let's go eat next-door at the Corridor." No. She wouldn't go in; she was afraid to, even then. We had hamburgers across the street at a little diner.

Word somehow came to P.K. Wrigley that Riccardo was letting blacks in. Ric was still Wrigley's tenant at the time. Wrigley called Riccardo: "I understand you have a certain element at your place. I think it's demeaning, the property will drop in value, and I suggest you be more careful about your guests."

Riccardo wrote a note to Wrigley: "I'll have whoever I want as a guest as long as they don't hurt anybody." He put up a sign in the corridor: ALL MEN OF GOOD WILL WELCOME. He said to Wrigley, "All are welcome, I don't care who they are. What do you propose to do about it?" Wrigley did nothing. Knowing Ric, today the sign would read: ALL MEN AND WOMEN OF GOOD WILL WELCOME.

22

Didn't Your Name Used to Be Dave Garroway?

There was a gala gathering of patrons—including the mayor and his missus—on the eve of the Lookingglass Theatre's adaptation of my book *Race*. It was front-page news; something *spess-i-al*, the Welsh would say; a tribute to two Chicago icons: the historic Chicago Water Tower, chosen as the new locale of the respected theater—and me.

David Schwimmer, the theater's founder, was director as well as co-adapter of this 2003 production. He was a national celebrity, a star of *Friends*, the most popular TV show at the time. His was a face familiar to millions.

He and I were the show horses of the evening. There was only one problem. I love martinis, dry. Two martinis, I doubly love. After three such martinis, I am a runaway slave seeing heaven's Milky Way as the drinking gourd—the sign of liberation. But in this instance the hosts, in the fashion of the day, were serving designer martinis. "*Designer* martini"! I had never heard the phrase before, let alone faced one. It was the equivalent of finding a bottle of Dom Perignon in the desert and spitting into it first. Nevertheless, I did manage to get smashed the old-fashioned way. David Schimmer graciously ushered me into a cab.

The cabbie, a black man, whose accent was foreign, stared at him for a moment and drove off. I am clinically deaf. I barely make out what the driver, no more than five feet away, is mumbling. His speech, to my drunken, defeated ears, sounds something like talking in tongues. "Name?" He appears to be addressing me.

I say, "Oh, my name?" My lowly spirits are somewhat lifted (*Studs' Place* is still remembered. In my stupor, I had somehow forgotten that it was au courant about fifty years earlier).

"No, no, no!" The cabbie sounds a touch querulous, but loud enough for me to hear every word. "No, no, not you—the man who put you in the cab. He looks familiar." Somewhat phlegmatically, I tell him of *Friends* and David Schwimmer. "Ah, yes," says he. "Of course I know him."

I lean back against the leather. Am I a faceless old man, a zero, caught in a moment of truth by Cartier-Bresson? Desperate, I'll play my ace in the hole. It usually opens doors and on occasion works wonders.

"How are things in Lagos these days?" It is not so wild a shot as you may think. Nigeria has a fairly large community in Chicago. Many are exchange students and drive cabs for the critically necessary fast buck. Here's one, a black African, non-American. He turns slightly, his eyes still on the prize, the road ahead.

"How do you know that?"

Much, much better. I sail on; the wind is with me. "Wole Soyinka, one of your countrymen, just won the Nobel Prize for Literature."

Once more, he turns: "You know that, too?"

I'm on my way to Canaanland with this guy now. I fire away, my words are as bullets from a Thompson submachine gun. "Oh," I murmur casually, "I've interviewed Soyinka several times." I'm fingering a fiver in my pocket as a tip to the good man, though the bill is no more than ten. He slows down momentarily and turns to really look at me.

As we near our destination, I apply the coup de grace, guessing which college in Chicago he has been attending. I hit it on the button: Truman College. As I'm about to hand him fifteen, I sense a touch of awe in his question. "Name again?"

"It's a crazy sort of name. Possibly you've heard of it. It is Studs."

He interrupts, this time completely out of patience: "No, no, no! The man who put you in the cab."

"Garroway. Dave Garroway," I say.

Why do I, for no ostensible reason, bring up an old acquaintance's name? As I hit the leather of the back seat, why am I humming "Auld Lang Syne"? It has in a zany way haunted me during the conversation with the cabbie. As he is referring to the current kid of our time, I am thinking of another kid of another time. I am thinking of the other Dave. I realize anew how quickly an icon becomes a face in the crowd.

LET'S BEGIN AT THE BEGINNING. Shortly after World War II had ended, a good five years before television came along, Garroway created a jazz program that began at midnight and ran for a couple of hours. The time was right, the circumstances were right, the show was a huge success. When Dave plugged an artist, lines formed for blocks around. He helped, say, Sarah Vaughan, immeasurably in this respect.

I was, in the meantime, conducting an eclectic sort of disc jockey hour. We often met on the nineteenth floor of the Merchandise Mart, where our studios were located. He was NBC's bright-eyed boy and I was with the ABC adjunct.

Remember now, this was 1949, 1950. There was talk of a new means of communication on the air, television. For some reason, it was Chicago that became the frontier city. It was in Chicago that three seminal programs had hit the air. This creative outburst was by the very nature of sudden circumstance spontaneous. It had no forebears.

There was *Studs' Place*, for however brief a time. And *Garroway at Large*, which with considerable advice from Charlie Andrews, scored in a mighty flash. Nothing could go wrong. If a stool or chair fell in view on screen, fine. There was no canned laughter or canned anything.

The third program, syndicated nationally, that caught the attention of John Crosby, the pre-eminent TV critic, was *Kukla, Fran and Ollie*. There was our one genius, Burr Tillstrom. Behind a little stage, the man himself was invisible, but his other selves—puppets who were really his hands and fingers, and his voices—were delightfully apparent. The only human face was that of Fran Allison, a thoughtful and endearing performer, who accepted Burr's creatures: Kukla, the ever-worried impresario; Ollie, the elfin, bad-boy, one-toothed dragon; Beulah Witch, the feminist on a broomstick; Madame Ophelia Oglepuss, the Kuklapolitans' matron of the arts; and the other wonders. It was a world of tenderness and gentle laughter. Its audience was more adult than child.

The hours for TV in those pioneer days were limited from 6:00 P.M. to 10:00 P.M. There was nothing on during the daytime. Out of the blue, Pat Weaver of NBC conceived the idea of daytime television, beginning early in the morning. Others thought it was an outrageous idea, people awakening in the morning to a strange face in the kitchen or bedroom. A test was made. Would people watch? NBC was overwhelmed with bushels of mail. So it was that a program called *Today* came into being.

It was obvious to all that Dave Garroway was a natural as a host. He already had an enthusiastic audience, as well as the personal attributes of ease and grace; and, in a strange way, with his specs, an FDR touch. *Today* was an immediate smash. And so it was that TV came into full growth; its performers became, for better or for worse, family familiars.

Dave of course became king of the hill; his face was familiar to more viewers than anyone else's in the world. Dave's offering of a Peace Salute as his daily morning adieu was an international ritual. I imagine his presence became as familiar as Charlie Chaplin's Little Tramp.

This was my earliest recognition of how a celebrity comes into being. In the electronic world, where technology had leaped exponentially, front and center, it was awe-inspiring. Perhaps a trifle disturbing.

How well I recall our Merchandise Mart encounters, when it was obvious that Dave was up, up to higher ground. He was euphoric. In describing General Sarnoff's★ phone call to him, he was deeply moved. "Never has any boss been so kind and thoughtful as he informed me of the new program, *day time.* And why they chose me." (In his exhilarated moments, he became somewhat formal in speech.) I suggested that he was a pretty valuable property to them, that they were not engaged in philanthropy. Dave chuckled; he knew all about my political crotchets.

For several years, Dave was TV royalty and then, bit by bit, there came some kind of decline. Charlie Andrews mentioned health as a problem; or perhaps he had irritated the network with a throwaway line about Southern Bell and its touch of racism. But, no, that wasn't it.

True, he had an eccentricity or two. The suicide death of his wife rattled him. That wasn't only it. Charlie was right: his health. Aging. I think Dave was touching sixty and, who knows, a wrinkle or two was showing. It was one thing and another. He disappeared. (Recently, when I touched ninety-three, Ted Koppel of *Nightline* had me on for an interview. He was remarkably gracious and hospitable, allowing me to say anything that came to mind. He wistfully pointed out that he was sixty-three, thirty years younger than I, yet it was obvious that Ted was nearing the end of his long and eventful course as a nightly fixture. And that it may not have been his decision to pull up stakes. The touch was more reflective than biting—and yet . . .)

A few years after Garroway left *Today,* I was on tour for my first book and being interviewed in Hollywood by a local young hotshot. "You're lucky. This is my first day back from vacation. My pinch hitter was someone named Dave Garroway. Oh, he was from Chicago. Did you know him?"

"Yeah."

★ General David Sarnoff, a pioneer in radio and television, eventually became the president of Radio Corporation of America (RCA).

Edwin Arlington Robinson was not only an esteemed American poet; he was as prescient as Nostradamus. I've a hunch he had someone such as Dave in mind when he, years before, wrote "Richard Corey."

> And he was rich—yes, richer than a king,
> And admirably schooled in every grace:
> In fine, we thought he was everything
> To make us wish that we were in his place.
> So on we worked, and waited for the light,
> And went without meat, and cursed the bread;
> And Richard Corey, one calm summer night,
> Went home and put a bullet through his head.

So, too, did Dave.

Sic transit gloria celebratum.

IN THINKING of Dave Garroway, Richard Corey, and all the touched and gone of celebrityhood, is there any enthralling memory worth it all? Oh, sure, I can name some remarkably rich souls, the great many anonymous I have encountered and commemorated on tape, but the one that came to mind in the backseat of that cab was a throwback to a key memory of my childhood: Bulldog's recounting of Wamby and his triple play. Remember, my mentor told me of the player's immortal moment in 1920.

Yet, back in that cab in 2003, some eighty-three years later, I recalled a letter I had received in 1951. Oh, God, how it all comes back. When *Studs' Place* was given the heave-ho by NBC, among the grieving notes was one scrawled on a piece of wrinkled, lined paper. Of course I lost it, but oh, baby, do I remember it.

It was obviously the scribbling of an elderly person. The note was from Cleveland.

"I feel so bad that *Studs' Place* is losing its lease. I have been watching it every week. There is an old Dutch word that tells you how I feel. It is *heimweh*. It means homesickness. It was just like my own neighborhood diner. I once played baseball. They called me Wamby." It was signed: "Bill Wambsganss."

Never mind my failing to impress the cab driver with "Lagos" and "Soyinka." I, at that moment, impressed myself with the memory of a wondrous note reminding me of a wondrous baseball play of eighty-three some years ago; an old man's scrawl written thirty-one years after it happened; that boosted my ego as well as morale some fifty-two years after the letter was written. You can't beat that. Oh, to be remembered—isn't that what this is all about?

THERE WAS A VARIATION on this theme several times, during my salt-mine years as a radio soap-opera gangster. From time to time, a strange elderly actor would appear for one or two stints at, say, *Ma Perkins* or *Woman in White* or *Kitty Keene*. During the tour of a play hitting Chicago at that moment, this actor would pick up a precious C-note or whatever was the fee before the American Federation of Radio Artists (AFRA), the union, was formed.

(I remember Tony Ross, while in town during the world premiere of *The Glass Menagerie*. He was the original Gentleman Caller. The play was being rehearsed in Chicago for several weeks. Laurette Taylor, who turned out to be magnificent as Amanda, was having a bottle problem, still grieving over the death of her husband, Hartley Manners. It was during those weeks that Tony Ross picked up a few checks in the soap opera *Woman in White*. He was playing a diamond in the rough. When they left Chicago, having made theatrical history by introducing us to a new young playwright, Tennessee Williams, I replaced Tony in the soap opera.)

The first instance I recall of my remembrance of an old-timey actor and its effect on him occurred during frequent runs in *Ma Perkins*. One day there appeared in the studios of CBS, Chicago,

for a three-shot role as a lumberyard owner in Ma's trials, a distin-
guished-looking old boy. I approached him. "I know who you are.
You're McKay Morris. I saw you as Pastor Manders in Ibsen's
Ghosts. You were great." He stared at me as though he had indeed
seen a ghost: a ghost of so many Christmases past.

"You remember me? That was so long ago. Did you really see me
as Pastor Manders?"

I assured him it was so and that I remembered it as though it were
yesterday. "Man, you were good."

He had at first appeared somewhat stoical in nature, a bit on the
stiff side. Not in this moment. He simply stared at me. It was then he
turned away, obviously fingering his eyes, trying to brush away a
tear as though it were something shameful.

For the next two days, he insisted on buying me lunch, while he
talked, talked, talked about Nazimova, whom I had seen as Mrs.
Alving in *Ghosts*, about theater, about everything. If I remember
correctly, he did send me a note from somewhere. A gentle, tender
note. Being remembered is what it was all about.

AGAIN, it was in New York. I was visiting my brother Meyer, who
had been attending CCNY. During my visit, we saw a revival off-
Broadway of Sidney Howard's *They Knew What They Wanted*. It
starred Richard Bennett as the old, Italian vintner, and Pauline Lord
(described by Ruth Gordon as America's Duse) who, in this instance, was the young waitress, Amy. The party of the third part, as
the young ranch hand, was Glenn Anders.

Years went by, as the calendar always did in Greer Garson–Walter
Pidgeon World War II epics. With their stiff upper lips, they, with
hardly a gray thread in their hair, gallantly weathered the Blitz
and all.

I forget the soap opera in which I appeared. It might have been a
children's evening program, *Little Orphan Annie*, or *Captain Midnight*, with Jim Ameche. Into the studio comes a face I find familiar.

I greet him. I don't know why; I am in a horsing-around mood: "Glenn Anders, I presume."

"Yeah. How'd you know my name?"

I told him about *They Knew What They Wanted*. The first legit play I had ever seen. If I remember, he did a hop, skip, and a jump.

"I'll be damned. You remember me?" That was the usual refrain. I didn't realize we were holding up rehearsals, but it didn't matter. The director of the radio show was stage-struck, so he simply listened, enthralled.

Now, I didn't know when to quit. "I saw you in the Blackstone Theatre as Dr. Ned in O'Neill's *Strange Interlude*. Judith Anderson was doing Lynn Fontanne's role as Nina Leeds." We later had a great dinner at Riccardo's, which he insisted on buying. To be remembered—that's what made you king of the hill. Not only were you celebrated in somebody's eye, you were remembered long, long afterward. That your hands trembled a bit was a small matter. You counted.

The third and undoubtedly most dramatic and traumatic encounter occurred in the early sixties. I had written a play, and a god-awful one it was. It was called *Amazing Grace* at just about the time there was an upsurge of pop-folk influence and the hymn of the same name had become popular. It was to be a professional production at the University of Michigan theater. Alumnus Arthur Miller's encouragement brought that theater into being.

My play was almost all cast, with Cathleen Nesbitt and Victor Bono as the leads. We needed a strong character actor as an old time Wobbly, a garrulous guest at a men's hotel. I immediately thought of an actor, James Bell. I haven't the foggiest idea why he came to mind. I had seen him in a play some thirty to forty years before and I had never forgotten his brief performance.

The play was *The Last Mile* by John Wexley. The locale was death row of a state prison and all were convicted and due for execution. The star was Spencer Tracy as Killer Mears. It may have been his last play before his explosive entry in the movies. But it was not he I most remembered in that play. It was a young actor, James Bell, who at the second-act curtain is led toward the electric chair. I was absolutely knocked out by that halting shuffle, absolutely mesmerized by this young actor.

I do remember seeing his name now and then in the theater section. During the forever-run of Jack Kirkland's adaptation of Erskine Caldwell's *Tobacco Road*, there appeared about a dozen Jeter Lesters: Henry Hull, Will Geer, James Barton, oh, God, too many to remember—and James Bell. A few years, uneventful, went by.

It was then, during the University of Michigan enterprise, that Bell's name so obstinately stuck with me. I figured he'd be about the right age: late sixties, early seventies. (My arithmetic was never any good.)

I was frantic; I had to find him; he was my man. Equity came through: a member, James Bell, had retired and was living in either Virginia or the Carolinas. I forget which.

I don't recall how many phone calls I made: I know that I did not impoverish Illinois Bell. Finally, a voice at the other end, a faltering, very, very fragile one, answered. Oh, I do remember the conversation, if you want to call it that. Let me paraphrase it as best I can.

VOICE: Yeah? (It was about four syllables).

ME: James Bell? Are you James Bell, the actor?

VOICE: Wha-a-at? I'm Jim Bell. Who you? What do you want? I'm not well. Make it snappy. [I tell him that I wrote a play and I'd like to cast him in it.]

VOICE: You—you wha-a-at? Listen, I'm an old, old man, sick as a dog, and got no time for jokes.

ME: I'm not kidding, Mr. Bell. I didn't have a chance to see you as Jeter Lester. I hear you were great. But I did see you in—

VOICE: (Cuts me short) Jeter Lester, yeah. A lotta guys did him. Look, I'm very tired. Say fast what you got to say.

ME: Mr. Bell, do you know why I remember you in *The Last Mile*? Spencer Tracy was in it. But it was you who knocked me out at the curtain of the second act.

VOICE: (Did he hear me?) Wha-a-at ya' trying to tell me?

ME: (Half shouting) I remember you as though it were yesterday. I'd like you in this part. (Now, I'm beginning to have my doubts.)

VOICE: (Apparently something registered with him) You remember somethin' that happened what? A hundred years ago. (It was only seventy or so.) You're not kiddin'? You remember that. Jeez, I can't hardly stand up. Ya' know how old I am. Eighty-something. I feel like a hundred and ten. Naw, I can't do it. Sorry.

ME: I am, too, Mr. Bell. One thing I know—I'll never forget you in *The Last Mile*. That walk . . .

VOICE: (long pause) I heard what you said. You remembered me for something I did five hundred years ago. Gotta go now before I collapse. (Before he hangs up, I hear what appears to be a funny cackle and a mumble.) "He remembers me . . ."

Click.

AMAZING GRACE received among the most horrendous reviews possible. Had James Bell, lame, halt, and blind, undertaken the role, it would not have hurt at all.

I still see him, young James Bell, in that second-act curtain, stealing the show from Spencer Tracy.

Yeah, Bell is up there with Wamby in my King Tut pantheon, forever young. I'm certain neither was ever asked: "Wasn't your name once James Bell?" Or "Wamby?" They had no need to be recognized by others, not while I was around . . . While I *am* around.

As for the lethal phrase, "Didn't your name used to be Dave Garroway?"—Charlie Andrews told me, as he kept company with Dave on his down, down, down ski-slide, he'd heard a curious cabbie ask it. I never had any reason to question Charlie Andrews, nor do I now. I still carry the fish-head cane that Charlie Andrews' widow, Amy, sent me. It helps this lame and this halt on his daily way to Canaanland. Each time I stare down at the fish-head cane he bequeathed me, Charlie says: Simply tell it as it was. Hang on to that cane.

23

Two Towns Called Girard

*History does not refer merely to the past. On the contrary, the
great force of history comes from the fact that we carry it within
us, are unconsciously controlled by it in many ways, and history is literally present in all that we do.*

—James Baldwin

Girard, Pennsylvania, 1982. It is an industrial town, thirty miles
out of Erie. Its people, mostly blue-collar, are experiencing
hard times. Since then, things have become much worse.

A controversy had arisen concerning the use of the book *Working*
in a high school class. A teacher, Kay Nichols, had made it manda-
tory reading, in conjunction with a course on American labor. The
parents of two students objected; they had discovered some four-
letter words in the book. It had been an assignment since 1978.
Until now, there had been no objections.

I was invited to the school by the Girard Board of Education.
There was to be a public discussion in the auditorium that evening.

I am visiting a classroom in the afternoon. The students range in
age from fifteen to eighteen.

HELENE: Our neighbor has the book. My mom looked at it and
said some of the words are unnecessary.

ME: How did she discover the words?

HELENE: She was glancing through, I guess.

ME: Have you any idea what effort it would take to find those words in a six-hundred-page book?

BOY: I found one. (General laughter.)

ANGIE: I could see the Christians' point of view. They don't think that language should be used. But we're not lookin' in it for smut words. We're readin' the book as a book.

JIM: A good book moves me. When I read one, it makes me think I should read more instead of just throwin' it back on the shelf.

PEGGY: I don't see why they're objectin' to it. They read worse every day. They speak the same language that's in the book. They're no better than what people say in there.

DON: Maybe some of those words could be changed and get the same meanin' across.

JIM: If he would have used any other words, it would have had a totally different meaning. Like Clark Gable in *Gone with the Wind*, when he said, "Frankly, I don't give a—."

Jim hesitated and didn't use the word "damn."

BETSY: If they use a word like "damn" all the time on TV, movies, people get used to it. Like this movie, Clark Gable said, "Well, I don't give a damn," that was really shocking back then. And then people got to thinking if they said it on TV screens and on the radio, you got used to it. So they started using more offensive words.

ME: What does "damn" mean to you?

BETSY: It's damning to hell. Think of the meaning behind that word. If somebody didn't look through that book, aha, they got away with it.

ME: You interpret the word literally, not as a piece of slang. The Bible, too?

BETSY: Of course.

ME: You don't believe in evolution?

BETSY: Of course not. Hardly anyone here believes in that.

ME: Does anyone in this class believe in evolution?

Silence. No one raises his or her hand. There are about fifty students.

JIM: Try to keep an open mind about things, not right away shuttin' it out.

BETSY: I know people read this book before and they don't want to read it again because they didn't enjoy it. They should have this choice.

TERRY: They're not required to read the whole book. They can skip the parts with the smut words.

BETSY: But if there's something I didn't believe in, I wouldn't want to read it.

STACY: Do you always believe in everything you read, evolution and all that? I think it's good to sometimes read something you don't believe in because you see other people's views and it helps you form your own.

THAT EVENING the school auditorium was standing-room-only, overflowing with parents and students. It had something of a carnival spirit rather than a girding for battle; not too dissimilar from the feel of a crowd at a high school basketball game.

There was a touch of tension when the objecting parents entered with twenty or so of their supporters, in tight formation. Yet there was something else, something poignant. It was not a Roman phalanx so much as a *laager*. They were in encircled covered wagons, surrounded by hostile forces about to overwhelm them. They were moms and pops who had worked hard all their lives so their children could grow up as decent, hardworking, God-fearing Christians in a world of woe. And Sin.

The image of Mrs. B. is still with me. A tough little sparrow, resembling the Irish actress Una O'Connor, she really let me have it. Constantly shushing her boy, Tom, who was wildly erupting with scriptural citations, she was eloquent in her wrath, her hurt, her terrors of something dark out there.★

★ *A Godly Hero: The Life of William Jennings Bryan* by Michael Kazin (Knopf, 2006).

It wasn't the language so much to which she objected. It was the spirit of discontent she found in the book. As, once more, she pushed her boy aside—he was now Jimmy Swaggart sailing into me with Colossians or Corinthians—she spoke of a hard life, heavy laden enough without still more sorrows burdening the young pilgrims at school. Why not show the happy side of people's lives, the cleansing and godly side? Isn't there enough trouble in the world?

> All the folks in Tennessee are as faithful as can be
> And they know the Bible teaches what is right.
> They believe in God above and his great undying love
> And they know they are protected by his might.
>
> Then to Dayton came a man with his new ideas so grand
> And he said we came from monkeys long ago.
> But in teaching his belief Mr. Scopes found only grief
> For they would not let their old religion go.
> —Fragment from a song by Vernon Dalhart, 1925

1960. John T. Scopes, middle-aged, is listening to the recording. We are seated in a Chicago radio station. Dalhart's voice comes through bell-clear, despite the record's scratch. I tell my guest it sold a half-million copies in 1925. "I didn't know I was that popular," he says.

Scopes, a young teacher in a Dayton, Tennessee, high school, a young teacher of biology, had been tried for having violated a state statute: No theory of the origins of man could be taught that contradicted the Book of Genesis. The trial lasted eleven hot July days in 1925. The contest between Clarence Darrow, attorney for the defense, and William Jennings Bryan, prime witness for the prosecution, is celebrated in folklore as well as history. The devastating effect on Bryan's life is also common knowledge.

Toward the end of our studio conversation, another recording by Vernon Dalhart is heard. He had written it as a tribute to Mr. Bryan, who died five days after the trial ended.

There he fought for what was righteous and the battle it was
  won.
Then the Lord called him to heaven for his work on earth was
  done.
If you want to go to heaven and your work on earth is
  through,
You must believe as Mr. Bryan, you will fail unless you do.

"Yes," says Scopes, "I think the tragedy is more man's than Bryan's. Because we haven't advanced too much."★

GIRARD, KANSAS, 1867 onward.

It was so named in honor of his hometown in Pennsylvania by Dr. Charles Strong, a deer hunter. As far as I know, and what a couple of old Wobblies at the Wells-Grand told me, this expectedly conservative town experienced some remarkable and strange happenings between the years 1895 and 1922.

A freethinking, American Socialist journal, *Appeal to Reason*, was published in this town. Though native as its base, it had many immigrant adherents who remembered their own dreams and the works of Thomas Paine and all those other visionaries. There was a time when its circulation approached a million.

John Graham of the University of Nebraska Press noted: "Although almost erased from our collective memory that was selectively focused on the American character, war, party politics, ideas, and great men to the exclusion of the faceless 'inarticulate' working people, those same Americans created a challenging movement as the twentieth century began."

With the Gilded Age, the growth of trusts, the powerful, "so ordained by God" as George Baer proclaimed; as World War I broke out, and the Palmer raids broke in, especially into the homes of outspoken immigrant militants—and don't forget the flivver and the

★ *The Great Divide: Second Thoughts on the American Dream* (Pantheon, 1988, pp. 47–52).

harvester—all these factors succeeded in breaking down these urges and movements. Reason was equated with treason in the quarters of the powerful. A danger to the status quo had to be exorcised. Some of the old boys in the lobby of the hotel still got a bang out of recounting that hopeful epoch, even though the falcon had already flown.

Every now and then, old Bill Brewer, whose gnarled hands intimated the jobs he'd had in the fields, on the railroads, and on the waters, would haul out of his hip pocket a little blue book. Let's not forget this informal library. E. Haldeman-Julius was the publisher. There were far more than a thousand of these nickel blue books published in, yeah, Girard, Kansas. They were published primarily for workingmen on the road, so they could read while they ran. You name it, they published it.

The first among the thousand little pocket-sized books that followed was Robert Burns. It is, I am told, still its bestseller, without any assist from Oprah. I challenge you to name one Scotsman, unlettered though he may be, who doesn't know a stanza, let alone, a line from Rabby Burns.

(Ironic note. How many can I call upon?) When I had that slight encounter in Pennsylvania's Girard, the wild-eyed boy, whose mother's case I found so moving, was named Robert Burns. The father, whose name was Robert, too, was silently standing by, addressing his knuckles. It was Mrs. Burns who was so overwhelmed by all the craziness and Godlessness that was holding sway and trying to hush-a-bye her lone child, Robert Jr.

When I discovered the name he bore, I felt so hopeful. Perhaps I could bring up the subject and tell him of his father's namesake. The more I tried "a man's a man for a' that" and "The best-laid plans of mice and men," the more furiously he threw Luke, Mark, Paul, and Peter at me, citing the book it was from and the numerical code. He didn't hear a word I said, and here is the moment that really destroyed me. As Mrs. Burns wiped her face with her apron, she urged him to listen. She did want him to know some things outside his sphere.

The next day, when the big papers, as she referred to them, the Pittsburgh *Gazette* and the *Los Angeles Times*, ridiculed her, I felt I had lost it all.

Namesakes: the two Girards; the two Burns families. There had to be some other more civil way than further hurting and humiliating these hard, hardworking people.

THANKS TO OUR ELDER GUESTS and my brother Meyer, I subscribed; that is, I replied to the full-page ads of the blue-book people in the alternative journals, such as *The Nation* and old-time prototypes of *The Village Voice*. For one buck plus postage you received twenty such marvelous works. To name a few of the thousands: Bernard Shaw, Tom Paine, Tolstoy's *Essays*, Darrow giving the literal interpretation of the Bible a hard time, Voltaire, Aristotle, Whitman, of course, down the line to Fabre's lectures on the Mason Bee.

After some seventy-five years, if I searched my messed-up closets arduously enough, I'd probably find a John Ruskin blue book. No Billy Sundays here.★ (Did you know that a long Sandburg poem, a polemic such as you never have seen, was held off publication for years, it was so inflamatory? And so direct: He called a fink a fink.) Oh, there was Frederick Douglass and old Abe's best speeches.

What it does tell us is that a yearning is there, expressed in one manner or another as to what we can be about, something of peace, grace, and beauty. The dreamer could be an autodidact, raised on nickel blue books, or a Harvard grad.

Girard, Pennsylvania, tells me one thing; and that one magic moment in Girard, Kansas, tells me another.

Claude Williams, a circuit rider (traveling evangelist) who I interviewed for *Hard Times*, comes to mind some forty years after we spoke.

★ Billy Sunday was an influential American evangelist during the early decades of the twentieth century.

I've used the Bible as a workingman's book. You'll find the prophets—Moses, Amos, Isaiah, and the Son of Man, Old Testament and New—you find the Pharaohs, the Pilates, the Herods, and the people in the summer houses and the winter houses. These people like John the Baptist are our people and speak our word, but they've been kidnapped by the others and alien words put in their mouth to make us find what they want us to find. Our word is our sword.

I interpreted this for the sharecroppers. We had to meet in little churches, white and black. It was in the tradition of the old underground railway. I translated the Bible from the vertical to the horizontal. How can I reach this man and not further confuse him? He had only one book, the Bible. This had to be the book of rights and wrongs. True religion put to work for the fraternity of all people. All passages in the Book that could be used to further this day I underlined in red pencil. The Book fell open to me.

The rabble-rousers hated me. I had the longest horns in the country because I was using the very book they were using. I turned the guns the other way, as it were. I interpreted as I thought the prophets would interpret it, given the situation.

We have a religious phenomenon in America that has its origin in the South. Established churches followed urban trends. People out here were isolated and delivered religion on the basis of what they saw. Store-brought clothes—which they could not buy out of poverty—became wordly and sinful: "We had rather be beggars in the House of the Lord than dwell in king's palaces." They were denied schooling. They were called rednecks and crackers and damn niggers. But the Bible was God's Book. Refused access to medical aid, faith healed the body as well as the soul: "We seek another world." It was a protest against things economically unavailable. I interpreted this protest and related it to the Bible—instead of calling them hillbillies and rednecks.

I translated the democratic impulse of mass religion rather than its protofascist content into a language they understood.

In Winston-Salem, when we went out to organize the tobacco workers, the leader said: "If you crack this in two years, it'll be a miracle." We went to the oldest church. It was a bitter night. The pastor was a white woman, Sister Price, sitting there with an army blanket around her shoulders and a little old hat. I knew she was the bellwether. Unless I got her, I got nobody.

I gave the gospel of the Kings: Good News is only good when it feeds the poor. This woman pastor got up and drawled: "Well, this is the first time I heard the gospel of three square meals a day, and I want in on it. I love to shout and now I know every time I shout, I know I need shoes." First thing I know, she was touching cadence and going way off.

I had to translate this emotion into action. But if I'd let her go on shouting, we'd never have made it. In three months, they called a labor board election. We won. We called on the Bible and the Son of Man.

Imagine Claude Williams meeting Mrs. B. in Girard, Pennsylvania. She has a Sister Price within her. If only Mrs. B. could meet Claude Williams, she could be one of the most stalwart of humanists.

24

Evil of Banality

When Hannah Arendt wrote *Eichmann in Jerusalem: The Banality of Evil*, she was referring to the trite, the trivial, the meaninglessness, and the lack of serious thought that leads to fascism.

Consider: KEEP OFF THE GRASS. That is an order. You may kill someone near the grass, i.e., a Jew or a lefty—but do not disturb the lovely symmetry of the lawn.

When Federico Fellini offered us in his tender and affectionate remembrance of his hometown, *Amarcord*, the lighthearted and light-headed exchanges between the villagers, he was also telling us of the vulgar, the flatulent brass of Il Duce's braying band in the background. The one dissenter was cleansed by the castor-oil treatment. Things went on as usual.

Let us reverse the phrase of Hannah Arendt. Let's call it, even more properly, the evil of banality. It has profoundly affected our language, and it has perverted our speech.

The word "liberal" today has replaced the word "Communist" as used in the high-flying days of Tailgunner Joe. When John Kerry, the Democratic candidate for president, Vietnam War hero, defends himself, "I am not a liberal," as though to be a liberal were shameful, less than American, we are deeper than Alice ever was in Wonderland.

I look up the word "liberal" in the dictionary.

Liberal: 1. Having, expressing, or following social or political views or policies that favor non-revolutionary progress and reform. 2. Having, expressing, or following views or policies that favor the freedom of individuals to act or express themselves in a manner of their own choosing.

I thought that's what Tom Paine was writing about when he said, "Reason is not to be confused with treason." Being a liberal, I had thought, is to believe in the First Amendment.

I think of myself as a radical conservative. Radical means getting at the core of things. Louis Pasteur was a radical. Some would have called him a nut. The physician Ignaz Semmelweiss, who said, "Wash your hands," was a radical. He *was* called a nut. I'm a radical conservative. Conservative: I want to conserve the blue of the skies, the potability of our drinking water, the First Amendment of the Constitution, and whatever sanity we have left. Labels mean *nothing*; issues mean everything. How do you stand on the issue of social security, or national health care, or the death penalty?

"Banality" is the operative word. We stare daily into our TV set, turn the dial on the radio, flip through the local tabloid. What do we experience?

Britney Spears, a pop singer, shaves her head and goes into rehab. Most Americans know her name. She is a celebrity. None of the contestants in a recent episode of *Jeopardy*, a popular TV quiz show, knew who Strom Thurmond was. For most of the twentieth century, on the floor of the Senate, he was the drum major of segregation. Not even his fathering a black child was within the ken of the *Jeopardy* participants. Nor did they know the name of Kofi Annan (the newly former United Nations secretary general).

There have been exceptions in the past. During the civil rights fighting days, TV did a good job. At least, it showed us the dogs of Birmingham. It did a decent job, to some extent, on the Vietnam War—The Television War, Michael Arlen called it, in *The New Yorker* magazine. Today, our commander in chief forbids the showing of caskets carrying slain American soldiers home from Iraq, and the networks comply.

Basically, there is an affront going on, an assault on our intelligence and sense of decency. We have a language perverted, a mind low-rated, and of course, the inevitable end result—forgetfulness. This is what haunts me at the moment.

The young know nothing about the past, nothing about the fight of abolitionists, nothing about Elijah Lovejoy, or Frederick Douglass. The gap is deep here between almost all generations.

We say "younger generation." What is a younger generation? Do I have to be ninety-four years old to remember these names? Are they otherwise erased from history?

Were you to ask the average kid today who our enemies were in World War II, they would know Germany and Japan, because of films if for no other reason. I've a hunch that 50 percent might say the Soviet Union was our enemy. During the Cold War that followed World War II, a phony "patriotism" took over. Forgotten was the fact that the Soviet Union army wiped out four out of five German soldiers on the Eastern Front.

Gore Vidal uses a phrase, "The United States of Amnesia." It's on the button. But we've got something even deeper than amnesia. If there is no past, we can *invent* our own past. And so we invent our own past.

In our political elections, we vote on the basis of *absence* of memory. What was the New Deal, what did it do? What is Social Security, what does it do? Why did it come into being? Has everyone forgotten something called the Great American Depression? The grandchildren, boys and girls whose granddaddies had their butts saved by big government, are the ones saying, "Too much big government!" They condemn the very thing that allowed their ancestors to carry on when the spine of the Free Market had shattered.

Memory itself is part of the brain. A brain is like a muscle, and unless it's used, it rots away and becomes useless. We haven't used our memory to call on the past because it's always the *present*, this

moment, that is it. We have the news today about what's the latest—
Iraq's got weapons of mass destruction. The next day we find it's
untrue. We, unabashed, go on to other matters. Our memory is also
determined by what we see and hear, and what we see and hear depends to a great extent on television, and bit by bit we've gotten a
media that's in the hands of fewer and fewer people.

We have been deceived so often, the memory of the past is the
memory of so much deceit. We erase it.

We want to be left alone and not to think of a past that might disturb us. Might disturb what? Might disturb our sense of compla-
cency, our sense of satisfaction.

Chester Kolar, technician, two-flat homeowner. "I'm cold to it,
these war photos. The only remark of me and my friends is, 'What
do you know about that?' What does John Q. Public know what
should happen? Let's not stick our nose into something we know
nothing about. We should know once a month, let's have a review
of the news: what will happen and what has happened. What will
happen these people should be worried about painting their rooms
. . . they should become industrious."

Fortunately, there is Stanley Cygan, a retired steel-mill laborer. "I
want to know, what is [speaking precisely, using all five syllables]
re-la-tiv-i-ty. I ask professor at Hull House, they can't explain to
me. I must know the meaning—I know it is important—re-la-
tiv-i-ty."

He is the next-door neighbor of Chester Kolar. He, too, lives in a
two-flat. Thus, we have two Americans.

I THINK ALL human beings want the same thing. They'd like a good
job, friends, happy family. They'd like to be undisturbed by things
and to live in an ideal world. If they could live in a vacuum, that
would be perfect.

We can't; we are related to the world whether we want to be or
not. And now, more than ever, we are a part of the world.

I have a memory of something in 1945, a very great moment, to me the most hopeful moment in my life and perhaps even in the life of the planet: when the United Nations was formed in San Francisco. It was such a fantastic moment! *That* is a memory.

After World War II, we had a boom period, things were easy, and all the talk about another world that could be, a world that was possible, was forgotten. I remember the words of the brilliant radio writer Norman Corwin: "Post proofs that brotherhood is not so wild a dream as those who profit by postponing it pretend." Although we were the strongest, the most powerful, the most generous of all the nations, at the same time we were *part* of the world community. The memory is now so warped that when the president said: "To hell with the U.N.!" thousands applauded. Fifty years ago, who would have dreamed of that occurring?

Memory. How can we have memory if we don't have any knowledge? If we have no history, no memory of what happened yesterday, let alone what happened fifty years ago?

It's ironic that a thing like the GI Bill, which greatly benefited World War II veterans, has fed into our forgetfulness. The GI Bill gave returning veterans money to go to college, and in the case of many, the GI was the first in the family to attain a college degree. The GI Bill helped them buy houses in the new suburbs, like Park Forest, or Levittown. As a result, something happens to this new American. He is a college graduate and a homeowner, and suddenly the term "middle-class" belongs to him. All his life he wanted to be something above that blue-collar guy. He is helped, of course. But at the end of World War II, something else happened: the Cleaver family and consumerism. He's now part of a new class, and he wants more.

Farmworker and organizer Jessie de la Cruz described one of the people most virulently against the Chicano workers' struggle to form a union as a guy who was once a Joad. He said: "I was an Okie. I own this! I worked hard." He could have been little Winfield Joad. Remember that little boy in *The Grapes of Wrath*? What happened to him after they found the camp? Winfield fought in World War II, got the GI Bill, went to college, and studied agronomy. And he bought a house! He became part of the affluent society; he made it. The result? All history is forgotten.

What happens to all Alzheimer's sufferers is tragic. What I'm talking about is what I call a *national* Alzheimer's—a whole country has lost its memory. When there's no *yesterday*, a national memory becomes more and more removed from what it once was, and forgets what it once wanted to be.

We're sinking under our national Alzheimer's disease. With Alzheimer's you forget what you did yesterday. With Alzheimer's finally, you forget not only what you did, but also who you are. In many respects, we have forgotten who we are.

We're now in a war based on an outrageous lie, and we are held up to the ridicule and contempt of the world. What has happened? Have we had a lobotomy performed on us? Or is it something else? I'm saying it is the daily evil of banality.

25

. . . And Nobody Laughed

A poll involving millions of viewers was recently taken by a couple of TV channels. Question: Who was America's best leader ever? Among the candidates were Abe, George, Thomas J., and Franklin D. The winner, hands down—Ronnie Reagan . . . and nobody laughed.

We declared war on Grenada. Most of us had no idea who or what Grenada was. Was it one of the Seven Wonders of the World? The dustup involved a number of American dental students who may have been experiencing bicuspid trouble. We triumphed over Grenada . . . and nobody laughed.

(1998: General Augusto Pinochet, the former president of Chile, was indicted in an international tribunal as a war criminal and mass murderer.)

February 15, 2006: A huge op-ed piece appears in the Chicago *Tribune*. It is headed: IRAQ NEEDS A PINOCHET. "I think all patriotic and informed people can agree; it would be great if the U.S. could find an Iraqi Augusto Pinochet. In fact, an Iraqi Pinochet would be better than an Iraqi Castro. Both propositions strike me as so self-evident as to require no explanation." The op-ed is signed: "Jonah Goldberg, Editor of *The National Review Online*" . . . and nobody laughed.

John Kenneth Galbraith told me a funny story. Several years ago,

Public Television featured Milton Friedman, the godhead of the good ship Free Marketry. There were ten or twelve hours weekly. Following that series was one featuring Galbraith, who expressed a wholly different point of view. Galbraith was given equal time. There was one difference: Friedman's lectures had no rebuttals. Every one of Galbraith's shows had a Free Market–driven rebuttal . . . and nobody laughed.

My old friend, Philip Clay Roettinger, CIA whistle-blower, came right to the point. "I got word in 1954 that we were planning to overthrow the government of Guatemala. A fellow came to my office and said: 'We're planning to overthrow a government.' Simple as that."

"Did he give any reasons?" I wondered.

"No, no, no, you didn't have to do that," Phil said, and laughed. He elaborated:

They sent me to Miami, where the headquarters of the operation was: the Marine Corps station in Opa-Locka, Florida. I didn't give it any thought because they said it was a rotten government, bad, Communist-influenced. Several of us went to Tegucigalpa in Honduras and set up a "contra" force. We didn't use the word in those days.

Boy, it worked fine, like clockwork. The president was a Communist, a bad guy. Actually, he was the best president they ever had. He was legally elected. Jacobo Arbenz, a professor. He's the one we overthrew. It wasn't that he was a Communist, nothing to do with it. He had a program for agrarian reform. A program of land distribution: unused land for the Indians to cultivate up in the mountains.

We've never had one that worked so well. We had a guy working for Arbenz who was our boy—the boy who double-crossed him. He'd be it. But we also had Castillo Armas. We owned him and told him he was it. It was our second coup. The first was overthrowing Mossadegh, newly elected in Iran. Armas was with us in Nicaragua, in hiding. He, their future president, was becoming a pain in the ass. I got so damned tired of him begging to get back to Guatemala, I said, "Go ahead," and he became the president.

Our boy who double-crossed Arbenz got sore, so John Puerifoy pulled a .45 caliber and told him to get lost. Armas, the guy we put in, got shot in the back by one of his guards. My friend at the embassy says, "What do we do now?" Well, this other boy wanted to be it, so we said, "Go ahead." He was our new boy. That's how we democratized Guatemala.

And nobody laughed.

26

Old Gent of the Right

Many of the readers are acquainted with the name of David Dellinger. But they never knew the man, nor his father, Raymond. We know of the celebrated Conspiracy 8 trial in Chicago as a result of the tumultuous happenings during the Democratic presidential convention in 1968. Governor Kerner, in a governmental paper, referred to it as something of a police riot as well as a study of the two Americas. It was a devastating report.

Hundreds of thousands of the country's young, as well as furious Vietnam veterans who felt betrayed by their leaders, did battle with Daley the Elder and his city's finest. Eight of the country's leading activists, objecting to the pursuance of our misadventure in Vietnam, were tried for encouraging violent behavior on the part of the many.

Of those eight, three were iconic in stature. The late Abbie Hoffman had become renowned for his wit, especially at the expense of the doddering jurist, Judge Julius Hoffman. Tom Hayden was involved in the Students for a Democratic Society (SDS) and author of the Port Huron Statement. The third was the eldest, Dave Dellinger, a lifelong pacifist and activist. During World War II, he had done time as a conscientious objector in a federal prison.

I was guest at a reunion between Dellinger and a group of seminarians he'd studied with at Union Theological Seminary. They re-called old times at the C.O. jail as they watched a number of ball games, all the while maintaining their objection to the killings in any war. The common sentiment: Whoever won in an armed struggle, it wouldn't be the people.

Dellinger was voted Wakefield, Massachusetts' top athlete of the half-century, as well as being awarded an Oxford scholarship. How-ever, in 1936, when he heard of the war in Spain against the Fascist Franco, he volunteered. By the time he returned, he was a commit-ted conscientious objector, no matter what the war.

From then on he knew his assignment in life. He had by the time of the trial become a figure of front-page repute. He was certainly the most stalwart of the eight. The trial was something of a farce and the journalists in town, especially the redoubtable Mike Royko, had a high old time of it. The result was that all of the con-victions were reversed on appeal. Dave went back to work again, objecting to all wars, wherever they might be.

Almost all of the above is known to the great many. But what about his old man, what about his father? Raymond Dellinger had been, all of his working life, a lawyer, a quite conservative and suc-cessful one. He was early on a close friend of Calvin Coolidge, who for a time was governor of Massachusetts, and later our president.

Ray Dellinger was more than simply conservative; he was ac-tively so. Yet folks in his community and beyond knew all about his son, who was vigorously against much of that in which his father believed. The father was far more than embarrassed; he felt humili-ated. You may understand that son and dad did not get along at all. The son was a cut to the father's heart.

The years went by. On special occasions, there would be family gatherings. Say it's Mrs. Dellinger's birthday. Dave's mother buys a special gown for the occasion. The father is in black tie, of course. Even Dave, who years earlier followed St. Francis of Assisi's exam-ple and traveled around in rags, would wear a tie for the occasion.

There is Dave's memory of his father, a formal gent, subject to all ritual. Yet there was something else Dave recognized in the man. Something wholly unexpected, yet often occurring.

During the sumptuous dinner, at one unbelievably horrendous moment, the young waitress, perhaps it was her first day, perhaps it was sheer nervousness—the dress, the patrons (they were all big shots) may have been too much—spilled a bowl of lobster bisque on Dave's mother's gown. Silence and embarrassment, a tightening of lips, a raising of brows. Not a second hand moved, not the semblance of a pause . . . Dave's father murmured in head-lowered fashion: "It was my fault. Did you notice what I did? I was holding forth and gesturing with my hands when they struck the tray and over it tipped."

He apologized to the trembling girl, who must have felt unbelievably relieved. She was the only one who knew, aside from Dave, that his father was lying. He wasn't within ten feet of that tray. Never once did Dave ever observe his father embarrassing, let alone bullying, a person serving their table.

Dave said, "That was not the first time, nor was it the last. I remember an elderly waiter, long past his prime years, goofing things up, making a mess of our order. My dad, the host, shouldered the blame as he always did, claiming he'd confused the waiter. This is how I came to know the vulnerable side of my dad. Never mind Cal Coolidge or whoever his Gibraltar may have been, my dad's concern was for the person serving."

Toward the end of our humiliating adventure in Vietnam, Dave's father lay dying. By this time, his rugged honesty and hard common sense had taken over. Of the gallantry and truth of his son's mission—as well as I can remember Dave's words—his father said, "Dave, I am so proud of you for standing up the way you have done for what you think is right. I have finally come around to agree with you."

There was a long pause as Dellinger told the story. Finally, Dave murmured as though his father were there: "Dad, I learned it from you."

27

Einstein and the Rest of Us

In my abysmal ignorance of recent technological advances, I confuse the meaning of "hardware" and "software." To me, hardware
is what I've always found it to be: pots, pans, kettles, metallic uten-
sils. Software has always been: pillowcases, sheets, bedspreads, towels. Today, I don't know half the industries. I knew what a spot
welder did, I knew what a tool and die maker did, a truck driver, but
what does a computer programmer do? What is a computer program? What is a startup company? It is more than a generation gap.
My reference is to what is a relatively new group. Technology has
played its Jester role to the Lear of making dough super-fast. There
are new phrases, new kinds of enterprises, that mystify me, but you,
the reader, most all of you younger than I by a long, hard, confusing
generation, would know.

We have technology, the pros and the cons. Where would I
be without a tape recorder? Sadly, my deafness is a challenge to even
the most advanced hearing aids. If there's noise in the background,
I can't hear a thing. I can't go to plays or see movies. My using
the telephone can be an ordeal, the fifth task of Hercules cleaning
out the Augean stables. The operators aren't bad. You say you're
deaf and they immediately help, but there's only so much they
can do.

I take some license with this story I always tell, I gild the lily a little—I always do that—but it's basically true. The Atlanta airport was very new at the time, and as I understand it, one of the first to have passenger trains. As you left the gate of the plane to continue, there were these trains that took you to the concourse that led to your ultimate destination.

You're walking to the train and it's silent, jammed. All you hear is a voice from up above. A human voice, a male voice, I remember it as a baritone. But the words are spoken robotically. "Concourse one, Fort Worth, Dallas, Lubbock." Done that way. That dead voice. Just as the pneumatic doors are about to close a young couple rush in. This couple pulls the doors aside and without missing a beat that voice up above says, "Because of late entry, we are delayed thirty seconds."

The crowd, not a word, looks at this couple. They're at the foot of Mt. Calvary about to be crucified. I'm standing there, having had a couple of martinis in preparation for an encounter of just this sort. I cup my hands around my mouth and I holler, "George Orwell, your time has come and gone!"

Dead Silence. Instead of laughter . . . dead, dead silence. I realize there are now three of us before the firing squad: the couple and me. I'm astonished that our hands aren't raised, awaiting the gunshots from Goya's soldiers in *The Disasters of War.*

I'm wondering: What's happened to the human voice? What's happened to Vox Humana?

I see a little baby seated on the lap of this woman who's Mexican or Latin American. She speaks Spanish. The baby is perhaps eight months old. I turn to the baby and I hold my hand over my mouth because my breath is a hundred proof. I say to the baby, "Sir or Madame, what is your opinion of the human species?"

And what does the baby do? The baby looks at me, and giggles.

I say, "Oh, my God, thank God. A *giggle.* The sound of a human voice. There's my hope."

I don't want to romanticize the past, become an old reactionary, an old fart saying, "In the good old days . . ." There were bad old days, too. I'm not saying factory life was a good life, I'm not saying let's bring back Dickens' world and the dark, satanic mills of William Blake.

Before, there was a noise, a *human* noise. In the old days, at the city desk of any newspaper, there were voices; there was shouting from desk to desk; a guy running back and forth with a news dispatch; someone on the phone hollering or whispering. Today there is silence in the city room. The young journalists are seated side by side, staring into their terminals. They are a foot away from each other, yet miles apart.

Yet, without the advances of technology, my own voice would long ago have been silenced. What is more of a personal metaphor for me than my being here now, approaching ninety-five? I should have been dead with my father and two brothers. A genetic problem: The men of the family all had angina pectoris. Ben was fifty-five when he died. My father fifty-six, and Meyer not quite seventy. Here I am, ninety-four. Here for one reason: the skilled hands of a surgeon and all manner of medical advance, especially in the field of cardiology. About ten years ago I had a quintuple bypass. The odds were in my favor. Nonetheless, an octagenarian was risking all. It worked. As a result, I have outlived my brothers by at least forty years.

More recently, trouble came again. When I was ninety-three, my primary care doctor, my cardiologist, and the surgeon all said I had to have a new heart valve. It was that, or a matter of months until I'd be impelled to ring the bell at the desk clerk's window—checking out.

In any event, there was a moment when I was deciding. At that moment, the odds appeared to be in my favor. Nonetheless, were I a bookie, it'd be six to five either way. I thought: "Oh, to hell with it, let it go, I've had a good life." Still, there was within me curiosity and ego. I was curious to know: What happens next? Finally my ego took over: "OK, let's do it."

The remarkable thing was that I wasn't scared. Oh, why do I lie to myself in this manner? I did have a shake or two, although I'm told I was cheerfully singing, "I'm On My Way to Canaanland," as they wheeled me down the hallway toward the operating room. As I came out of surgery, the surgeon, still wearing his rabbinical cap, looked down on me and said, "It's all over."

I said, "You mean I'm dead?"

"No, no. You've got a new valve and at least four more years."

I said, "I don't want four more years. One more year is enough." But there it is and here I am.

THERE'S THE TECHNOLOGY of saving lives, and there's the technology of death, mass death. Technology's worth depends on who is in charge and for what purpose it's used.

That technology, that same machinery made by what Mark Twain called "the damn human race," the very machinery that gave us Hiroshima and Nagasaki, can destroy the whole human race in one moment. "Bring 'em on!" We can knock off the world tomorrow. You know something funny? They can knock us off, too. They, too, can say, "Bring 'em on!"

We can no longer talk about the world in old historical terms, of how an empire comes to an end. With the technology of destruction such as never envisioned before, one bomb can knock off what years of battle once took. I don't know how many we lost in the Battle of the Somme, the great horrendous battle of World War I, or the Battle of Passendale. But I know the losses are nothing compared with what can happen when one bomb drops now.

Who is the hero, the villain, the god of all this? Who is the one above all most responsible for the state of the world today? Albert Einstein: the greatest heart and mind of the twentieth century.

It was a colleague of Einstein's, Leo Szilard, who convinced Einstein that he was the only one who could persuade President Roosevelt to make the atom bomb. There was Lisa Meitner in Sweden, demonstrating to her nephew, with grains of sand, the theory of relativity. There also was Niels Bohr in Copenhagen. And there at my alma mater, behind the University of Chicago's abandoned football field, was the distinguished physicist Enrico Fermi and his gifted colleagues who split the unsplittable. The phrase "Italian navigator lands safely" came to President Truman and he knew we had succeeded in splitting the atom. Our young chancellor, Robert Maynard Hutchins, wryly observed: "We should never have given up football."

We come to a new leap, in Los Alamos, New Mexico. Here, a colony was set up of the most advanced scientists in the world, headed by the brilliant physicist J. Robert Oppenheimer. There in the Alamogordo desert, Oppenheimer saw the mushroom cloud. He raised his hand in triumph like a winning prizefighter, and then immediately dropped his hand in despair, for he saw death everywhere. From then on, he devoted himself to stopping the loonies from working further on the nuclear bomb. For this he was destroyed, along with his colleague Robert Maynard Hutchins.

Sadly, our own physicists, brilliant though they were, miscalculated. They had assumed that the German scientists were way ahead. The truth is, they were far behind.

The world changed inexorably on that sunny Sunday summer afternoon, August 6, 1945, in Hiroshima. When Einstein heard that a bomb had been dropped on human beings, the bomb for which he was responsible—not simply because he convinced Roosevelt to do it, but because his very equation led directly to the splitting of the atom—he tore his hair. Einstein never dreamed the bomb would be dropped on Hiroshima or Nagasaki. He thought it would be dropped somewhere over the wide-open Pacific.

Sometime in 1962, I interviewed the Russian playwright Nikolai Pogodin. He spoke of having been invited to Princeton by Einstein: "I felt like a pilgrim going to Mecca. Einstein's one fatal flaw," the Russian said, "he came out of the future, and we, his contemporaries, were not ready for him. He, the richest in vision, the most generous of heart, and the most hopeful toward the making of a better world, has caused so much trouble. Science and its exponential advocates and its advances have so threatened us."

After the bombings, deep in grief, Einstein said: "If there's a World War Three, I don't know what weapons we'll use, but I know the weapons of World War Four: sticks and stones." Meaning that our children's children's children will be back in caves.

We talk about neo-conservatives and neo-liberals, and their kindergarten debates, but we never mention neo-Neanderthals, which is the end result of all of the other neos. The end result will be thousands and thousands of years of knowledge and culture gone, because out of these caves will come not our *ancestors*, but our *descendants*. Our great-great-great-great-grandchildren with bull hides on their backs and clubs in their hands. They'll come out and they'll be *terrified*, but somehow out of their tribal memory will come words . . . "Sh-hh-hh-Shakespeare. Who dat? Ode on a Grecian urn. What dat? Mozart. Ahhhh . . . who?"

Einstein had precisely the opposite in mind. He and Bertrand Russell corresponded on several occasions. Their messages were imbued with hope for a world such as there never was. With all the labor-saving devices, all the broken backs unnecessary, man would be ready for a new adventure in which his work would be the living of his life. Russell spoke of a new paradise on earth.

THERE WAS A THIRD VOICE to be heard: Buckminster Fuller. Designer. Architect. Visionary. Aside from his original thinking, he was known for the arcane aspect of his language—the geodesic dome. Spaceship Earth. Synergetics.

Buckminster Fuller was the grand-nephew of one of the most remarkable American women of the nineteenth century, Margaret Fuller. She, our country's leading literary critic for Horace Greeley's paper, helped us in the discovery of Melville, Hawthorne, Poe. She was a conversationalist like no other. In fact, males paid two bucks a head to listen to her talk. In her travels, she met George Sand,

Thomas Carlyle (whose great-man theories she abhorred), Robert Browning and his wife in Italy, and Giuseppe Mazzini.★ Fuller and her husband and child drowned off Fire Island. But her visionary traits lived on in her grand-nephew Bucky.

We think of Bucky Fuller's language and it is here that I must, as we near the end of my reflections, include this man of prescience. Most often, his listeners were professors and grad students—academics. Imagine him, then, in an unthinkable situation to which I had unintentionally contributed.

On one occasion, the one that, to me, represents what my books are all about, he spoke to a gathering of the unmatriculated. This occurred one fiercely cold Sunday afternoon in 1965. As we drove through an old Chicago neighborhood that had gone through many ethnic changes, and which was then primarily Puerto Rican, he said: "This is where I lived during my worst days. I was flat broke, my child had died, and I was thinking of suicide. It was at that time I realized I was thinking other people's thoughts and not my own. That this world was in a state of change technologically, and thus humanly such as never before."

I mentioned to him that later that afternoon there would be a gathering at a local church. No heat. No electricity. All would be cold and dim. The church was holding a gathering of protestors against evictions. Cha-Cha Jimenez, the leader of the Young Lords, who rode with us that day, told us that his family had been kicked out and forced to move six times in one month; that they felt like checkers on a checkerboard. It was then that Bucky suggested the unthinkable: "Let me talk to these people."

I thought to myself: "Oh, my God. What crazy thing have I suggested? If professors have a tough time understanding him, how will it be with working people who've gone no further than fifth grade?" Nonetheless, he insisted.

★ Giuseppe Mazzini was an influential Italian philosopher, patriot, and politician whose efforts were instrumental in creating the *Risorgimento* of Italy, its unification as one nation.

This moment, this event, was a key one in my life in under-scoring a belief. It is a simple one: that people *can* understand what is necessary for their well-being if it's explained to them. Honestly.

Consider this most incongruous of occasions. The cold church, filled with men, women, and children bundled up in coats and blankets. There on the stage paces this old man with his crew-cut white hair, no hat, an old overcoat with two buttons missing, a tiny lapel mike pinned against the warm wool. Imagine Bucky Fuller's arcane speech and the chilled, downcast assemblage of Puerto Rican working people and their families. My head was spinning at the burlesque aspect of the situation.

What was the reaction? I closed my eyes fearing the worst. I opened my eyes and I saw something wondrous. These people, of such limited academic training, listened intently to Bucky take off on the nature of housing. He spoke of gentrification and urban re-newal and of the devastation it caused the have-nots and have-somewhats. He spoke of a world in which, thanks to technology, or as he called it, "technology-*for*-life" (rather than *against* it), there would be enough to go around.

I speak about an utterly new world, a world in which it is assumed there's plenty for all; a world in which you don't have to have a job to prove your right to live. Where the first thing you're going to think of is not 'How am I going to earn a living?" but "What needs to be done? What am I interested in? Where might I make a contribution?" What an extraordinary new preoccupation of man! Work will be the most privileged word we have. The right to work will be not with the muscle, but the right to work with your brain, with your *mind*. You are born with that, but just getting ac-credited by the other man to be allowed to use that tool, and get-ting credit enough so he helps you, and cooperates with you, and you make a breakthrough on behalf of your fellow men, is the next thing. That's the work. Work will be the most beautiful thing we can do.

The funny thing is, after he spoke, they asked him all the right questions. They had understood everything he said and exactly what he meant.

Bucky Fuller has been dismissed in some quarters as a hopeless utopian. But others have found out that his ideas are a *thinking* man's ideas, and that some of his notions are right on the button. This revelatory afternoon proved for me that the intellectual and the Hand (an old-fashioned term for a workingman) *can* understand one another, provided there are mutual self-esteem and mutual respect. As Tom Paine put it, we must be not just men but *thinking* men.

Remembering that afternoon reminds me also that Bucky Fuller, Bertrand Russell, and Albert Einstein were and are on the same wavelength—yours and mine. That's the big one. Are we ready for what the man of the future has requested of us?

Again, the journalist Nick von Hoffman's observation on what being part of a movement, no matter how local, can mean: "You, who thought of yourself up to that moment as simply a member, suddenly spring to life. You have that intoxicating feeling that you can make history, that you count."

"You count." What the little boy in Flannery O'Connor's "The River" had in mind.

It was Mary Lou Wolff who sounded a more personal note. She was the wife of a telephone lineman, a mother of eight, and fighting to save her neighborhood from destruction during the sixties. The cement lobby and the mayor had plans for a new expressway, so that cars could go faster, of course. The neighborhood would be wiped out, but no matter, the cars would fly by the nothing left in their wake.

As Mary Lou spoke to a tumultuous and terrified gathering, things all fell into place for her. Something of a revelation, she called it. The Big Boys who had planned this local wreckage were one and the same as those who had planned the Vietnam War (which she had earlier favored). "I realized I was saying things I never even dreamt about." Her short speech was a classic. "I began to realize rules are made by some people and the purpose of these rules is to keep you in your place. It is at times your duty to break some of these rules. This is such a time." The crowd roared its approval, and the expressway project was abandoned.

From that moment on, Mary Lou became the spokesperson for much of Chicago's blue-collar discontent. She said it all when she observed: "If it could happen to me, it could happen to anyone. I now believe in human possibility: in things all of us can do publicly and politically. That's where the excitement is. You become aware and alive. It's not a dream. It is possible every-day stuff."

She counted. As I think of Mary Lou, of Peggy Terry, of Nancy Jefferson, of Rose Rigsby, of Florence Scala, of James Cameron, of Saul Alinsky, of Dave Dellinger, and so many others—we may be ready for Einstein's hopes and dreams. After all, he is a man of the present. There is no alternative. Are we ready for it?

Yes. No. Some of the less celebrated of Einstein's perceptions deal not with the sciences, but with human behavior; especially here in the United States. Though it is embarrassing to mention Ayn Rand in the same sequence with Albert Einstein, I do so to make a point. After all, there may be more readers of *The Fountainhead* than there are of *The Grapes of Wrath*. In Rand's world, we equate the individual and independence. The Lone Ranger, John Wayne, who on his own wins and sits on top of the hill. The former Federal Reserve chief, Alan Greenspan, was a fan of Ayn Rand. They appear to share an allergy to collective action. This, they maintain, causes a loss of individuality. Barbara Branden, Ayn Rand's biographer, puts it this way: a Rand hero is "the man who lives for his own sake against the collectivist, who places self above others."

Einstein, on the contrary, believed that an individual working with others in assemblage strengthens his individuality. In recognizing that there are others who dream, hope, and work as he does—for a better world—he is not alone.

Haven't we learned anything from the Great Depression of the thirties? Haven't we learned that the Free Market (read: individual) fell on its face and begged a benign federal government (a gathering of minds) to help?

It is time for a reprise from Jimmy Baldwin: "History does not refer merely to the past. On the contrary, the great force of history comes from the fact that we carry it within us, are unconsciously controlled by it in many ways, and history is literally present in all that we do." It is time for us to overcome the malaise from which our society had been suffering: a national Alzheimer's disease.

During all my commencement addresses, I have "borrowed" from William Sloane Coffin Jr. His invocation during a commencement exercise at Yale University serves as a touchstone. At the time, in the early sixties, he was chaplain at the university and a passionate, eloquent resister to the Vietnam War. This prayer was addressed to the students of the graduating class.

> O Lord, grant us grace to have a lovers' quarrel with the world we love. Come out and have your lovers' quarrel with the world, not for what it is, but for what it still can be, so that there will be a little more love, a little more beauty than would have been there had you not had your lovers' quarrel. Number us, we beseech Thee, in the ranks of those who went forth from this university longing only for those things for which Thou makes us long. Men [today, read "men and women"] for whom the complexity of issues only serve to renew their zeal to deal with them. Men and women who alleviated pain by sharing it.
>
> And men and women who will risk something Big for something Good, who will recognize others for what they are rather than from what they are told these others are, who will regard that which ties us together rather than that which trivializes and separates us, who are willing to have a lovers' quarrel with the world not for what it is, but for what it still can be.

Let Bill Coffin's closing words to his invocation be my benediction:

> O Lord, take our minds and think through them, take our lips and speak through them, take our hearts and set them on fire. Amen.

Postscript

After I became known, a local celebrity, a woman said to me, "Aren't you Ben Terkel's brother?" I said I was.

She said, "He was wonderful. My little child had a clubfoot and he was so good to her. He treated her as though she were a princess." When Ben worked for DeWitt Shoes, he handled kids with clubfeet and other problems. A number of women spoke about him with a great deal of affection, about how good he made the kids feel.

When he died, I got a phone call from a woman, weeping. "I never worked with your brother Ben but I loved him very much. My little girl with deformed feet felt like Miss America." Suddenly it occurred to me, I should be proud of him, because he had a generous nature. He had such a gentle, easy way with people.

Not too many years ago, another old survivor spoke of my brother Meyer as having been his best and most favorite teacher. Was I related, too? Again I had that feeling of uplift and pride. These two brothers of mine were without my self-centeredness, and were doing their work and making no bones about it. My brothers were better persons than I in their thoughtfulness toward others.

In a way, my son Dan reminds me of my brothers in their generosity of spirit. And of course, he reminds me of Ida, with his kindness and concern for others.

I'm the guy who's supposed to be full of concern for people. But there is a lot for which I feel regret. Letters I've not replied to, people I've not followed up with, favors I've not granted, book blurbs I've not written. I was going to get to it and didn't. "Rueful" is the word. Knowing you've caused hurt by things you've not done can haunt as deeply as the reverse. And you remember it. There's a lot of that for me. Which, of course, involves neglect of family at times, too.

It's ironic that an irreparable loss, with the death of Ida, whom my son and I both loved, has also resulted in some gain. What happened is that I became dependent on him as I hadn't been before, and that's brought us much closer. Through all my various ailments, he's become a caregiver. He has his own work, but he makes time to take care of all manner of things for me. My appreciation is boundless.

When asked what the secret to my interviewing is, I always say, "to make people feel needed." Learning from those I interviewed that I needed *them* helped me when the time came, when Ida died, when I needed my son, and in many ways, when we needed each *other*. To feel needed. It's the most important thing. Dan has played a tremendous role, being there, like a fireman with a net. In *Will the Circle Be Unbroken*, the book I finished after Ida died, I talk about a *lied* Lotte Lehmann sang, of a mountainside against which you lean when weary or bereft. He continues to be that source of strength and comfort.

My mother hung up her gloves at eighty-seven.

As for me, curiosity is the one attribute that, for better or worse, has kept me going. My consciousness of this may have begun at that New York café, eighty-six years before, with my father and "Natacha Rambova." Curiosity. So my epitaph has already been formed: Curiosity did not kill this cat.

Index

NOTE: ST refers to Studs Terkel.